THE IMPORTANCE OF FEELING INFERIOR

Other books by Marie Beynon Ray
HOW NEVER TO BE TIRED
DOCTORS OF THE MIND
HOW TO CONQUER YOUR HANDICAPS
THE BEST YEARS OF YOUR LIFE

THE
IMPORTANCE
OF
FEELING
INFERIOR

by MARIE BEYNON RAY

Foreword by MANFRED J. SAKEL, M. D.

HARPER & BROTHERS PUBLISHERS NEW YORK

THE IMPORTANCE OF FEELING INFERIOR

Copyright © 1957 by Marie Beynon Ray

Printed in the United States of America

Library of Congress catalog card number: 56-8773

1584287

TO MY BELOVED DAUGHTER

TABLE OF CONTENTS

FOREWORD

by DR. MANFRED J. SAKEL, Fellow of the American Psychiatric Association and Life Member of the New York Academy of Science

The Importance of Feeling Inferior seems, from the point of view of a psychiatrist, to be a book which should be of particular interest at this time. It would seem that the public has reached the point of saturation for books in the field of pseudo-psychology and pseudo-psychiatry, of books written *for* neurotics *by* neurotics. But here is a book of common-sense, down-to-earth psychology which normal people can understand and apply. It is definitely not a book in the field of psychiatry, which is a medical specialty devoted to the treatment of nervous and mental disorders.

What makes this book on the inferiority complex particularly timely is that the public is beginning to recover from its long enslavement to the fascination of Freudian theories and from domination by the overwhelming personality of Freud himself as well as from the hypnotic attraction of the psychoanalytic couch. The Freudian doctrine is compounded of a few *facts* and much fancy. Freud himself never claimed that his ritualistic therapy was designed for mental illnesses.

Too little attention has been paid to the field of normal psychology, and too little research done in it. Not everyone who has an emotional problem is abnormal. Normal people, too, have their problems presented by everyday life situations. This book, with its practical approach to the problems which constantly arise in relation to their work, to sex and marriage and to society, may help these individuals to resolve them with no one officiating at the couch head. In some cases it may even serve as a substitute for the advice and guidance that can be given by an experienced doctor.

The world is also beginning to recover from the pessimism of Freud and to turn toward the more optimistic view of man and his possibilities taken by Adler, the advocate of the inferiority complex. Adler's Individual Psychology, more oriented toward social and spiritual values, is more in line with our thinking today than is Freud's one-sided animal-instinct-based, purely earthy psychology of disillusionment. It holds out hope of the possibility of self-betterment. Adler's emphasis on the inferiority complex is an indispensable counterweight to the outworn and never valid Freudian theory of pansexuality, the theory that in the last analysis sex is the sole motivation of man. The drive to survive is a more fundamental and much more potent force in human nature than the sexual drive. Adler's insistence that *self*-preservation precedes and supersedes the preservation of the species, the premise on which he based his "drive to power," is incontrovertible.

Finally Freud overlooked, as Adler did not, too many of what I call the "ultimate causes," neglecting completely man's inherent and perpetual desire and quest for intangible values, such absolutes as justice, co-operation, self-sacrifice, compassion, etc.

It is not a question of one school superseding the other, of the Adlerians finally winning out over the long-dominant Freudians, but rather of the two interpenetrating. Thus psychotherapy becomes, as it should, more eclectic, taking the best from both schools as well as from later practitioners who recognize the social and environmental forces, such as Stekel, Fromm, Horney. In this new psychotherapy the Adlerian orientation is assuming a deserv-

edly greater importance. Freudian psychoanalysis has had
the disadvantage of being a ritualistic routine, varying
little to suit the needs of a given individual. Adler's *Individual Psychology,* or the psychology of the individual, is
far more flexible. To the classic Freudian ritual many psychoanalysts have now added another ritualistic practice,
that of giving tranquilizing drugs, which too many doctors,
psychologists and psychiatrists are administering perfunc-
torily today to keep their patients quiet while they try to
think what to do for them. Some even quite erroneously
hope to cure their patients with these tranquilizers.

The Importance of Feeling Inferior, lucidly and inter-
estingly written, with many convincing examples of the
stimulation to achievement sparked by feelings of inferiority—such outstanding cases as those of Lincoln and Alexander the Great, the despised Macedonian, Agnes de Mille
and Dr. Norman Vincent Peale, and its many case histories
of less-known individuals—can enormously assist the normal person to understand himself and others and to order
his life more happily. It seems to me that it could be read
with some profit by specialists in these fields.

ACKNOWLEDGMENTS

ACKNOWLEDGMENTS ARE MADE to the following books and periodicals:

By Alfred Adler:
What Life Should Mean to You.
Understanding Human Nature.
Problems of Neurosis.
The Education of Children.

Dance to the Piper by Agnes de Mille, published by Little, Brown and Company.

Lincoln's Sons by Ruth Painter Randall, published by Little, Brown and Company.

The Best Years of Your Life, by Marie Beynon Ray published by Little, Brown and Company.

Doctors of the Mind by Marie Beynon Ray, published by Little, Brown and Company.

R.S.V.P. by Elsa Maxwell, published by Little, Brown and Company.

Discovering Ourselves by Edward Etrecker and Kenneth Appel, published by the Macmillan Company.

The Natural Superiority of Women by Ashley Montagu, published by the Macmillan Company.

A Star Danced by Gertrude Lawrence, published by Doubleday and Co.

How to Be Happy Though Human by Beran Wolfe, published by Rinehart.

Motivation and Personality by A. H. Marlow, published by Harper & Brothers.

Love or Perish by Smiley Blanton, published by Simon and Schuster.

Somebody Up There Likes Me by Rocky Graziano, published by Simon and Schuster.

Life, for quotations from Robert Wallace and Bertha Trujillo.

The Reader's Digest for quotations from Carlos Romulo, Farnsworth Crowder, Mme. Vijaya Pandit.

Flying for quotation from Howard C. Kurtz, Jr.

The New York *Herald Tribune* for quotations from Bertrand Russell, Carlos Romulo, Art Buchwald, Hy Gardner, Somerset Maugham, and Margaret Parton.

The *New York Times* for quotations from Kim Novac, Tennessee Williams, Albert Einstein, and Robert Moses.

THE IMPORTANCE OF FEELING INFERIOR

CHAPTER I

Have You an Inferiority Complex?

It's a June day that has been on order for a long time and that has only just gotten delivery.

The new streamlined Broadway Limited stands flashing its flanks in the Sunnyside railroad yards in Long Island.

Suddenly bulbs explode, cameras click, the crowd surges. A man in trunks steps out on the tracks, hitches a chain to the observation car, braces himself, pulls. The whole seventy-two tons of steel quiver and follow him along the track like a dog on a leash.

He is forty-seven years old and his name is Angelo Siciliano.

Never heard of him? Wait.

Angelo was born in Brooklyn, the son of Italian immigrants. He lived in the slums, but worst of all, even at sixteen he was, in his own words, "a 97-pound runt, pale, nervous, and a prey to bullies."

One Saturday he went with a group of boys from the Italian Settlement House to the Brooklyn Museum. Angelo never got beyond the main lobby. All afternoon he sat transfixed by the statues of the Greek gods and goddesses, gazing a little at Apollo but mostly at Hercules. He had

1

no idea that he was held spellbound by the highest expression of art man has ever attained. He thought it was the biceps of Hercules.

Angelo almost fell off the bench when the group leader informed him that these statues were actually the likenesses of men. The great sculptors of antiquity, he explained, had always used young Greek athletes for their models.

These, then, were men! Not gods, but men! And if men—!

That evening Angelo Siciliano clipped a series of exercises from a newspaper and began making himself over in the likeness of a Greek god.

Month after month he kept at it, convinced that what man could do Angelo could do.

He never gave up. Not when everyone sneered at his feeble display of muscle. Not when he stepped swaggeringly up to a bully and said, "Wanna wrastle?" and the fellow just put out a hand and pushed him over. Not when he saw pictures of Bernarr flexing the famous MacFadden muscles and learned he could never hope to achieve this state without all sorts of fancy gymnasium equipment.

No, he just started in inventing his own exercises, pitting one muscle against another, a system he was later to call Dynamic Tension. Presently there was no doubt about it, even when someone else took the measurements—Angelo was beginning to bulge in all directions.

On top of the Atlas Hotel at Rockaway Beach, where Brooklyn boys went to swim in those days, stood a wooden statue of Atlas supporting the world on his back. One summer day a member of the gang suddenly pointed and shouted, "Hey, lookit! Ain't Tony the spittin' image of ole Atlas? Lookit the chest on him—and the legs! He's Atlas!"

Now, of course, you know him—Charles Atlas, "the

world's most perfectly developed man," "the possessor of
the true classic physique, in perfect proportion, smooth,
harmonious, a blend of Hercules and Apollo."

These are not empty phrases. They are titles he has
won in every major world-wide contest. His is not the
typical strong-man physique with vast swellings and out-
croppings of levators and flexors, but the easy flow of
muscle beneath a smooth sheathing of flesh. In our day no
one has come so close to the Greek ideal of manly beauty
as he.

Almost certainly you have seen statues of him. He posed
for the statue of Alexander Hamilton in front of the
Treasury Building in Washington. For George Washing-
ton on the Washington Square Monument in Manhattan.
For *The Dawn of Glory* in Prospect Park in Brooklyn. For
Sorrow on the banks of the Marne. For many others.

Isn't it obvious that Angelo Siciliano became Charles
Atlas because he was once a 97-pound runt, the prey of
bullies?

Every Sunday a stocky man, looking totally unlike
a prophet of the Lord and very much like a Wall Street
banker, ascends the pulpit of the Marble Collegiate
Church in New York City and preaches to congregations
totaling four thousand.

And every Sunday the miracle occurs. At some unpredictable moment he ceases to be a man and becomes
an electric charge between his audience and some super-
natural power. At such moments, he is no more conscious
that he is speaking than a bird is that it is flying. During
that period his listeners live on another plane, almost on
another planet. Afterward they remember this moment
and try to be again what they were then.

This is the man who, all through school and college,
called upon to recite, blushed, stammered, trailed off into

incoherence or semicoma. More than anything in the world he longed to hold vast audiences spellbound with his oratory—but he was paralyzed with self-consciousness.

This is the man of whom it has been said, "He is never truly himself except when he is speaking before an audience"—Norman Vincent Peale.

"In my childhood," he will tell you, "I had three goals in life. Because I was a skinny little runt, I yearned to be a two-hundred pound football hero or a pugilist. Because I was a p.k.—preacher's kid—I had to prove I was a tough *hombre*. When any skulduggery was afoot it was young Peale they sought, and young Peale they usually found. Because I had been frightened almost into convulsions when I got up to speak my first piece in school by a perfidious female who screamed, 'Look how his knees shake!' I longed to be a Chautauqua lecturer or an actor or an auctioneer—anything that would afford me the opportunity to hear the tintinnabulation of my automatic jaw. Three things I knew I must be when I grew up—tough, fat and an orator. At various times in my life I've accomplished all three."

It is doubtful if any other clergyman has ever reached so large an audience. With radio, television lectures, syndicated columns, periodicals and books on how to live confidently and think positively, his public is roughly the size of the national debt. Once called "The No. 1 Go-Getter for God," he was pleased as though he'd just been handed a halo.

It is half an hour before a party to which two hundred celebrities have been invited and two hundred celebrities are coming, drawn by the fame of a hostess for whose parties Cole Porter has composed music, Lauritz Melchior has sung, Charlie Chaplin has performed, palm trees have been set ablaze in the Sahara, and George Copeland has played "Clair de Lune" as the moon rose over Venice.

In the hostess's suite the telephone rings.

"It's Mrs. Cornelius Vanderbilt," murmurs her awed secretary. "She says she's heard so much about your parties she wondered if she might drop in with a few friends this evening to watch the festivities."

For a moment, silence, then a burst of laughter so raucous that the secretary, shocked, hastily covers the mouthpiece. The laughter ceases and the hostess drops into a chair. A scene from the past rises before her.

She is a child of twelve, living in San Francisco, and today is to be the most wonderful day of her life. At the big house across the street they are giving a birthday party for her friend. All day long she hangs on the fence, watching the preparations. The marquee goes up, the caterers arrive, then the florists, the orchestra, brought all the way from New York, delivery boys with presents, messenger boys with telegrams, dressmakers, waiters—a glorious hubbub.

"Mama, mama, what dress am I going to wear?"

"You? You're not going to the party, my dear. We're not invited."

"Not—invited—mama?"

"No. We're not grand enough, it seems."

That evening she sat in her window watching the carriages drive up, the dresses trail up the path, hearing the gay chatter, the laughter, the music. Even when she was an old woman, this would remain the cruelest memory of a lifetime.

"Mrs. Vanderbilt is holding the line," her secretary reminds her . . . Mrs. Vanderbilt, the queen of New York society, the leader of the Four Hundred! The most intoxicating sense of triumph she had ever experienced sweeps over her.

"Tell Mrs. Vanderbilt the party is restricted to my friends," she says. "You may add that I do not include her among them." . . . She has learned her snobbery in a hard school.

It is obvious to anyone why Elsa Maxwell became the party-givingest woman in the world and a hostess of international fame. She herself, in her autobiography, *R.S.V.P.*, says:

"What makes Elsa run? I believe my major motivation can be traced to my first exposure to snobbery when I was 12 years old and Senator James G. Fair gave a birthday party for his daughter. I can still feel my burning resentment when my mother told me we were too poor to be asked to the party. I swore to myself then that I would give great parties all over the world. Subconsciously, I suppose, I have been trying ever since to prove my social equality with the Fairs. Whenever I achieve a small social triumph today, my memory invariably darts back to that first exposure to snobbery and the feeling of resentment that choked me."

Because of that childhood wound, this woman, who says herself that she is without beauty, social position, money, education, glamour, and who had only gaiety and persistence and a small talent for playing the piano, became the most famous hostess on three continents. In her seventies she could say:

"I have associated with artists and creative geniuses all my life. I have entertained a dozen kings and been on a first-name basis with half the title-holders in the Almanach de Gotha."

Here are three people, all with very different goals, who achieved those goals because of a strong feeling of inferiority in their childhood.

This is not the exception. It is the rule.

No one succeeds *without* an inferiority complex.

No one succeeds *in spite* of an inferiority complex.

Everyone succeeds *because* of an inferiority complex.

Fortunately everyone has an inferiority complex.

You doubt it? You yourself have none?

Perhaps at this point it would be well to consider just what an inferiority complex is.

Let us admit at the start that we expect to use the term with considerable looseness. There are sticklers who would have us use the words "inferiority feeling" or "sense of inferiority" or "feelings of inadequacy" instead of "inferiority complex." Does anyone ever refer to his "sense of inadequacy"? Yet "inferiority complex" is on the tongues of taxi drivers and manicurists. Needless to say theirs is not the sense in which psychiatrists employ the term. And yet even psychiatrists are pretty loose in their definitions. Whenever you get four psychiatrists together you have at least eight opinions. After years of semantic wrestling, the American Psychiatric Association has only recently begun to put together a provisional glossary of psychiatric terms.

There are those who insist that if one is conscious of it, it isn't a complex, just a feeling, since a complex is, by definition, unconscious and suppressed. To which others retort: "Nonsense! Any group of interdependent ideas charged with emotion is a complex, whether it is conscious or unconscious." Some maintain that, as with any complex, one is conscious of the *feeling* but not of its cause, at any rate not of the original childhood situation which precipitated it. At which others snort, "Ridiculous! A person can be conscious of the whole situation—feelings, causes, childhood episodes—and can react consciously to them."

You are deafened with their clatter, not to say confused —but scarcely more confused than they. What you would like to know, for example, is whether having an inferiority complex makes a person a neurotic. Here is some of their contradictory thinking on this point.

Dr. A.: One may have a *feeling* of inferiority and be perfectly normal. But once it is forced into the unconscious, with all its attendant circumstances, it is a complex and one is neurotic.

Dr. B.: Not at all. It is not a question of whether or not one is conscious of all the circumstances that makes the difference between being normal and neurotic. It is how one reacts to the situation. If a man reacts negatively to an inferiorizing situation, he has a complex and is neurotic. If he reacts constructively, no complex, no neurosis.

Dr. C.: My working thesis is that an inferiority complex is a chronic affliction caused by residues of inferiority feelings of a more evanescent nature—not necessarily suppressed, not necessarily neurotic.

Dr. D.: Look, what are we arguing about? There *is* no cut-and-dried definition. We all use different terms to express the same concept, we even use the same term in different ways at different times. Let's face it, psychiatry, not without reason called "the nasty little science," is one part science to three parts intuition with a dash of art. That's *good* psychiatry. Bad psychiatry is one part ignorance to one part stupidity with a dash of charlatanism.

In all this confusion, it is well to remember that Alfred Adler himself, the discoverer of the inferiority complex, didn't coin the phrase or use it in the beginning. Not until he came to the United States on his first lecture tour and heard himself everywhere referred to as "the father of the inferiority complex" did he finally adopt it. Previously he had spoken only of "inferiority feelings." Actually he shifted ground many times, making no clear distinction between feeling and complex. On one occasion he wrote that "Only if a child uses his feeling of inferiority to avoid contributing to the community does the feeling become a complex and prevent normal development."

Many psychiatrists consider the whole subject pretty academic since the public has taken the matter into its own hands, insisting on understanding the term in its own way and ignoring professional hairsplitting. The average man knows exactly what he means by the term. Whereas the professors may define a complex as "a group of memories and ideas with a strong affective charge, cut off from any normal connections with the psychic development of the person and remaining always outside it like a foreign body," to the man in the street it is no such complicated thing. It is quite simply that feeling he sometimes has of being at a disadvantage in certain situations or conditions or with certain people. This, frankly, is something he prefers not to discuss, feeling rather sheepish about the whole thing. But if you can draw him out, you will discover that sometimes he knows why he feels as he does and sometimes he doesn't; that sometimes this feeling is confined to certain phases of his personality but at others it pervades his whole being. Occasionally he may even admit that his feeling borders on the abnormal, being at times grossly exaggerated and resulting in unreasonable attitudes and reactions such as extreme hostility, aggressiveness, or shyness.

The daddy of the inferiority complex himself bowed to this freehand definition. Any fair-minded psychologist will do the same. So shall we.

This is not the Freudian notion of a complex. To Freud a complex is an unconscious and repressed system of desires and memories which, in disguised form, exerts a dominating influence on the personality. This is why the discoverer of the inferiority feeling at first refused to use the word *complex*. To him the inferiority feeling was not necessarily repressed nor unconscious nor disguised. That it did, however, exert a dominating influence on the personality, he spent his life proving.

The question now is: Have *you* an inferiority complex? You are inclined to think not. You may even feel that if you have any complex at all, it is a superiority complex. Let us consider the case of a man who felt just as you do.

I was the guest at the Stork Club one evening of a man reputed to be the highest paid commercial artist in the world. For over twenty years his income has run from $10,000 to $150,000 a year. You may remember him as the illustrator of the Alexander Botts stories in the *Saturday Evening Post*—Albert Dorne.

I knew him well enough to ask, during the evening, "Tell me, have you an inferiority complex?"

For a moment he looked blank.

"That's a strange question," he said at last, "and a difficult one. Well, I'll answer it frankly." He considered a moment. "No. I would say quite definitely that I have none. Probably the opposite."

Later I slipped another question into the conversation. "Do you always invite your guests to the Stork Club?"

"Either here or to '21.' "

I complimented him on a tie he was wearing.

"I get my ties at Knize," he said. (Ties up to $50 at Knize's.)

I remarked the tiny hand-embroidered monogram on his shirt.

"I have my shirts made to order at Sulka's," he explained. (Nothing like it under $40 at Sulka's.)

"The color is perfect with your suit," I observed.

"Well, as a matter of fact, it was ordered for this suit. De Gez makes my suits." (Nothing made to order at De Gez under $300.)

I smiled.

"What are you driving at?" he asked. "Has all this something to do with that question you asked me a while ago—about the inferiority complex?"

"Maybe."

"You mean—you mean all this 'putting on the dog' is an effort to wipe out some sort of feeling of inferiority?"

"It often is."

"I see what you mean. Damned interesting idea!"

Silence. Then suddenly:

"Look, I'm going to tell you something. You've seen my studio?"

(I had—one of the most de luxe duplex studio apartments in one of the most fashionable sections of Manhattan.)

"Well, from my windows I can see the cold-water tenement where my mother was a janitress, took in washing, and slept on the floor. We were always cold, we were always hungry, we were always in rags. I can still remember one suit I had when I was eight. My mother had mended the seat of the trousers so often that they would no longer hold a patch. I leaned over backwards as I walked—like this"—he rose to show me—"so that the jacket would hide the seat. . . . Today I have $300 suits to make up for that. And monogrammed handkerchiefs. And made-to-order shirts. And Cavanaugh hats at $60. I can remember as a boy swearing to myself, 'Someday I'll have the finest clothes in the world—I'll show them—I'll show them.'"

He paused.

"A few moments ago when I said I didn't have an inferiority complex, I believed it. I have a lot of self-confidence. Then when I began to suspect that maybe I had one, I asked myself what there was to be ashamed of. Because of it I became one of the highest-paid commercial artists in the world.

"Come to think of it, I've reacted to all the handicaps

of my childhood in the same way. I was the unhealthiest kid in several square miles of slums. In addition to all the regular diseases, I managed to acquire malaria, pneumonia, tuberculosis, and heart trouble. So, of course, being sickly, I had to prove I was Superman. I swam in the East River where the rats came out from under the wharves to snarl at us. At twelve I was smoking bigger cigars than Churchill, which I was hard put to it to conceal at home and at school. I boxed in the toughest fight clubs. Gradually I built up a physique which only alcohol has ever threatened.

"As a boy I wanted desperately to be an artist, but I couldn't pay for lessons. So I taught myself. I've never been inside an art school in my life—except to lecture. On the whole, I think my inferiority complex has paid off."

All right, you say, Dorne had an inferiority complex but all his life he got along just fine without realizing he had one. So why know?

Because if we refuse to admit it, it's a blind force, as likely to be working against us as for us. If we recognize it for what it is, we can use it intelligently.

But then, you may ask, what did people do before the inferiority complex was discovered? To which the reply is, what did people do before the causes of malaria or diphtheria or polio were discovered? Some lived and some died, without benefit of science, as some will succeed and some will fail without benefit of psychiatry. But more live and more succeed today because the causes of these disabilities have been discovered.

So suppose we now inquire into the origin of the inferiority complex and its possibilities for good and for ill in human affairs.

Psychology, up to the end of the nineteenth century, was a pretty academic science, primarily a study of mind, conscious and static. But, as we know today, mind is seven-eighths beneath the surface and it is dynamic. That we have today a dynamic depth psychology is primarily due to one man, a man whom some call God and some Anti-christ—Sigmund Freud.

Freud began his great work with the discovery of the unconscious, that reservoir of memories forced into oblivion because they are too painful to be tolerated in consciousness. He noted that in *all* his cases it was not just *any* repressed emotion which produced neurotic symptoms—it was always a repressed sexual desire.

Say a man has a compulsion to be constantly washing his hands. Why? Because since boyhood he has been repressing the shameful memory that he then practiced manual masturbation. The thought, forced into the unconscious, is forgotten. Only the feeling that his hands are unclean remains.

This was merely the prelude to Freud's doctrine of pansexuality. From then on what he discovered about human nature became ever more unacceptable to doctors, to ministers of the gospel, fathers of families, and all respectable citizens. For it is not only neurotics, Freud soon announced, who harbor these buried sexual memories and desires, but even apparently normal individuals. In their mounting tension, symptoms such as anxiety, apprehension, a sense of guilt, or extreme nervousness develop. All this, countered the medical men of Freud's day, was not only purely presumptive and without scientific proof, it was a very nasty reflection on human nature.

Freud, unmoved and undeterred, continued to dredge from the unconscious even more unpleasant facts. Not only in adolescence, he discovered—and Freud himself, a respectable husband and father, was as much shocked by this as any of his mid-Victorian readers—did these psychic traumas originate, but frequently far back in childhood, even in infancy. Many of his female patients could recall attempted seductions, invariably by a father or brother, from their childhood. (With male patients it was a nursemaid.) But, reasoned Freud, not possibly could there be so many depraved fathers and brothers. These seductions, he discovered, were not memories at all but pure fantasy, representing the wish fulfillment of the child.

Such theories, even after half a century of exposure to Freudian psychology, still seem revolting to many people. But Freud pushed relentlessly forward to turn up even more distasteful notions.

Even the infant in his crib, he announced, has a rich sexual life, manifested in its frank play with its sexual organs, its sensuality, its enjoyment of all its physical processes. As he grows, his curiosity concerning sex increases, bringing a Niagara of questions as to the differences between boys and girls. His questions being evaded, he comes to understand that these subjects are taboo.

Repression begins. Nothing is forgotten; it is merely forced into the unconscious. He is not less curious, only more cautious.

Still further proof of the sexuality of children is the boy's strong attachment to his mother, the girl's to her father—the boy's resentment toward his father (whose privileges he covets) and the girl's toward her mother, and the reciprocal feelings of the parents. A whole life pattern may be built on these early incestuous impulses. Here are the origins of Freud's famous Oedipus and Electra complexes.

In all his thousands of cases, Freud claimed, he never discovered *one* where the neurosis could not be traced back to some sexual frustration. All were rooted in the sexual tensions of adult life, the repression of sexual fantasy in childhood, or the failure to pass emotionally from an earlier to a later stage of sexual development.

This is Freud's doctrine of pansexuality. It is the foundation of his whole theory of psychoanalysis, which was blasted root and branch by the entire medical profession, clergymen, scientists, and all right-thinking people.

But there was a suspect minority to whom it made sense. They were willing to admit that they could see traces of this sort of thing in themselves and others, and that Freud offered a plausible and coherent explanation of much in human nature that had heretofore been incomprehensible. One by one the medical men, who had never had the slightest success in treating their nervous patients anyway, began to accept certain of his less distasteful theories. Finally even religion yielded an inch or two. After all, the clergy pointed out, Freud went right along with revealed religion in the doctrine of original sin and the innate sense of guilt in man.

One thing was certain. Psychology would never be the same again. The discovery of the unconscious alone would have revolutionized it. Before Freud, psychology took into account not much more of mind than appeared on the surface. After Freud, consciousness was recognized as being only a small part of the psyche. Not reason, but the dynamic emotional energy of the unconscious, initiates most human behavior. For in the unconscious is preserved not only our own past but the past of the race, the primitive drives which are as much more powerful than reason as a tiger is than a kitten.

But there were many psychiatrists and psychologists who, while accepting Freud's theory of the unconscious, were unwilling to subscribe to his doctrine of pansexuality.

"At the bottom of every neurosis is a sex conflict," Freud had said, and, "Without processes having their origin in sexual life the greater part of human activity would cease."

Among those who disagreed with him was a young Viennese psychiatrist and an associate of Freud's—Alfred Adler. Suppose we listen in on an imaginary conversation between the two men. Similar conversations we know took place in pre-World-War-I Vienna, where both men practiced.

"I don't find it explains everything—this theory of pansexuality," says Adler. "On the contrary, I often find a quite different force at work."

"This 'different force,'" we may imagine Freud asking, "what is it?"

"The aggressive instincts. The law of the jungle. The primitive, ruthless drive to power. No prettier than incest, I admit. These, too, must be thrust down into the unconscious. We dare not acknowledge them even to ourselves.

"These aggressive instincts lead to the desire to assert ourselves, to be important, to dominate others. At the very core of the human ego is the unshakable belief in its own value and the desire to demonstrate it. Hence the drive to power and the will to dominate. Without this drive the human race could not survive. It is a corollary to the will to live. It exists in the lowliest of human beings, in the charwoman equally with the queen, in the beggar equally with the dictator."

"And how does this 'drive to power' explain the neuroses?"

"The inner conflict between our self-assertive drives and the repressive forces of morality and society is what engenders the neuroses. The drive for superiority is so powerful that if a man cannot outstrip his fellows in actual performance, he will do so in dreams and fantasies. He will, if necessary, resort to madness, becoming in his own mind Christ or Napoleon."

"Very interesting. But have you gone deep enough? We strive to outdo others, yes. But why? Exhibitionism to attract the opposite sex. In the last analysis, it all comes down to sex."

"I can't see it that way," says Adler slowly. "Actually

I see very little of the Oedipus Complex, the Electra Complex, castration fears, and so on at the bottom of neurotic difficulties. No, sex is by no means our only motivation. It is only one among many—and I don't even believe it is the most important."

"Isn't that perhaps because you have a moral disgust for the idea?"

"I don't think I'm squeamish," smiles Adler. "No, it is simply that it doesn't satisfy me. It doesn't cover the facts. It is plausible and it explains many things—but not all. It is partially true but not wholly true. To maintain that all children harbor an innate love for the parent of the opposite sex and an innate hate for the parent of the same sex, is not borne out by reason and experience. When we find it, it seems to me far more likely that it is fostered by the parents."

"Your theories will prove far less distasteful than mine. You've got hold of a very plausible notion. You should be popular—and you like that."

"Yes, I like to be liked," says Adler. "And I like people. I don't think you do."

Freud shrugs.

"Why should I love my neighbor?"

"Because that is the goal of man—to be a good neighbor to his fellowmen."

"That is ethics, not psychology. Unfortunately, I am merely a scientist—not a theologian."

"You are a man. Being a scientist is only part of being a man."

"I find no evidence in the psyche of any high destiny for man. A man's unconscious is an inferno of unfulfilled desires, too hideous for him to contemplate."

"I find much good there, too—impulses of self-sacrifice, tenderness, the desire to serve, gropings toward ideals. This is the mysterious genius of man, present in no other animal. After all, men do lay down their lives for their brothers—and for ideals, too."

"I think you will be an excellent pedagogue—but scarcely a scientist."

"What significance has life if it is not to make some contribution to humanity?"

"Who says it *has* significance? No, my dear Adler, I cannot go behind the scenes and play God. My work is simply the analysis of the psyche—work enough for one man."

"But you are a doctor of sick minds. It is a doctor's mission to heal. I agree with you that it is our job to acquire as much knowledge of the psyche as possible, but chiefly for the purpose of healing. We must give these troubled souls who come to us a chart to steer by so that they may sail as safely as possible through the rough waters of life to their goal."

"There *is* a goal?"

"There *must* be a goal."

"And what, may I ask, is it?"

"The good of the community."

"You're out of my depth, my dear fellow. I repeat I am not a philosopher, only a humble scientist."

As time went on the difference between the two men became sharper, the quarrel more bitter. Finally they broke completely. Freud continued to develop the revolutionary science of psychoanalysis. Adler went on to build up a totally new psychology, fundamentally different from psychoanalysis though stemming from it. He called it Individual Psychology, meaning *the psychology of the individual.* The cornerstone of that psychology is the inferiority complex.

The psychology of both men is founded on the study of sick minds. While both are primarily contributions to abnormal psychology, both do explain much concerning the behavior and motivations of normal people. But of the two, Adler's theory of the inferiority complex is more readily understandable, more acceptable, and more easily applicable by the layman of his own life and daily problems. It is not an either-or proposition—a case of Freud being right and Adler wrong. It is rather a matter of both being right to a certain degree. Neither system alone explains all human behavior.

Adler placed more emphasis on helping the normal individual to understand himself, to solve his own problems, to regulate his behavior and to achieve his goals. Freud had little confidence that the average human being could or would do anything of the sort. Freud thought and wrote as an intellectual for intellectuals. Adler spent a lifetime simplifying his psychology so that all might comprehend. As an approach to understanding and regulating human conduct, Individual Psychology can be used by the least sophisticated. It holds that the average normal human being can dredge up from childhood memories of inferiorizing situations, of competing for the place of top dog or of the lion's share, of flights from reality into daydreams or books, or withdrawal from the society of others to uncritical solitude and to feelings of resentment for the injustices of those in authority, and of disparagement and inferiority. Adler also pointed out that we all recognize that our activities are unmistakably in pursuit of a goal and that therefore the mind is dynamic, not static and mechanistic. Since it moves, it must be either forward or backward, either from a minus to a plus or from a plus to a minus, always under pressure of an inferiority complex.

An inferiority complex is not necessarily a neurotic symptom, according to its discoverer—and who should know better? It is, on the contrary, standard equipment. To lack such a complex would be abnormal. Ordinarily, therefore, having an inferiority complex is not a matter for the psychiatrist. By and large we can handle it ourselves—in fact, we have to. But there is a certain knowledge and skill to be acquired first.

Adler made all this so simple and so clear that those who held that psychology is for the psychologist accused him of letting science down.

"I have taken forty years to make my psychology simple," Adler replied, "and I might make it even more simple by saying, 'All neurosis is vanity.'"

Adler believed that a grain of common sense is worth a ton of intellectual verbiage. Truth, he held, is not truth unless it can be explained to practically everyone. We all have some ability to run our own lives and can be helped to do so in many ways—by lay therapists and religious teachers, by books and by friends, not only by Viennese psychiatrists.

Right here is where he lost the medical profession and the psychiatrists, who naturally do not believe in a do-it-yourself type of treatment. The psychoanalysts had built up a flourishing practice on the basis of five treatments a week for a minimum of two years at twenty dollars per treatment. Except financially, Adler pointed out, a long cure is no better than a short one. He added that this same charge of oversimplification was also brought against Socrates at his trial. He went right on simplifying things so that even a child could understand.

Many of the more common-sense psychiatrists are today advocating Adler's realistic approach.

"For heaven's sake," they plead, "let's limit our psychiatric services to those who exhibit at least a certain degree of true psychiatric illness. Let us try to persuade people to handle the minor discomforts of living themselves."

To give the man in the street—and even the child in the schoolroom—some knowledge of his own soul and of human conduct and how to regulate it was Adler's aim.

He was the first to offer a psychology that would enable us to evaluate ourselves and others. In this it is more practical than Freud's, which requires the services of a psychiatrist.

It was Adler's contention that if we are to understand ourselves and others, achieve our goals and be reasonably happy, we must:

Admit, first of all, that we have an inferiority complex.

Recognize its symptoms in ourselves and others.

Discover our own inferiority complexes.

Realize that an inferiority complex can be either a liability or an asset.

Learn how to use our inferiority complexes as a springboard to success and happiness.

So suppose we visit Dr. Adler in his old office in New York and question him on some of these points. He is no longer there, of course, having died in 1937. Indeed, he may quite possibly be the psychiatrist to whom, on his arrival at the pearly gates, St. Peter is reported to have said:

"Glad you're here, doctor. Come right in. We're having a little trouble with God. You see, He thinks He's Roosevelt."

CHAPTER II

Just a Minute, Dr. Adler!

HE SITS AT his desk in an office just large enough for his books and the two people usually found there—the doctor and his patient, intimate as conspirators, knee to knee, often smoking like chimneys. Here is no pontifical couch with high priest and human sacrifice. This is rather the meeting of two human beings on a footing of friendly equality, trying to figure out what is wrong with the world in general and one individual in particular.

The doctor himself is a casual sort of fellow, brimming with high spirits and twinkling humor. As he advances to meet you, hand extended, you feel at once that he likes you. Everyone feels at ease with him—the rich and the poor, the proud and the humble, the good and the bad, the sane and the insane. He lacks completely any sense of superiority or inferiority. He does not admit that distinctions of race, religion (he himself is a Jew turned Protestant), wealth, social position, education, birth, age, or sex make a difference in the value of a human being. Before the doctor, as before God, all men are equal. To him the insane are people who have lost their way. Criminals are those who have become confused and are not sufficiently intelligent to resolve their difficulties. So close did he feel

22

himself to these outcasts of society that often, after a few minutes in his presence, a raving manic grew calm, fascinated by being with a person who communicated with the humanity in him.

For children he had an irresistible charm. "Come back and stay forever," the most intractable among them would plead as he left. For him a child could do no wrong.

"If you do not believe in corporal punishment," a mother once asked him, "then what punishment *is* suitable for a child?"

"No punishment is suitable for a child," Adler replied firmly.

It wasn't that he didn't approve of discipline ("If no difficulties exist for a child," he said, "then we must invent them")—he just didn't approve of ignorance.

So extraordinary is his influence with all kinds of people that it seems as though he must be acting on some special principle known only to himself.

As indeed he is.

Alfred Adler was born to be a doctor.

When he was a very small boy, he awoke one morning to find a brother dead in bed beside him. To this terrible experience he reacted in character with the man he was to become. He decided to be a doctor so that he might fight death.

Early in his medical career, Adler stumbled upon a sequence of phenomena which was to lead to his becoming one of the greatest discoverers of facts concerning the human mind who has ever lived. Poking into the chinks and crannies of cadavers, he noted certain conditions which had never before attracted any particular attention. He discovered a heart enlarged to three times its normal size and noted that the obstruction of a valve had prevented blood from reaching the lungs in sufficient quantities. Had the heart perhaps increased in size in order to make up this deficiency?

In a body from which one diseased kidney had been removed, he noted that the other kidney was considerably larger than normal. Why? Could it be that it had increased its activity in order to do the work of the missing kidney?

Where one lung was weakened by injury or disease he might find that the other had developed supernormal power. Wasn't it logical to suppose that it was endeavoring to make up for the lost efficiency of the other?

Or he would find a heart with a leaky valve, and the muscles of this heart would be unusually large. In order to help the heart pump the normal amount of blood?

Upon broken bones he remarked that heavy callous bone had formed. Was this to make the bone stronger than before?

These phenomena, he decided, occurred too often to be mere accident or coincidence. They happened so regularly as to make it appear that the body had a law of its own: to replace a minus with a plus in its blind instinct for self-preservation.

Now he grew excited. He decided to push his searches further. He would investigate living organisms and see if this rule held good there, too. It was common observation that when a man had lost one arm, the other arm often assumed athletic proportions; if he had lost both legs, his arms and torso frequently became unusually powerful, more powerful than they otherwise would have been. In such cases, not blind nature alone but the central nervous system had played a part.

Following up this lead, Adler, who was an eye specialist, began visiting art school's and testing the eyesight of the students. As much to his surprise as theirs, he soon discovered that over seventy per cent of them had more or less serious deficiencies of sight. Why, he wondered, had they elected to build a career around a defective organ? Poking back into their childhood, he discovered that as children they had sensed their inadequacy and had made a special effort to see as well as, or better than, others. They had trained their sight, their observation, their pleasure in seeing to the point where they took a more than average interest in the visual world.

Adler now dug into the biographies of the great artists of the past and discovered that many of them had suffered from deficiencies of sight—that Albrecht Dürer squinted, Matejko was myopic, and Adolph von Menzel so short-sighted that he was forced to bring his canvas to within a few inches of his eyes; that Manet and El Greco had severe astigmatisms and von Lenbach only one eye. Naturally it takes more than poor eyesight to make an artist and of course there can be no doubt that for an artist good eyesight is preferable to poor. The curious thing was that so many individuals with poor eyesight had elected to become artists. Was this perhaps the same law at work that he had observed in his dissections: that nature endeavors to compensate for a bodily deficiency?

He went on to study the blind and confirmed that their hearing, touch, and smell were unusually keen. He examined deaf-mutes and attested that their powers of observation were far above the average. Then he inquired into the lives of gifted individuals of the past. The fresh observation and visual imagination of such creative writers as Goethe, Schiller, Milton, Gustav Freytag, Jules Verne, and so on, would seem to have had a very definite connection with their defective eyesight, and the aural deficiencies of such musicians as Bruckner, Franz, Mozart, Smetana, Dvoràk, and Beethoven seemed at least in part to account for their extraordinary intentness on the beauty of sound.

Beethoven was a startling example. Afflicted from childhood with an organic hearing deficiency, at twenty-eight he was already quite deaf. From then on he grew steadily in power, his genius keeping pace with his increasing deafness—and with nothing else. Four years later he could just barely hear a full orchestra with the aid of an ear trumpet. That was the year he composed his incomparable *Second Symphony*, only to be surpassed, as his deafness reached totality, by his *Eroica*, his *Moonlight Sonata*, his *Fifth Symphony* and finally, when he had been almost completely deaf for twenty-five years, his *Ninth Symphony*, one of the most glorious ever written. To have composed the *Ninth Symphony* and never to have heard it—that was the fate of the greatest deaf man and the greatest musician who ever lived. Since he could scarcely have been greater, it would appear he could only have been less great had he not been deaf.

Adler, in his investigations, had passed imperceptibly from biology to neurology and from neurology to psychology—from compensation for organic deficiencies on a biological level to compensation for bodily defects on a psychological level. But so far the types of compensation he had noted had all been made unconsciously. The human will had played no part.

He now began investigating less obvious cases. There was the famous neurologist who, following a stroke, had been paralyzed on one side of his body and rendered speechless. One day he wrote on a slate, "I *will* recover. I *will* walk. I *will* speak." Like a child he had learned to walk, a step at a time. He had learned to talk, a word at a time. In the end he was as good a man as he had ever been.

"I *will* recover." On that an uninjured area of the cortex had taken over and learned to perform the task the injured area could no longer carry out.

Pasteur had done the same. With the speech areas

of his brain destroyed by a stroke, he had slowly and painfully fought his way back to speech, by a powerful effort of the will developing new speech centers in the brain.

There could be no doubt that such recoveries as these were accomplished through an effort of the will. A man who did not make this effort would lie forever paralyzed and speechless.

Now let us go a little further, thought Adler. Let us examine some of the great figures of the past and see if any part of their greatness can be traced to a conscious compensation for a deficiency. What of Demosthenes?

As a boy Demosthenes had a marked shortness of breath, a feeble voice, and a terrific stutter. So naturally he wanted to be an orator. He not only wanted to be—he was determined to be.

He began training himself by running up hills, declaiming all the way; by standing on the seashore, his mouth full of pebbles, and shouting down the roar; by posing before a mirror and reciting the great Greek tragedies, complete with gestures.

Dissatisfied with his progress, he retired to a cellar and shaved one side of his head to make sure he wouldn't emerge until he had accomplished his purpose. Eight times, with only brief interludes for sleep and meals, he copied in their entirety the eight volumes of Thucydides' history of the Peloponnesian Wars in order to improve his style. He hired the foremost actors of the day to train him in voice production, diction, delivery, gesture, poise.

At twenty-eight he emerged from his enforced retirement to compete for the Athenian alm of eloquence, which he won handily. He went on to defeat every great orator in an age of great orators. For two thousand years orators have been compared to him, always unfavorably. In his own day it was written:

"He is a torrent which sweeps everything before it. We can neither criticize nor admire because we have not the command of our faculties."

This, thought Adler, was surely an *I will*. Demosthenes owed a part of his greatness at least to an initial handicap.

Continuing his investigations, he turned up hundreds of similar cases—famous strong men who had been weaklings in their youth, record-breaking milers who had been cripples, prima ballerinas who had had polio, great singers who had been consumptives. Struggling desperately to overcome their disability, they had developed a superior ability. This was not blind nature at work—this was the human will.

It began to look—it really did—as though this were some sort of law, as though human beings often accomplished what they did because of an initial disability, as though humanity needed a hurdle in order to jump—and that the higher the hurdle, the bigger the jump. This idea of a psychological compensation was a long way from the biological compensation with which he had started. Adler had at last put his finger on the exact point at which a purely physical fact is transformed into a psychic fact. This discovery of the psychic axis threw a brilliant new light on the whole field of psychology. But the discoveries which were to give an overriding importance to Adler's system of psychology were still to come.

So far he had demonstrated only that human beings tend to compensate for physical disabilities, sometimes consciously, sometimes unconsciously. He had not shown that *psychological* disabilities may likewise impel a person to compensate.

Now he took a long, hard look at the human race.

From the first day it draws breath right on through its entire childhood, the child is a helpless specimen of humanity—and he knows it. Compared to the adults around him, he is the very embodiment of insufficiency. He experiences a deep feeling of insecurity. Not only is he born inferior to others but every day the list of his inferiorities grows. He can do nothing that those around him can do. He cannot stand, walk, warm or feed himself—he can only yell. He knows what he wants long before he can get it. This is not conducive to a feeling of self-confidence. The desire to be on a par with others or even to outstrip them is born in him and becomes a paramount force in shaping his character. This state of dependency continues until he is an adult ready to support himself. A sense of his inferiority, physical and psychological, is thus firmly established in his ego.

Freud believed that every child is born to sin; Adler that it is born to a sense of inferiority. It is difficult to deny the first; impossible to deny the second.

What is true of the individual is true of the race. How could it be otherwise? Man is among the weakest of animals, lacking the strength, the speed, the fang, the claw that enables other animals to survive. As an animal he is *inferior* to other animals. Therein lies his strength. Because of it he forged the most powerful weapon possessed by any animal. Out of his sense of inferiority developed the greatest phenomenon in nature—the human brain. The race, like the individual, owes its survival to an initial inferiority.

Man alone of all the animals is conscious of his own inadequacy. He alone has an inferiority complex. He alone attempts to compensate for it.

That is why he is man.

Thus Adler reasoned from organ inferiorities to a system of psychology based on the inferiority complex.

This is no minor theory of a minor psychiatrist. It is one of the most important contributions to the understanding of human nature ever made. As we watch Adler developing his psychology, we will see that in some ways he goes beyond Freud, beyond Jung, beyond any of the men of our own day. He envisioned for man a higher destiny, a more immense horizon than did any of the others. Freud looked upon man *as he is*—and found him pitiful. Adler looked upon man as he could be—and found him inspiring. True, as Freud pointed out, Adler took flight from psychiatry to invade the realms of pedagogy, philosophy, ethics, even religion, where Freud refused to go. For what, Freud very logically asked, have ethics and religion to do with the science of psychiatry more than with astronomy?

But Adler obstinately continued to follow his own nose and, as we shall see, it led him from the first casual observation that an enlarged heart may be nature's way of compensating for a leaky valve to the proposition that all human beings harbor a sense of inferiority based on physical or psychological inadequacies for which they endeavor to compensate. To understand the role of the inferiority complex in human affairs, suppose we now take that chair opposite Adler's and ask him first—well, why people so often refuse to admit that they have an inferiority complex.

"Because," smiles Adler, "it is every human being's fond hope, if not his unalterable conviction, that there is nothing inferior about him. Yet an inferiority complex is as much standard equipment as a nose. We are born inferior. We are inferior to our parents, to our older brothers and sisters, to our nurse. We couldn't survive a day without some superior power saving our lives at every turn. All through life we continue to acquire superiors— teachers, playmates, fellow students, bosses—all those who surpass us at work or at play. If a person says, 'Far from having an inferiority complex, I have a superiority complex,' you may be sure he has an unusually strong feeling of inferiority. These are not two different complexes but two sides of the same complex.

"Another reason for denying we have an inferiority complex is that very often we are unaware of it. It is so painful that we have thrust it deep down into the unconscious. Even though their success and happiness may depend upon it, many people cannot bring themselves to admit an inferiority complex, even to themselves."

"You consider this complex to be the motivation for the greater part of human activity, just as Freud believed that the sexual instinct was, don't you?"

Something that might almost be called a dimple flickers at the corner of his mouth.

"Sex is certainly one of the most powerful instinctual drives. I would merely say that it is not my favorite complex. Self-preservation is an equally strong instinct. The struggle for life and the survival of the fittest implies the destruction of the unfit—the inferior. But what most people do not understand is that the inferiority complex, far from being a liability, is one of our most valuable possessions. For a person not to know that he has an inferiority complex, and how to use it, is like going through life in poverty, not knowing that someone has left you a million dollars."

"These feelings of inferiority may be due to many things, even imaginary defects, may they not?"

"To *absolutely anything*. What makes one man feel inferior may make another feel superior—a brilliant wife, for example, or inherited wealth, or a large family. The *fact* is nothing; our attitude toward it is everything."

"Although the causes are infinite, for the sake of simplicity we may classify them under four main headings—physical, intellectual, moral and social—or, broadly, complexes relating to our bodies, to our work, to love and marriage, and to the community. Does this seem like oversimplification? If I speak in a way that everyone can understand, you must realize that it has taken me a lifetime to learn to do so. It would be very easy to say these things so that only my fellow psychiatrists could understand them."

"Take the physical category. Our egos cannot tolerate the slightest physical blemish. History affords thousands of examples of men scourged to greatness by some physical defect, often quite minor. Rostand's play, *Cyrano,* is based on the intolerable sense of inferiority of a truly heroic man because of a grotesque nose. No more than actual deformity can a man bear to be puny or undersized. Bonaparte may very well have become Napolean because of his small stature. Being a little man, he was driven to prove he was a big one. Nietzsche was sickly, and as a compensation he developed his superman philosophy—the deification of the strong man, the 'master race,' the tyrant, what he called 'the lords of earth,' by whom he meant those who have not been enfeebled by Jewish and Christian ideals. He relegates to a quiet and humble domesticity and obscurity those whom he calls 'the herd people,' the meek and poor in spirit. Napoleon was his hero. No doubt a Mussolini or a Hitler would have been today. As for actual deformity, it is not farfetched to say that the first World War was precipitated by the withered arm of an egomaniac, Kaiser Wilhelm.

"In the intellectual category the sense of inferiority is often due to a lack of education, which has goaded many men to extraordinary achievement. Not only did some of the greatest men who have ever lived have no schooling but many of them actually were dullards at school. Charlemagne couldn't learn to read or write. Napoleon graduated forty-second in his class. Of Hegel, the great German philosopher, it was said at the university, 'He was of middling industry and knowledge but especially deficient in philosophy.' Schiller was constantly being hauled on the carpet because of his low scholastic grades. One of Oliver

Goldsmith's teachers reported that he was one of the dullest boys she'd ever taught, and a special tutor hired to jack him up in his studies pronounced him not only ignorant but stupid. James Russell Lowell was forever being reprimanded at Harvard because of his unsatisfactory marks. President Wilson had a low academic standing at Princeton.

"Not all of this can be laid to the nonconformity of genius. A lot of great men just don't seem to have been very bright in their youth. It needed the spur of a burning sense of inferiority to rouse them to action. And when it came—!

"Take Newton. For two years he attended the grammar school at Grantham without making any impression as a brain, without causing a single headmaster's eyebrow to rise a hairbreadth. Indeed, for a long time he balanced precariously on the brink of failure. Then one day he was doubled up by a blow in the solar plexus from the school bully. He could not retaliate, he could only brood. And all his brooding led to one conclusion: he must in some way show himself the superior of the bully. Difficult, since the bully not only reigned supreme in the schoolyard but in the classroom, as far ahead of him in his studies as in physical prowess.

"But here at least he had a chance. He began to study, slowly passing his classmates until only the bully outranked him. In the end he passed even him. That was Isaac's start as an Intellect. He went on to become one of the greatest mathematicians and philosophers who has ever lived. His contributions to science have been called 'pre-eminent above all the other productions of the human intellect.' "

"You have made a study of great men to discover their inferiority complexes and how they compensated for them, haven't you, Dr. Adler?"

"I recommend the reading of biography and especially of autobiography to anyone who is interested in the dynamics of the inferiority complex. From this point of view biography becomes utterly fascinating. The self-portraits of great artists are equally revealing. Botticelli was an invalid from his early youth yet in his self-portraits he painted himself, not as he was, but as he wished to be—a swashbuckling young Florentine who could stand up to any of the swaggering, handsome young Medicis. Artists were always painting themselves into great religious pictures, idealizing and romanticising themselves. Dürer used himself as a model for the head of Christ. All this is self-aggrandizement to cover up a feeling of inferiority.

"The other way of betraying an inferiority complex is by self-derogation. No man can tell the truth about himself, try as he will. Rousseau, brutally outspoken, shockingly frank, completely distorted the picture of himself in his *Confessions* by dwelling on his vices. It was probably also very enjoyable—like living them all over again.

"The reading of biography, especially for the layman, who has not the psychiatrist's opportunities for delving into the soul, gives a real understanding of the inferiority complex at work. Take the case of Leonardo da Vinci.

"At first it might appear that there is no flaw in this luminous personality, no chink in this shining armor, no crevice for the smallest inferiority complex to hide in. Here is a man who can be anything he desires—painter, sculptor, architect, musician, mechanician, mathematician, scientist, engineer, philosopher. He was among the best of his era—one of the most brilliant civilization has produced—in all of these fields, among the best of all time in some of them.

"Science? He knew long in advance what Bacon, Galileo, Newton, Harvey would one day discover, and set him-

self problems which scientists ever since have been endeavoring to solve.

"Inventions? It would take a museum to house them—
aerial bombs, two-level city highways, helicopters, machine guns, air conditioning, and so on.

"Art? He painted—and this was perhaps not his finest
achievement—some of the greatest pictures ever created,
among them the "Mona Lisa" and the "Last Supper."

"He possessed in addition so many great qualities of
heart and mind, such extraordinary beauty, such winning
charm, so many unsurpassed social gifts and accomplishments, that 'unbelievable' was the word most frequently
applied to him. It still is.

"Where in such a man is there room for an inferiority
complex? One looks in vain—until at last one comes upon
it in his bastardy.

"There is no more terrible word in the language to a
proud nature. It is in every man's eyes and on many men's
tongues. Nothing can ever wipe it out. It has led men to
the gallows and to the throne. Without this goad, it is
doubtful that da Vinci would have risen to the heights he
did.

"It was Robert Burton who wrote—I think I can quote
him correctly: 'Almost in every kingdom the most ancient
families have been at first princes' bastards, their worthi-
est captains, best wits, greatest scholars, bravest spirits in
all our annals have been base born.' There you have the
sense of shame that drove Erasmus to become the Prince
of the Renaissance; that spurred the Bastard of Normandy
to become William the Conqueror; that made the Bastard
of Orleans, victor over the English under Joan of Arc,
one of the most brilliant soldiers France has ever produced.

"Bastardy comes under the heading of a social inferiority complex. For an example of a moral inferiority com-

plex at work, take a man like Robert Burns. Burns made a fetish of the purity of womanhood. Why? Because he was a rake. Rousseau wrote his most famous books on the moral training and the education of children—he abandoned his own on the doorsteps of foundling hospitals. Wordsworth, one of the severest moralists in all English poetry, had behind him a youth of sexual debauchery. Bunyan, a terrific young rake, became a terrific old moralist. Hypocrisy, fanaticism, bigotry, self-righteousness, the holier-than-thou attitude—these are the compensations for a sense of moral guilt.

"Read the lives of the saints. Frequently the bigger the sinner, the greater the saint. Loyola, Assisi, St. Augustine, St. Paul—what sinners, what saints!

"When you find an individual overrating or underrating a particular moral quality, be sure that is his Achilles' heel. In all his work, Edgar Allan Poe deifies the human will. 'Man doth not yield himself to the angels nor unto death utterly save through the weakness of his feeble will,' he quotes. Yet he himself was the weakest of men and a confirmed drunkard. Henley, the man who wrote in his magnificent 'Invictus,' 'I am the master of my fate; I am the captain of my soul,' drew from his friends the jeer, 'The hell you are!' "

"You believe, Dr. Adler, that most of us have more than one inferiority complex?"

"Naturally, since we are inferior in so many respects. I know of no more extraordinary example of this than Lord Byron. In every one of the four categories I've mentioned—physical, intellectual, social, moral—he had one or more complexes.

"Take the physical. He was so handsome that he was constantly compared to the Apollo Belvedere. Charles Mathews said of him, 'He is the only man to whom I could apply the word *beautiful.*' And Coleridge wrote, 'If you

had seen him you could scarcely believe him. His eyes
were the open portals of the sun—things of light and for
light.' . . . *But he had a clubfoot!* To compensate for this
disability, he became an outstanding athlete, a masterly
horseman, a dead shot, the greatest swimmer of his day,
finally accomplishing his famous feat of swimming the
Hellespont.

"Intellectually he was a genius . . . Yet in life his
countrymen rejected his poetry and in death they refused
him burial in Westminster Abbey, even so much as a bust
in Poets' Corner. To compensate for this treatment Byron
made himself the leader of a whole continent of poets.
'The English may think of Byron as they please,' said
Goethe, 'but this is certain, that they show no poet to
compare with him.'

"Socially he was of noble birth. There at least you would
have thought he'd feel secure. Not at all. He was so
hypersensitive to social slights that the inadvertent failure
of a host to bid him good night could bring on a fit of
melancholy. Finally, a social outcast in his own country,
he escaped to Europe and, by his brilliance, beauty, and
charm, placed a whole continent at his feet.

"Morally he showed a complete lack of desire to conform to any code of morals but his own. Wild passions,
youthful excesses, a year of marriage ending in a disgraceful divorce, an endless succession of mistresses, rumors
of incest—all this was the fabric of his life. Having exiled
himself from England (on the ground that if reports of
him were true he was unfit for England; if false, England
was unfit for him) he took up the cause of Greek freedom,
became a Greek patriot, fought for Greek liberty, and died
with the words on his lips, 'Follow me, men! Don't be
afraid! Follow me!' Devotion to Greek patriotism, love
of truth, kindness to the unfortunate—these were his compensations for his sexual immorality."

"You have sometimes referred to your own feelings of inferiority, Dr. Adler. What of that?"

"Naturally I have inferiority complexes, being a member of the human race. First, I am a Jew—and it would be difficult for a Jew not to have inferiority feelings in the world today, or in any day for that matter. For centuries the Jews have been a rejected people. I once heard a Jewish prayer—'Oh God, we have been Thy Chosen People for so long, now please choose someone else!' It is this rejection that has made them a strong people.

"Then again, I was a younger son. Nothing is more calculated to arouse a feeling of inferiority than an older brother, always a little taller, always a little stronger, always smarter, always a class ahead—the first born, the head of the nursery. No matter how I tried, I could never catch up with him. He was always ahead of me—he still is ahead of me. To the lifelong effort to pass him, I owe whatever success I may have had.

"It is not the complex that counts, it is our reaction to it. That is what determines our success or failure. Being a psychiatrist, I am chiefly interested in those who fail. Those who succeed are the individuals who face their inadequacies honestly and try courageously to overcome them. The failures are those who grow discouraged and early withdraw from the struggle. At the bottom of every neurosis is an inferiority complex, the result of an attempt at compensation that has not entirely succeeded.

"Although I have never seen a single case of neurosis that did not have its origin in an inferiority complex, normal human beings also have painful feelings of inferiority. A sense of inferiority is the normal state of man. The dynamics of psychic life, based on these complexes, are the same for both.

"The person who fails in life, equally with the person who succeeds, is trying to compensate. Of the two, he is probably working the harder at it. The neurotic, the psychotic, the criminal, the pervert, the prostitute, the drug addict, the alcoholic, all have the same ultimate goal as the saint—absolute individual superiority, the attainment of godlike power. Only in insanity does anyone ever achieve it. In our insane asylums are many God Almighties, Jesus Christs, Jehovahs, Mohammeds, and, among those who do not aim quite so high, Napoleons, Dalai Lamas, emperors of America or China. Once a man takes seriously the goal of godlikeness, when nothing less will satisfy him, he is compelled to flee reality. Nietzsche, when he became insane, signed himself *The Crucified.* To what else could the doctrine of the superman lead?

"What we have here—and in dictators and business tycoons—is *over*-compensation. The natural desire to excel has become the Nietzschean 'will to power.' The aggressive drives are necessary to survival, yes, but they cannot, as with a Napoleon or a Mussolini, be allowed to ride roughshod over mankind. In dictators, in all ruthlessly successful men, the twin goals of superiority and power eventually dominate all their thinking and are pursued with ever increasing violence. Gradually they lose the sense of reality. They become exclusively occupied with their personal triumphs and the impression they create. Individuals, even great masses of human beings, appear unimportant to them; they think of them as pawns, to be used for their own ends. Finally, completely controlled by these drives, their state of psychic tension reaches a point where they are no longer normal—if they ever were. They have made their world over to conform to their own requirements.

"Crime is invariably the result of a strong feeling of inferiority. The great creative writers have always understood this, from Euripides to Dostoyevsky. Long before we psychiatrists were around they intuitively employed it as motivation, though they never called it an inferiority complex. If I had never read the Bible, I would still understand something about Cain, once I learned he was the first-born of two sons. For a while he was the only baby on earth, just as every first-born feels *he* is—unique in the universe, the center about which it revolves. Suddenly—an intruder. When Abel appeared on the scene, Cain suffered a psychic trauma from which he never recovered. He became moody and sullen. Even God favored his younger brother. There was only one way to re-establish himself in his rightful position in the world. He must get rid of Abel. When he'd killed him, God set the mark of a murderer on his brow. Once again he was—unique.

"That is how most murderers feel—unique. The criminal has an overwhelming inferiority complex for which he is too weak, too stupid, and too discouraged to compensate constructively. Instead he blames his environment for his difficulties and builds up a shoddy superiority complex by defying authority. This, he feels, proves him to be exceptional. 'Few men would dare to do what I do,' he thinks. 'I am strong. I can kill. I am clever because I can break the law and escape it. How many men can do that?' Yet at the bottom of his soul he knows that he is an outcast from society. That is why criminals so often welcome capture and death.

"No human being can long tolerate a feeling of inferiority without being thrown into a state of psychic tension. Criminals and psychotics are reacting in a violently negative way to an inferiority complex. But there are also those who react in a timidly negative way, and these are the run-of-the-mill failures.

"Frequently if an individual believes he cannot improve the situation, he will attempt to *appear* superior by such devices as boasting, alibi-ing, assuming airs of importance, posing, pretending, bullying, and otherwise inflating his ego. Many people care more about the impression they create than about the actuality. In any large organization the 'big shots' contend among themselves for the biggest office, the biggest yacht, the biggest country estate. President Wilson described this attitude perfectly when he said, 'I've brought a lot of men to Washington and some of them grow but most of them merely swell.'

"The failure in life, instead of pressing forward, vacillates, stands still, or retreats. His strategy is to achieve a feeling of superiority without improving either himself or the situation. Naturally the painful sense of inferiority remains, always provoked by the same conditions, and a permanent undercurrent of neurotic feelings and behavior results. This is the true pathological inferiority complex. On his way to failure, he gradually narrows his field of action and becomes more occupied with avoiding defeat than in pursuing success. Totally unlike Napoleon, he is incapable of saying, 'I make circumstances.' "

"It's easy to see that failure is due to inferiority feelings, Dr. Adler, but most people would find it difficult to believe that success is."

"The whole theory of the inferiority complex is so obvious that I never cease to wonder that it wasn't always known, leaving nothing for me to discover. Discover? Can one be said to discover the nose on one's face? I discovered nothing. I merely called attention to it. Almost at once everyone recognized that it was true. Success and failure are merely two different reactions to the same thing. The successful person sets about ridding himself of his feelings of inferiority by the only direct, realistic, and satisfactory method there is—improving himself and the situation. No one ever reaches his goal of total superiority. Our interest in living derives chiefly from our uncertainty as to the outcome. The nearest humanity ever comes to this goal is in the genius—and there never was a genius who wasn't riddled with inferiority complexes. In his struggle to rid himself of them, he contributes more to mankind than any other class of human beings."

"Does anyone ever completely overcome his inferiority feelings?"

"Never! What would keep us going? But we can recover to a great extent and can lessen the pain of them. We can get over feeling self-conscious when we enter a roomful of people or address an audience. We can come to feel at ease with people or in situations which formerly made us uncomfortable. But we can never, this side of insanity, rid ourselves of every shred of inferiority feelings."

"If a person is honestly convinced he has no inferiority complexes, what should he do?"

"Dig one up. Being human, he certainly has one, and if he's not too far gone in neurosis, he can generally unearth it. I don't say everyone, always, without help. I do say most normal individuals usually can. I am not one to believe that practically everyone is neurotic. I am more inclined to believe that many even of the insane are more or less normal. In normal people the cause of the feeling of inferiority is usually close enough to the surface for them to discover it themselves. The neurotic will need help. With him the situation in the past which produced the complex has been so painful that it has been thrust deep into the unconscious. The last thing in the world the neurotic wants is to get over being neurotic. He has, at considerable pains, devised a strategy admirably adapted to getting what he wants. Why should he abandon it? He dare not, he *cannot,* admit his inferiority. But the normal person will, once convinced it is better to fight it in the open rather than in the dark, endeavor to unearth it. There are three major classes of problems in life which we must all solve—those connected with work, with love and marriage, and with society. It is in one of these three spheres we must look for the cause of inferiority feelings."

"Your theory of compensation for an inferiority complex has been called the most important key yet found to understanding normal people."

"It seems to me to illuminate large areas of human conduct. It is the source of all improvements in social conditions, in culture, even in science, which is man's attempt to throw off his weakness and to control his fate. I don't see how it would have been possible for man to develop a soul without it.

"It is the basis of my psychology that we can compensate for our deficiencies in all four categories and thus transform a minus of our nature into a plus. I believe it is to this universal ability to compensate for his weaknesses that man owes his unique human character, his survival, and his hope for the future."

This is Adler's psychology. Does it appeal to you? Does it fit in with what you already know of the nature of others? If so, you will no doubt want to know how it fits in with your own, how it explains you as a person, how it can help you to transform a minus in your life into a plus.

But first you will need to discover just what your inferiority complexes—if any—are. So suppose we look you over in a bright light to see just what inferiority complexes you may have come down with, all unknown to yourself.

CHAPTER III

What Are Your Symptoms?

THE WINDSHIELD OF the car streams with rain; her face streams with tears. From Philadelphia to Trenton she sits numb and dazed. From Trenton to New York she sobs continuously and loudly. The man beside her, driving, her dancing partner, makes no effort to comfort her.

She has just been thrown out of the biggest job she's ever had—the choreography for a big Broadway musical. It was her own fault. She had failed . . . why had she failed?

Because—

Because she was incapable of asserting herself. Because she couldn't shout, "Clear the hall!" Because she hadn't the courage to refuse dancers who couldn't dance, costumes that couldn't be danced in, and stages that couldn't be danced on. She couldn't even stand up to a bleached-blonde chorine posing a Petty-girl leg at her, smiling maddeningly, and tell her to go get lost.

But why? What was the *cause* of that dreadful docility? She went back in memory, far back into her childhood. Father . . . Her adored father, the famous William

44

de Mille, author of countless Broadway successes. As a child she had lived to earn his favor. He told her what to read—she read it. He told her what not to read—as of today she hadn't read it. He ordered her to write—she wrote. He sang—she accompanied him. He played brilliant tennis—she took tennis lessons. He was a superb photographer—she studied photography. He talked—she listened. His wit, his charm, his genius made poor Uncle Cecil, clambering over sphinxes, directing his spectaculars in his riding breeches and boots, seem a pretty drab character by comparison.

And Mother . . . Even Father didn't dare to oppose Mother. She ruled with a moonbeam—a smile, a nod, a glance. Mother was always right. Anyone who went against her invariably turned out to be wrong. When she and her sister were well on in their teens, Mother still dressed them for parties, arranging their hair to suit herself, though it seldom suited them.

A soul-racking sob.

"Why didn't I disobey Mother?" she cried inwardly. Not once, after the age of ten, could she remember disobeying her in the smallest matter. Every time she had said *yes* when she meant *no,* she was preparing for the day she would go down limply before Norman Bel Geddes. Every time she had let Mother choose her hair ribbon, she had made it impossible to throw the bloody costumes back in the teeth of the costumer. To this day she was the obedient child. She was framed for failure.

She had reached the storm center of her grief. Suddenly she was still. Now she knew. Now she understood *why* she had failed—and in that stillness she solemnly resolved that, so help her, she would cease to be a child and become a person in her own right.

From that day she began to unlearn her submissiveness. She severed the umbilical cord. She threw her childhood out of the window. Every break with authority increased her self-confidence. It took over a decade before she could shout, "Clear the hall!" but today she can trample a costume under foot or rock a producer back on his heels with a curare-tipped compliment.

Thus did one girl, Agnes de Mille, whom you know as the choreographer for *Oklahoma! Tally-Ho! Fall River Legend, Rodeo, Carousel, Three Virgins and a Devil, Bloomer Girl, One Touch of Venus,* discover one of her inferiority complexes (we shall see that she had many) and digging deep into the past, unearth its beginnings.

You think it is difficult? I know it is difficult. It is so painful that few will undertake it until, like Agnes de Mille, they are face to face with failure. Then only will we ask ourselves, "*Why* did I fail? What is there in me that accounts for this catastrophe?"

Only a ruthless tracking down of symptoms, tracing them back into childhood to discover their genesis, will give us the answer. I suggest for this purpose the technique of the famous Professor Bryng Bryngelson of the University of Minnesota who does a psychological striptease act that would put Gypsy Rose Lee to shame.

Professor Bryngelson is Director of Speech Pathology and Professor of Speech at the university. His classes (clinics would be a better word) are attended by students (patients) with speech defects, usually a neurotic symptom due to, or conducive to, an inferiority complex. Each term, at an early session (autopsy), Bryngelson stands up in the classroom (operating theater) and pulls himself apart, complex by complex, till he stands unashamed before them, a man stripped of every rag of psychological camouflage. Thus does the professor (surgeon) establish an atmosphere of scientific objectivity and give his patients an example of what they must do to be saved.

Then, one after the other, he calls upon them to do

the same. None has ever refused . . . You at least can undress your psyche in the privacy of your own room.

It is the simplest thing in the world to recognize the symptoms of an inferiority complex in others; it is almost impossibly difficult to recognize them in ourselves. Had we watched Agnes de Mille at rehearsals we would have seen at once that her failure was due to timidity, lack of self-confidence, deference to authority, the desire to please, the inability to stand on her rights—all those qualities which mark the "good child." But when we ourselves are defeated by these same qualities we are apt to think of them, not as the marks of a subordinate nature, but as amiability and co-operativeness.

We know exactly what it reveals when we hear Elsa Maxwell say, "I have a standing invitation to be the guest at the most magnificent places on the Côte d'Azur. At one typical affair there were the Duke and Duchess of Windsor, Clark Gable, Tyrone Power, Lord Milford-Haven . . . I was on first-name terms not only with kings but with statesmen . . . The greatest artists of our day have performed at my parties without charge."

But do we realize what we are betraying about ourselves when we refer to celebrities whom we have barely met as "Kit" (Katharine Cornell), "Bart" (Herbert Marshall), and "Doug" (Douglas Fairbanks, Jr.), or when we casually mention a castle in England or a swimming pool in Beverly Hills where we have been entertained, or when our conversation drips with famous names, oozes foreign phrases, and leaks anecdotes culled on our foreign travels?

We have no difficulty in diagnosing the case of others who indulge in such antics as these as a galloping inferiority complex for which they are all too obviously attempting to compensate by boasting. But have you never caught yourself edging into a group of celebrities at a cocktail party, feeling resentful of someone obviously your inferior in charm or importance who was being made much of while you went unnoticed or mentioning, apropos of nothing, that you were to play golf with the chairman of the board next Tuesday? Of course you have! We all have. We just didn't know that this sort of thing was symptomatic of a feeling of social inferiority. We are so mercifully blind to our own shortcomings, so mercilessly aware of those of others!

Boasting, equally with self-deprecation, arrogance, equally with humility, bullying, equally with timidity, talkativeness, equally with tongue-tied silence—all betray a sense of inferiority. We recognize shyness as a mark of a feeling of inferiority, but do we realize that excessive aggressiveness is also? We concede that hostility indicates a sense of inferiority, but are we aware that extreme amicability may too? The chap of whom it was said, "No one could love anyone as much as Bill loves everyone," is overcompensating for a feeling of social rejection which the man who eats alone every evening in an automat is quietly accepting.

Oversensitivity to social slights is a symptom which afflicts those in high places equally with those in low. The woman who was almost queen of England gave as her reasons for wishing to write her autobiography the desire to prove that she was born "on the right side of the tracks" and her conviction that she had been very shabbily treated in being refused permission to be addressed as "Her Royal Highness." How, if the Duchess of Windsor can feel so affronted, can the rest of womankind escape an occasional twinge of social inferiority? This feeling betrays itself in many ways and seeks many types of compensation.

One evening some years ago an excessively pretty woman entered the gaming rooms at Monte Carlo on the arm of Gordon Selfridge, English multimillionaire, her diamonds increasing by several thousand watts the candle-power of the room. She marched straight to the table where the Aga Khan, ex-King Manuel of Portugal and Prince Esterházy of Hungary were playing *chemin de fer* for unlimited stakes. She played against them and consistently won. At last the King and the Aga Khan, wishing to retain a part at least of their rapidly dwindling fortunes, dropped out. Only the Prince remained.

By this time the table was surrounded by a hushed crowd. Everyone sensed that this was a duel in which more than money was at stake. Finally, when the lady had more than 10 million francs piled up before her (in the days when a franc was really a franc, not the price of a postage stamp) the Prince rose and bowed. The lady swept up her winnings and turned to face the crowd.

"I won't say I'm sorry," she announced. "On the contrary, I'm delighted to have cleaned out the great Prince Esterházy." She rose and looked straight at him. "My grandfather was a serf on his estate and was often whipped by his overseer."

Thus did Jenny Dolly, of the famous Dolly sisters, reveal her galling sense of social inferiority—and take revenge for it . . . Who among us has not at some time felt this overwhelming desire to humble those who have humbled us? Revenge is the natural and almost universal reaction to inferiorization. Feeling this desire, we should recognize that the cause is a lurking sense of inferiority.

Now what would you say was the inferiority complex of a man who, from youth to old age, makes a career of the conquests of women, up to and including the most coveted woman of his day, the adored Eleonora Duse, and who constantly brags of these conquests, not only at his club but in the public press, relating the details of their suicide, their retirement to a convent, or confinement to a mad-house when he left them?

Wouldn't you say that here is a man driven to prove his virility over and over again?

And if this same man must play Caesar as well as Don Juan—go to war when he is over fifty; raise an army, conquer Fiume, and rule over it as almost-king; erect a monument to himself before his death; court death on every occasion, always with a suspicious lack of success—and talk, talk, talk about it?

Wouldn't you say that this is a man who must demonstrate his courage at every moment, and first of all to himself?

You wouldn't be surprised to hear then that this D'Annunzio was a miniature man, only 5 feet, 3 inches tall, who eternally sought reassurance of his manhood because of his inferior physique.

When we read in the papers, as we did some years ago, that a little Austrian sergeant named Hitler, an untrained military man and a bad soldier, risen to be the head of an army and of a nation, screams at a general staff meeting, "I demand that my generals, just as ordinary soldiers, carry out every one of my orders with instantaneous, blind, and unquestioning obedience!" we have no difficulty in diagnosing his case as a chronic malignant inferiority complex. But do we recognize our own will to dominate in the home, at the office, in society, as symptomatic of the same thing? Not at all. We regard it as the mere rightful exercise of authority or the expression of superior judgment.

A man may go through life haunted by a vague sense of inferiority without ever recognizing the cause. But if he can discover it and come to grips with it—no need to become a couch case. Just take yourself apart, admit the most damning facts about yourself, and try to put the pieces together again in a more satisfactory pattern. Admittedly it's difficult. You're a pretty complicated piece of work. You are, you sometimes think, a shambles. But in the labyrinth that is you, you can still find your way about—if you hold a clue.

And there is a clue. The way Adler put it was this: Ask yourself, "What is my goal in life?"

Every human being, he held, has a goal. Formulated in infancy, it is at first no more than a vague desire to dominate. Throughout life the ultimate goal remains the same for all of us—superiority, prestige, the esteem of our fellowmen. But to attain this end, we set up intermediate goals, different for all, even different for each one of us at different times. The child successively wishes to be a cowboy, a policeman, a sheriff, a judge. Our goals always represent a compensation for some real or fancied deficiency. The cripple will aspire to be a great runner—and Glenn Cunningham was. The ugly duckling will yearn for adulation—and Katharine Cornell got it. The deaf and dumb child will long to speak—and Helen Keller did. The poor boy will want to be rich, the uneducated child cultured, the social outcast popular, and the orphan loved.

So ask yourself what is it you want most in life? What is your goal? It is, naturally, what you most feel the lack of, what you feel inferior without, what you will make every effort to get.

Adler arrived at this conception of a life goal through a step-by-step advance from biology to psychology, just as he had with the inferiority complex itself.

Motion, he begins, is a characteristic of life. All motion has an objective. Things move in order to get somewhere.

The soul—spirit, psyche, mind, as you will—is an attribute of living things. It bears an innate relationship to free motion. Psychic life could only develop because of the possibility of motion, of change—and of change for a reason and with a purpose. Psychic life begins with motion, is directed toward an end, and involves striving in an effort to adapt to the environment. This striving implies an objective. When it is attained, the organism will be in an improved situation. No evolution, physical or psychological, would be possible without this concept of an objective.

"We cannot think, feel, will or act," said Adler, "without the perception of some goal . . . All the temporary and partially visible objectives, after the short period of psychic development of childhood, are under the domination of an imagined terminal goal . . . Every psychic phenomenon, if it is to give us any understanding of a person, can only be grasped and understood if regarded as a preparation for some goal."

It is impossible to conceive of the psyche except as a force striving toward an objective. All the manifestations of the human spirit are directed toward that goal. The psychic life of the individual as of the species is determined by an ever-present goal. Granted this goal, every psychic tendency follows with a certain compulsion. All a man's actions, thoughts, emotions, dreams, desires are dictated by it. The goal itself may change; its inner essence never. A style of life directed toward achieving it gradually develops. The goal makes the man. He will be a worthy or a worthless human being according to whether his goal is or is not useful to the community.

But what *is* useful to the community? Who decides what is right? To be out of step with the majority does not necessarily mean to be wrong. True, the criminal is out of step—but so is the genius. Often those who are out of step are the very ones who bring about progress. Customs and traditions exist for the individual, not the individual for them. When, where, and by whom may they be broken? Criminal and genius are both in rebellion against the *status quo*. Both are compensating aggressively for severe inferiority complexes. Both think nothing of breaking the law. Nothing pleases them so much as the raised eyebrow, the shocked expression. The difference is that while the criminal will sacrifice the world to his own self-interest, the genius will sacrifice his whole life to force society to accept his gifts. The apparently most antisocial geniuses who have ever lived (and there have been plenty of them) are seen by their work to be the greatest benefactors of the human race. What they did they did for all mankind *forever*.

This question of conformity is one of the most fertile sources of inferiority complexes, more so today than ever before. For this is *the* age of conformity, particularly in America. The individual by nature detests conformity. It subtracts from his individuality. It decreases him. It shrinks him. It makes him feel inferior. And yet he conforms. Why?

Because if he doesn't he feels a louse. He is called antisocial, accused of being against the greatest good for the greatest number. Ride him out of the herd!

He's an enemy of society if he doesn't conform, an enemy to himself if he does. What is the poor devil to do?

As he looks about him for an answer he grows steadily more confused. He hears arguments on both sides. He sees that all progress, whether in science, art, religion or any other field, is made possible only because of leaders of strong individuality. But individuality is compounded of originality and rebelliousness. Originality presupposes a deviation from the normal, and the abnormal is suspect by the community to which "nothing is good but mediocrity."

He learns a lot at the office about the value of co-operation. The bad old days of the buccaneer in business are gone. The topmost executive, like the lowliest clerk, is the faithful slave of the organization. The dog-eat-dog scramble to success has given way to the organizational crawl. All that is asked of anyone is that he be a good member of a team. The army of workers must be as uniform as an army of goose-steppers, as co-operative as a colony of ants, as subordinate as Univac.

America, our man reads, is becoming a nation of robots. The uniformity of Americans makes Europeans nervous. Their writers find in us, for all our mixed blood, a deadly similarity in bearing, dress, manners, ways of standing, walking, listening, telephoning, even of waiting. The monotonous similarity in our hotels, cooking, gas stations, which we find reassuring, they find stultifying. America, they conclude, is now mass-producing Americans.

Even here in America we are at last beginning to sense a danger in this will to conform. *Fortune* magazine makes a survey and finds that even the wives of executives in large organizations must follow a pattern, even to their drinking habits—and woe to the executive who can't produce such a wife!

William Whyte writes a book attacking "the bureaucratization of modern society," which has spread from industry to higher education, to the detriment of the liberal arts and sciences. Everywhere it produces the corporate mind. Everywhere it demands declarations of dependence. Everywhere the techniques of "social engineering" are applied to guide men to "group belongingness" and not the individual is the best means to decide all things and to create all things. Everywhere the idea of dominating men has given way to the doctrine of manipulating them into "self-co-ordinated and cheerful subordinates"—packaged white-collar, gray-flannel men and women.

All this, our man reads, is contrary to the course of civilization. Since the days of the Renaissance, men have believed in competitive enterprise, a daring conception which rescued the world from feudalism. Now that success depends on conformity and on everyone co-operating with everyone else, we are headed for a bee-hive society—no rebels, no nonconformists, no rugged individualists, no leaders. If we are to be saved from this dreary prospect, we must rediscover the creative and independent individual and give rein to his initiative.

Our confused observer goes out socially. He sees that everyone wants to be liked and accepted, to be absorbed into the group to the point where they become as inconspicuous as a single drop in a glass of water. They display an unbridled desire to get along with one another. In vain does he listen for some such wild outburst as Gauguin's, "I don't want to like anyone and I don't want anyone to like me!"

Addressing a graduation class at Smith College, Adlai Stevenson, commenting on this neurotic desire for conformity, said:

"One looks back with dismay at the possibility of a Shakespeare perfectly adjusted to bourgeois life in Stratford, a Wesley contentedly administering a country parish, a George Washington receiving a barony from George III."

Nonconformity, he continued, is what the Communists constantly try to brainwash out of people's heads. What America needs, he concluded, is more "ornery" characters.

Our confused American next turns for enlightenment to the psychiatrists. To conform or not to conform—which will save him? He finds the psychiatrists in a state of confusion almost equal to his own.

Psychiatric treatment has always had as its aim to adjust the patient to society, but recently Dr. Robert Lindner, author of *Prescription for Rebellion* and *The Fifty-Minute Hour*, very sensibly propounded the question of why psychiatrists should endeavor to adjust their patients to a maladjusted society. Norbert Wiener commented that "one of the curses of modern psychiatry is its facile assumption that passive conformity is the ideal goal of psychoanalytic treatment." And Bertrand Russell added: "I have been myself all my life a rebel with just sufficient cunning to escape serious punishment by the herd. I have been struck, especially in America, by the very thing he [Dr. Lindner] deals with, namely the passion of psychiatrists and psychoanalysts for making their patients ordinary. The passion for uniformity which Dr. Lindner attacks is, I think, much more rampant in America and Russia than in other countries, but the tendency exists everywhere."

What is this poor devil to conclude? High-pressured on every side to conform, exhorted by leaders of thought *not* to conform, what is he to do? That is the problem that is making neurotics of us all, driving us in our thousands to the psychoanalytic couch while the French, who don't even try to conform, have nothing wrong but their livers. A psychoanalyst couldn't get couch space in France—the place crawls with liver specialists.

To conform and be damned or to rebel and be damned is the question. For some it is no problem—they love to conform. For some others it is no problem—they couldn't possibly conform. But for the average American it is a daily tussle between himself and his conscience. This is where Adlerian psychology intervenes with a solution.

The touchstone of our value as a human being is not whether or not we conform but whether or not we contribute to society. Gauguin neither could nor would conform. For him it would have been fatal. There would have been no Gauguins for the rest of us to admire. Genius cannot conform—and it is doubtful if the rest of us should to the extent that we do today in America. The least gifted among us resent the shackles that conformity puts upon us. It is mass psychology, such as we witnessed in Nazi Germany, not individual initiative that we have to fear today.

So what we should ask ourselves is not whether we should conform but whether we are contributing. Put it to yourself this way:

What is my goal in life?

Is it of value to the community?

Is the good of the community more important to me than my own?

Does the work I am doing contribute in some way to society?

If the answers are in the affirmative, you're headed in the right direction.

For the gifted individual to conform in any way that prevents the flowering of his gift is anti-social. Even if the gift is pure venom, it is wrong for him to conform. *Gulliver's Travels* is a cup of poison—should Swift have withheld it?

I knew a gifted girl, an orphan brought up in a Catholic boarding school, where docility and demureness, which were not in her nature, were imposed upon her. She came out dripping honey, all convent-bred manners, submissiveness, sweetness. But conflict and rebellion simmered within her. One day the brew finally exploded in a series of poems called *I Hate Women, I Hate Men, I Hate Editors.* Ever since, Dorothy Parker has been distilling the hostility, not unmixed with pity and humor, which was generated in her in her childhood. An inferiority complex, bred of loneliness and rejection, of being half-Gentile, half-Jew, of the pressure to conform exerted upon an original and rebellious nature, finds compensation in her writing. Antisocial as Dorothy Parker feels and acts and no doubt believes she is, her work is a contribution that proves her otherwise.

The test of the value of our "style of life" is therefore not whether we are like everyone else with no sharp corners and no rough edges, not whether we fit into a mold and are universally approved of, but whether the achievement of our goal will contribute to society. Certainly those with the most to contribute, the leaders of men, do not fear to be "different," are not worried about what others think of them, and are not concerned with "keeping up" with anyone. They do what they think should be done and hope that others will try to keep up with *them*. If even in a small way a person is serving the community, his actions and emotions will form a harmonious pattern, he'll feel at home on the crust of the earth and even unfortunate experiences will not mislead or discourage him.

If his goal is antisocial he will never be at peace either with others or himself. If he has set his goal too low he will experience a lurking sense of guilt and inferiority. If he has set it so unrealistically high that he is, and always was, incapable of reaching it—if he set out to be a surgeon and is only a veterinarian, if he wanted to be a judge and remains a court clerk, if he yearned to be a statesman and never rose above ward heeler, or if she tried to be an actress and can't get beyond modeling—then he will know inferiority to the dregs.

As early as the age of five or six we have set our goal, we have created our prototype and established our style of life. If we have little real interest in others, we will develop an unco-operative strategy of life, find it impossible to establish good relationships, and in consequence fail in solving our three major problems. Result—a welter of inferiority complexes.

Now let us see how, once we have discovered our inferiority complex, we can—not get rid of it, heavens no—but use it to the best advantage. What is the technique for turning this liability into an asset?

CHAPTER IV

Springboard to Success

HE WAS BORN to poverty—and became one of the richest men in America.

He started life as a printer's devil—and became a great writer.

He had only two years of schooling—and became one of the most learned men of his day.

He was of lowly birth—and rose to be our first ambassador to France.

He had no training as scientist, inventor, statesman—and became a leader in all these fields.

He was without experience as a courtier—and he became the idol of the court of Louis XVI.

Benjamin Franklin not only wrote, he *lived* the first American success story.

How did this boy, a nobody and the descendant of generations of nobodies, accomplish this?

By a completely honest, ruthless approach to Ben Franklin, Nobody, and an unalterable determination to make him a Somebody. To that end he launched a direct, head-on attack on every liability he possessed with the intention of turning it into an asset.

His schooling ended at the age of ten. At night, after

work, *at that age,* he studied arithmetic, at twelve he added formal exercises in writing, in his teens began the study of foreign languages, eventually including French, Italian, Spanish and Latin. All his life he studied to fill up the Grand Canyon of his ignorance—and was honored with degrees from Yale, Harvard, William and Mary, even the university of Oxford, in none of which he ever set foot.

He advanced from printer to editor to publisher to writer, steadily perfecting his literary style till eventually he wrote *Poor Richard's Almanac,* which made his fortune, his *Autobiography,* which established his reputation as wit and philosopher, and the many epistles which placed him among the supreme writers of familiar letters.

Intellectually, socially, financially he was not dissatisfied with his progress but he looked with a jaundiced eye upon his moral status. He has come down to us as a man of high principle, whose virtues and maxims on virtue are quoted even among the head-hunters of the Upper Amazon. Yet all his life he had a tough time of it with Ben Franklin, sinner. His attitude toward women prepared him for the manners and morals of the dissolute French court long before he ever went there. Founding Fathers are not supposed to have illegitimate children nor to make bawdy remarks about all cats looking gray in the dark.

So, he one day asked himself, why go around feeling morally inferior any more than socially or intellectually inferior?

"I conceived the bold and arduous project of arriving at moral perfection," he wrote. "I wished to live without committing any fault at any time. I would conquer all that either natural inclination, custom, or company might lead me into. But I soon found I had undertaken a task more difficult than I had imagined. While my care was employed in guarding against one fault, I was often surprised by another; inclination was sometimes too strong for reason. I therefore contrived the following method."

In a notebook he allotted a page to each of the thirteen virtues he considered most important, ruled each page into seven vertical columns, one for each day of the week, and into thirteen horizontal columns, one for each virtue. At the end of each day he put a black mark opposite each virtue against which he had transgressed. Later, deciding it was beyond human might to practice all thirteen virtues every day, he decided to practice one each week, leaving the other twelve to take their chances. In a year he could thus go through each of the thirteen virtues four times. This practice he kept up for many years, until the pages were almost free from black marks and virtue became a habit. Thereafter he went through the course only once a year and, late in life, only once in several years.

"On the whole, though I never arrived at perfection, but fell far short of it," he confessed, "yet I was a better and happier man than I otherwise should have been." To this artifice, he continued, he owed "the felicity of his life—his long-continued health, the early easiness of his circumstances and acquisition of his fortune, with all the knowledge that obtained for him some degree of reputation among the learned, the confidence of his country, and all the evenness of temper and that cheerfulness in conversation which makes his company still sought for."

Only some such device as this, he concludes, will ensure a man's steady progress toward virtue.

A modern sophisticate might smile at the naïveté of this artifice. But what would chiefly prevent him from putting it into practice, is not its naïveté—but its strenuousness.

It was the very strenuousness of his attack on his liabilities that enabled Franklin to retire at forty and devote the second forty years of his life to public service, feeling that he had done enough for B. Franklin, private citizen. Thereafter he helped draft the Declaration of Independence, founded the University of Pennsylvania, represented his country in England and France. Leaving Paris after nine years as ambassador, he was carried by royal litter, cheered by the entire populace, all the way to the coast and returned home "the most famous private citizen in the world."

This is the purpose of the inferiority complex—to spur us to compensation. In Franklin's case compensation was direct and deliberate. Lacking wealth, he made a fortune; lacking schooling, he acquired an outstanding education; lacking social position, he achieved an unparalled one; lacking honors, he became one of the most honored men of his day; lacking in virtue, he became one of the most virtuous of men.

But there is another way to achieve compensation—the way of another great American.

He was a man of such striking ugliness that people turned to look after him in the street. He never made the slightest effort to improve his appearance, to the end of his days remaining careless in dress, wearing, as though to emphasize his ungainly height, awkward gait, and dangling hands, narrow black trousers, a coat like an umbrella sheath, and a stovepipe hat.

He was from the backwoods—and to the last, even when he rose to high position, his manners remained those of the backwoods. He still answered the door in his shirtsleeves, still wore black gloves to the opera, invariably told the wrong stories to the right people, and often, at public affairs, withdrew into sudden fits of gloom. Everywhere he looked out of place—at the bar of justice, on the speaker's platform, in Congress, on the farm, even in his own home.

His birth was not only lowly, it was crossed by the bar sinister, his mother being an illegitimate child. Another man born to poverty would have sought wealth. Not this man. He was not indifferent to money—he scorned it. All his life he remained acutely aware of his social short-comings, especially in the presence of women. Faced with a woman, he was overwhelmed with a sense of his poverty, his awkwardness, his ill-fitting clothes, his lack of breed-ing. He made no attempt to fight this painful self-con-sciousness—he simply retreated in utter disorder.

No one could have started lower, no one could have risen higher.

He became the President of the United States.

How was it possible for a man who made no effort to compensate for such heavy liabilities to achieve what Abraham Lincoln achieved?

The answer is that he *did* compensate, not directly like Franklin, but indirectly, not by replacing each liability with an asset, but by using his great qualities of mind and heart to rise above them. In only one respect did he make a direct compensation—education. And here he worked desperately hard to overcome an initial handicap. His ignorance was abysmal. Never, until he was twenty, did he hear a preacher who didn't believe the earth was flat. By candlelight, by firelight, by lamplight, he read his eyes deeper and deeper into their sockets, always disheart-ened by the little he knew in comparison with what remained to be known. When filling in his Congressional blank, opposite *Education* he wrote, "Defective." He com-pared himself with every better educated man he met, always to his own detriment. Pitted against an orator like Douglas, he recognized that he was completely outclassed. At once he put himself through an intensive course in oratory until one day even Douglas was outclassed.

For all his other deficiencies he compensated indirectly.

His whole life was an over-all compensation for everything he lacked and knew that he lacked and went right on lacking. He lived without wealth, social position, success in love and marriage, and bent his whole effort toward one goal—to become President of the United States. From the first he knew what he wanted. He was not a child when, asked what he intended to be, he answered, "I am going to be President." Nothing less than the highest office in the land could satisfy him. He was as ambitious as Caesar.

Herndon, his law partner and biographer, said of him: "He was a man of great ambition. He wanted office, always wanted it, and when in office always wanted a higher office. Ambition was the mainspring of his whole life." Of him Hay wrote: "It is absurd to call him a modest man. It was his intelligent arrogance and unconscious assumption of superiority that men like Chase and Summer could not forgive."

Lincoln's was, however, no narrow, selfish ambition. He yearned to place all the qualities of an original mind and a noble character at the service of mankind. He bent an unconquerable will, not on overcoming his liabilities, but on using all his great qualities of mind and heart to rise above them and prove himself worthy of high esteem. What other men had that he didn't have could be acquired—or done without. What he had that they didn't have, they could never get. That, like any poor, under-privileged child, he felt intensely his early deficiencies and strove desperately to compensate for his feelings of inferiority, only makes him more human and understandable.

On his deathbed, his bitterest enemy, Stanton, said of him, "There lies the greatest ruler of men the world has ever seen . . . Now he belongs to the ages."

Two ways of compensation—direct and indirect. One consists in turning our liabilities into assets; the other in adopting an over-all strategy that leaves the liabilities unchanged and develops other resources to rise above them.

This is Adler's law of compensation. It flows as naturally from the inferiority complex as the inferiority complex flows from the child's helplessness. It is one of the greatest contributions ever made to psychology.

In the case of Franklin and of Lincoln it is not difficult to see how this law works. But there are personalities so complicated, so twisted or so murky, that it is almost impossible to grasp the fact that, in their own distorted way, they too are compensating. And such cases likewise we should try to understand for we ourselves may be among them.

Consider Schopenhauer.

Here was a man hated and hating. He quarreled violently with his father; he was banished from the house by his mother; he never married, never loved, never made a friend nor lost an enemy. Only in his own company, he announced, could he associate with an equal. Even Goethe, Hegel, and Kant were unfit to consort with him. A poor conversationalist, he insisted that no one was worth talking with.

Behind this insistence that no one was fit to associate with, lurked the suspicion that *he* was not fit to associate with anyone. Behind the hostility lurked a furious sense of inferiority. He was ugly, partly deaf, fearful of the family insanity, ashamed of his mother's infidelities and of his own unbridled sexual passions.

He never attempted to change any of these things. He never made the slightest effort to like people, to forgive his mother (he never saw her for over thirty years), to understand his father, to be a tender lover or a good friend, to appreciate the work of others, or to cultivate a single social grace.

Yet he knew himself for a genius and he was determined to force mankind to accept the gifts he bore. Strangely enough, he desired above all things the admiration of those he despised.

"All men's efforts," he wrote, "have in the end no further object than to raise themselves in the estimation of others." This was as true of Schopenhauer as it was of Lincoln.

In the end he gave the world one of the great philosophies of modern times, a philosophy that is the complete antithesis of Schopenhauer the man. He who was incapable of being just to any man formulates the sum total of virtue as justice and benevolence. He who reveled in sex orgies and wallowed in creature comforts, extols art and asceticism. He who lived without ideals, built his whole philosophy on an audacious idealism erected upon an equally audacious realism.

Here is a personality so complicated and so devious that it is almost impossible for us to understand that he was—and subconsciously longed to be—a benefactor of mankind. His compensation for his profound sense of inferiority is as incredible as it is unexpected. For this sort of devious compensation, also, we must look in ourselves.

But, you may say, these are geniuses and I'm just an ordinary human being. I can't possibly compensate in any such extraordinary way.

It's amazing the compensations that many not exceptionally gifted people can make.

What would you say were the principal requisites for the Editor in Chief of *Vogue*?

Good taste, a sense of chic, social background, education, culture, writing ability, wouldn't you say?

Yet the woman who held that position for almost forty years possessed none of these.

An editor, her "autobiography" was largely written by her daughter.

Head of a staff of college graduates, she herself had only the sketchiest of educations.

A fashion authority, she came of Quaker stock (only a nudist cared less for clothes) and was herself not fashionable.

Editor-in-chief of a magazine of international society, she came from a small town, an undistinguished family and a modest home.

An arbiter of taste, the walls of one of her apartments were decorated with cover girls from *Cosmopolitan* magazine and photographs of French bathing beauties.

How then was it possible for Edna Woolman Chase to become editor of *Vogue?*

Her whole life, from the age of seventeen, was dedicated to *Vogue.* Her private life was tucked away in some unimportant corner. She employed every resource of a clever mind, an intensely ambitious nature, a personality kept constantly on dry ice, and a will relentless as a dentist's drill to build an organization that would supply her deficiencies without threatening her position. Thus she worked out a style of life which, in its entirety, was a compensation for all her deficiencies and feelings of inferiority.

No one need worry that he *won't* compensate. Death and taxes are not more sure. To convince yourself of this, you have only to glance for a moment at the genesis of this drive—and the place to look is in the cradle.

The most pampered infant in the world does not feel completely secure. With the first slap and cry, we know insecurity and will never again know security. It is a commodity which does not exist in nature. In order to feel some measure of security, the infant demands a plus factor of safety. Thus there arises in his soul a movement toward domination. Well fed, dry, and sleepy, he will still cry in the middle of the night for the sole purpose of exercising his power over that humble creature who will come running. This satisfies him so completely that he repeats it every night. He is on his way toward domination of his mother. Later he will try similar devices to cut out rivals for her attention—his brothers, father, all who threaten his position.

Then comes the desire to grow up and to become as powerful as the adults around him. This goal of superiority and domination presents grave problems. If he fails in solving them he will feel inadequate and will try to rid himself of this painful feeling either by increasing his efforts in the area where he has failed or by turning to some other activity where he feels he may have a better chance of success.

We can no more escape this sequence of events—desire for security, domination of others in order to achieve it, compensation for failure—than we can avoid breathing. All that falls to choice is *how* we'll compensate.

Without the whiplash of the inferiority complex all talent would lie dormant. It is the spark that disturbs our clod. For the compensation to be satisfactory and thus allay our painful sense of inferiority, it must fulfill certain conditions.

It must be positive, not negative.

It must be energetic, not passive.

It must be an expression of our own independent thinking and acting.

It must be conducive to self-esteem and the esteem of others.

It must be socially responsible and valuable.

It must give us a normal sense of power and a feeling of "goodness."

The compensations of the criminal do not meet these requirements. They may be energetic, and they may be an expression of the criminal's own independent thinking and acting. But they are socially harmful; they bring only a temporary feeling of superiority, an easily toppled sense of security and power, and a fundamental conviction of wrongness. The criminal actually desires to cut himself out of the body of the community, knowing himself to be a social cancer.

"Thanks, fellows, that's what I wanted," said a murderer to the policemen who fatally shot him. And, "Catch me before I commit another murder, I cannot stop myself," pleaded another in the notes he left on the scenes of his crimes. "The criminal has a right to his punishment," is the way one psychiatrist puts it.

Human beings, complicated and inconsistent creatures that they are, frequently make both negative and positive compensations. This dual mechanism is often clearly marked in genius.

Edgar Allan Poe was a seething mass of inferiority complexes. He was the child of an actress—in a day when acting was disreputable. He was left an orphan at three. He was adopted by people of wealth who alternately spoiled and neglected him. He had an organic lung disability. He was neurotic.

His negative compensations were:

That he carried his spoiled-child attitude into manhood, gambling when he had no money, defying the authorities at West Point, getting himself court martialed and dishonorably dismissed, drinking to excess, and everywhere demanding special treatment and privileges. Finally he entered the dangerous world of fantasy and toward the end of his life, "I became insane with intervals of horrible sanity," he wrote.

The superiority complex he built up to counteract his agonizing sense of inferiority reached a point where he could say, "My whole nature utterly revolts at the idea that there is any Being in the universe superior to myself."

His compensations on the positive side were equally drastic.

His daydreams were like none ever dreamed before and he was able to translate them into literature. Not only did he invent the detective story (clues, corpse, eccentric detective, surprise solution, and the like), but he created a style of poetry which, original and startlingly beautiful, influenced a whole continent of poets—needless to say not our own. Everything else may have been on the useless side of life; the poetry and prose of this man put the world into his debt forever.

Second, the compensation must be energetic.

Whereas escape into the world of fantasy may sometimes be the only way in which the genius can accomplish what he came into this world to do, for the average human being it is neurosis without the bonus. In the world of daydreams, every girl is a ballerina, a glamorous debutante, a movie star, an opera singer; every boy is a test pilot, an orator, a foreign correspondent, a criminal lawyer; and all these glittering goals are achieved effortlessly, through the dreamers' natural gifts, which they never doubt they possess, rather than by hard work, which they hope to avoid. They choose the goals which flatter their egos without ever considering their ability to attain them. Since they are incapable of reaching them, and make little effort to do so, their sense of inferiority steadily increases. The remedy? To shift the goal. It may be humiliating to admit that one is never going to be a Lindbergh or a Garbo but that, with hard work, one can become a darn good public accountant or private secretary—in the end it is far more satisfying than a dream that never comes true.

A puny lad can no more help dreaming of being a pugilist, a strong man, or a football hero than a diabetic can help dreaming of processions of slaves bearing platters of rich foods and sweetmeats, but, unless he is willing to work like an indentured slave to build up his miserable physique, he had better give up the whole idea and settle for something less glamorous.

A puny lad named Carnegie dreamed of being a football hero. A college football coach finally convinced him that he was more the type for a water carrier. Digging around in the ruins of his dreams, the young man came up with the surprising discovery that what he really wanted was the applause and popularity attached to being a football star. He switched to public speaking, for which he had a small talent, and eventually founded a famous school of public speaking and wrote a book called *How to Win Friends and Influence People*. By shifting his goal from the impossible to the attainable, Dale Carnegie not only overcame his own inferiority complex but helped millions of others to overcome theirs.

Unrealistic goals lead to what one psychologist, Wendell Johnson of the University of Iowa, calls the I.F.D. disease. By I.F.D. he means the sense of failure that arises when goals are set impossibly high, in which case we pass by slow stages from idealism to frustration to demoralization. Psychologists recognize this process as fertile soil for all sorts of mental and nervous disorders. No other ailment, Johnson declares, is so common among university students. Fixing our goals beyond our abilities to reach, we soon find ourselves dropping behind schedule, become discouraged, begin to doubt our ability, develop acute inferiority feelings. This negative self-evaluation is the basis of the inferiority complex. Continued failure leads to apathy, then to boredom, to loss of energy, finally to depression.

The remedy is to adjust our sights to meet the realities of the situation. We must be fluid and adaptable. The Maginot Line type of personality can only mean defeat. Life changes constantly—we must change to meet it. One never steps into the same river twice.

The other extreme is as bad. The weather-vane mentality is a rudderless compassless, anchorless ship. Between these two extremes is "optimally adaptable." Like a Damascus blade, he can be bent to a circle—but he always springs back. He changes his mind enough but not too much, when indicated, but not constantly, readily, but not quickly. He is adaptable but not flighty. Very often it is necessary to admit that our adolescent goal is unrealistic and to shift to one more practical. If the new goal is well chosen, energy is generated and what might have become a neurosis will be only an occasional twinge of inferiority.

Third, the compensation must be an expression of our own independent thinking and acting. No dictated life, no carbon copy, no reasonable facsimile, no echo of another's life can ever give us that heady feeling of independence, that complete satisfaction in making our own mistakes that is the basis of self-respect. Love no more than fear is an excuse for doing as we're told.

Fourth, the compensation must be conducive to self-esteem and the esteem of others. Since the ultimate goal of all our efforts is not so much to reach heaven as to raise ourselves in the estimation of our fellowmen, this condition is axiomatic. Any time we fail to win this dual approval, we can fairly feel the cold ripples of inferiority beginning to lap around our feet.

Fifth, our goal must be socially responsible and valuable. A purely personal goal distorts the whole strategy of life. We concentrate on that one of the three problems of life where we feel we have the best chance of success, to the neglect of the other two. We become a business tycoon, a pleasure seeker, a minor Casanova, a saloon-recking Carrie Nation—a caricature of a human being, out of Dickens by Daumier. Not self-interest but social interest must be the aim.

The final requirement for a satisfactory compensation is that it bring a normal sense of power and a feeling of "goodness." Power we all crave, even godlike power, but we'll settle for a reasonable control over our own destiny. We fear nothing more than to be the tool of another's will or the pawn of another's whim. To achieve this sense of being in control of the situation we must select goals not beyond attainment and employ all the resources at our command to reach them. We will also conduct ourselves so as to arouse as little opposition and as much co-operation as possible.

As for goodness, that is the point at which the Freudians accused Adler of wandering off into religion and ethics. Since the moral and social values are so important a part of Adler's psychology, a later chapter ("No Man Is an Island") will be devoted to them.

Compensation, the psychiatrists point out, can be effected in one of several ways.

The defective organ or faculty may be trained to function as well as, or better than, the normal one.

Following an accident, George B. Sutton was left with only stumps for arms. What game did he elect to play? Billiards, naturally. Without artificial attachments of any kind, manipulating the cue with his stumps, he became champion of two continents and at one time held the world's high run (799) at 18.2 balkline billiards.

The function of a healthy organ or faculty may be substituted for the defective one.

A Frenchman named Jean Périer, wanted above all things to be an opera singer. The fact that he had very little voice and that what he had was a calamity, uneven, hollow, and forever on the verge of cracking—or cracking— did not deter him. With that voice he became one of the great baritones of the Paris Opéra, a singer for whom the great composers clamored to write operas and for whom audiences rose shouting, while the boys with the big rotund baritones cowered in the wings.

How did he do it?

By substituting acting for singing. He filled a role with such beauty that strong men wept. He gave a moving, unnamable magic to such parts as that of Pelléas. He created a moment of unbearable beauty in *Le Chemineau* when the paralytic old father, in an incredible demonstration of will power, lifts himself from his bed to denounce the man who has dishonored his house.

A situation may be developed in which the defect becomes an advantage.

Another Frenchman, billed as Bétove (French for Beethoven) used to play the music halls in the character of an old-fashioned music professor. In a shiny Prince Albert, dangling tie, the owlish, tortoise-shell eyeglasses, with frayed red hair and whiskers, he crept out on the stage with an air of wistful ineffectualness that convulsed his audiences.

He imitated the great composers and the stars of opera and concert hall with a murderous satire that reduced them to rubble. He could have withdrawn then and left his audience weak with laughter. He remained to hold them spellbound with some of the most exquisite music they would ever hear.

He entered as a clown and left as a master musician, the composer of many beautiful operas and songs—Michel- Maurice Lévy. And the reason for this was—his ridiculous appearance. From youth he had been misshapen and obliged to wear a heavy steel brace. His hair spurted wildly in all directions and his shortsighted eyes were concealed behind glasses like the bottoms of beer bottles. Only by making himself a figure of fun could he catch his audience off guard and then take it by storm. He was a man named Bétove whom everyone came to laugh at— and remained to revere. His whole career was founded on maneuvering himself into a position where a defect became an asset.

A "psychic superstructure" may be constructed so that the total personality assumes a pattern which is a compensation for all one's complexes, regardless of their genesis.

Which method one will choose will depend largely upon the nature of the individual. The cautious person will proceed realistically, compensating in a practical way. The rebellious individual, stimulated by his disability, will attempt the impossible. This damned-if-anyone-is-going-to-dictate-to-me type, losing an arm, will go in for games which can't possibly be played without two arms. If he loses a leg or two—

Two legs off? Charles Zimmy, being what most people morbidly refer to as a basket case but what Zimmy himself describes as being "unusually buoyant," became a swimmer. At forty-six, well past an athlete's prime, he swam the Hudson from Albany to New York, 145 miles in 149 hours. With this single performance he won the world's distance and endurance records.

The question is, not *if* we will compensate, but *how* we will compensate, for compensate we must.

Up to this point we have produced proof that somewhere about our personality we all conceal an inferiority complex or two. We have indicated the symptoms by which you can recognize your own and (much more delightful) other people's inferiority complexes. We have shown how compensation can help eliminate a complex and be used as a springboard to success.

Now suppose we take up the various types of inferiority complexes one at a time and show how they can be used to our advantage. Let us begin with those due to physical disabilities, inadequate physical performance, and unsatisfactory personal appearance.

CHAPTER V

Deformity Is Daring

HE WAS BORN Dzhugashvili but he called himself "Steel" to indicate his determination to revolutionize Russia and to conquer the world through the power of the sword, the plowshare, the machine, and the human will.

His father was a drunken shoemaker, his grandfather a serf. Expelled from a theological seminary for Marxist propaganda, he became a revolutionist, thereafter spending much of his life either in prisons or fleeing from them.

He became the most powerful figure in the world. He built up a colossal empire. He constituted himself a one-man government, ruling over 200,000,000 people. His whim was law. A nod from him liquidated millions of human beings. A gesture launched strikes and insurrections in distant lands. A word converted a scientific fallacy into a scientific law. "I will shake my little finger," he once said, "and there will be no more Tito." One sixth of the world owed him allegiance.

He lifted his nation from a fifth-rate power to one of the Big Four.

What was the source of the inferiority complex that generated this indomitable will to power?

Low birth, lack of education, a sordid childhood, but

most of all, physical deformities. Only 5 feet, 5 inches in height, with drooping shoulders, stubby neck, pock-marked face, a grotesque nose, blackened teeth, his crowning disfigurement was that one arm was noticeably shorter than the other.

> Deformity is daring.
> It is its essence to o'ertake mankind,
> By heart and soul, and make itself equal—
> Ay, the superior of the rest. There is
> A spur in its half movements, to become
> All that others cannot.

To a physical deformity, a rebellious, aggressive nature reacts with such violence as sometimes literally to shake the world. Psychiatrists, analyzing the character of Kaiser Wilhelm, point out the dynamics of his deformed arm. One has called it "the most dangerous deformity that European civilization has ever known." It engendered in that arrogant personality a sense of inferiority and a consequent drive for superiority that precipitated World War I. Of Talleyrand's deformed feet, Benjamin Constant says, "Talleyrand's feet were the decisive element in his character"—and what was decisive in Talleyrand's character was decisive in the destiny of France.

Into the mouth of Richard III Shakespeare put these words:

> I, that am curtailed of this fair proportion,
> Cheated of feature by dissembling nature,
> Deformed, unfinish'd sent before my time
> Into this breathing world, scarce half made up,
> And that so lamely and unfashionable,
> That dogs bark at me, as I halt by them;
> Why, I, in this weak piping time of peace,

Have no delight to pass away the time;
And therefore,—since I cannot prove a lover . . .
I am determined to prove a villain.

Not that deformity inevitably leads to villainy. It leads
in many directions. Toulouse-Lautrec, with his deformed
body, lived a wildly dissipated life, mostly in a bordello,
but he painted like an angel. William Wilberforce, a pint-
sized man, sickly, fragile, kept going only by the constant
use of opium, which he had the will power never to
increase beyond the doctor's prescription, put up a lifelong
fight against the slave trade in Great Britain, winning it
a month after his death.

A physical defect is the more galling because it is there
for all to see. The urge to prove that though deformed,
one is powerful, though ugly, strong, though undersized,
important, though crippled, athletic, though puny, brilliant, though plain, charming, is a powerful incentive. It
accounts for some of the greatest men and women who
have ever lived. We cannot read the biographies of men
like Darwin, Heine, Keats, Stevenson, Pope, Parkman,
Kant, Byron, Chopin, Wagner, Massenet, Dostoevski,
Bacon, Aristotle, without realizing that their characters
and lives were molded by their physical defects or disabilities; that men like Alexander, Caesar, Napoleon, Nel-
son, D'Annunzio were stimulated to seek military glory
because of their small stature; that men like Socrates,
Mirabeau, Voltaire were goaded into developing their
extraordinary abilities by their extraordinary ugliness.

Whosoever hath anything fixed in his person that doth
induce contempt hath also a perpetual spur in himself
to rescue and deliver himself from scorn; and therefore,
all deformed persons are extremely bold . . . It stirreth in
them industry . . . Layeth their competitors and emu-

lators to sleep, as never believing they should be in possibility of advancement till they see them in possession . . . Deformity is an advantage to rising Kings.

Thus Francis Bacon. Could a psychiatrist have put it better? It is one more proof that the creative writers have always anticipated the psychologists. Centuries before Adler discovered the inferiority complex, Bacon recognized its workings. Centuries before Freud discovered the Oedipus Complex, Sophocles was building his dramas around it; and Plato, two thousand years before psychoanalysis, was delving into the unconscious and interpreting dreams in the Freudian manner. Shakespeare knew intuitively much that modern psychologists have only recently "discovered."

The same or a similar physical defect can produce diametrically opposite results. Richard III reacts to deformity by becoming a murderer; Steinmetz, by becoming an electrical wizard. "Schnozzle" Durante, with a nose that was a calamity, adding to it his many other liabilities— a raucous voice, a Lower East Side accent and a general hell-raising propensity—parlayed it into fame and fortune. "Baldy" Jack Rose, from childhood hairless as a billiard ball, played hooky to escape ridicule, became a juvenile delinquent, later a gambler and stool pigeon, eventually the man who lured the murderers of Herman Rosenthal.

His deformity is the outstanding fact in the mind of the deformed man. From childhood it is what marks him off from everyone else. He is always conscious of it and believes that everyone else is. He is convinced that they see only his hump. He must prove he is more than his hump. He must demonstrate that he is superior to those who are straight.

There was Alexander Pope. Born with a crooked spine, always encased in a canvas jacket, often "taken at a distance for a small windmill," he became the English poet with more quotations in Bartlett's *Familiar Quotations* than anyone but Shakespeare. Self-educated, at the age of twenty-five—such is the daring of the deformed—he translated the *Odyssey* and the *Illiad* from Greek into English. Continually lashed by his feelings of inferiority, he drove himself relentlessly from obscurity to fame, eventually reaching such a pinnacle that he thought nothing of falling asleep at table while the Prince of Wales discoursed of poetry.

Crippling humiliates a man beyond bearing. The amputee, even if he has lost no more than a finger, feels it as a kind of castration, lessening him as a man. Many men are not satisfied with a moral or intellectual victory. They feel a compulsion to prove themselves *physically* the equal of other men—nay, the superior. In a questionnaire sent to two hundred college and secondary-school athletic coaches, one question was: "What types of sports are chosen by the handicapped?" The answers were astounding. More boys, it seems, prefer to attempt the impossible than to win an easy victory over the possible. Many will settle for nothing less than a physical triumph over their disability.

A Peg-Leg Bates, a one-legged Negro, not only ran the 100-yard dash in 11 seconds (Olympic champion Jesse Owens, a famous biped, set a record of 9.4 seconds) but made dancing his career, becoming a world-famous tap dancer.

A Count Zichy, minus his right arm, became a brilliant pianist, often playing with Liszt his arrangements for three hands and making extended concert tours with works especially composed for one hand.

A Jean Yves Gosselin, with one leg gone above the knee, could execute all the intricate twists and turns in skiing, including the brilliant high *gelandesprung—on one ski.*

Some of the greatest runners and dancers were, as children, physically handicapped by rickets, polio, weak, spindly legs, burned or broken legs, among them Glenn Cunningham, Nana Golner, André Eglevsky, Ted Shawn, Tatiana Riabouchinska, Alicia Markova. In love with mobility, they could not rest until they had achieved the utmost physical virtuosity.

Such a man was Dug Hepburn.

In 1955, at the Empire Stadium in Vancouver, Canada, Dug lifted a 370-pound weight, the heaviest single lift ever made to that date, after which he announced that he had no intention of being merely the strongest man in the world, he fully intended to be "the strongest man in history." Asked how he came to have such extraordinary strength, Hepburn replied, "I was born with a withered right leg and I took up lifting to compensate for my weakness."

The kind of compensation we make for a physical disability depends on our temperament. Where the prudent man very sensibly goes in for activities where his disability will not count against him, the rebellious individual says, "I've lost an arm—so what? No one is going to dictate to me what I can and can't do! I'll show the cockeyed world!" And instead of compensating along the line of least resistance, he chooses the line of greatest resistance. Where some natures are crushed by overwhelming difficulties, such natures are stimulated by them. The conservative person is encouraged to make an effort only when the goal is within reach and within reason; the hypermanic type is stimulated by the impossible.

A chap named E. G. Neely was that type.

Neely was an easy-going, apathetic youth until one day, in a shotgun accident, he lost an arm. When a man loses a part of his body, he suffers a spiritual as well as a physical loss. Part of his manhood goes with it. Until then he has taken his masculinity for granted. Now he must prove it.

A kind of fury, divine or hellish, drove Neely to prove himself a man physically superior to other men. One after the other he went in for college athletics, always the least likely for a one-armed man. He played guard on the 1919 Dartmouth football team and made the All-American team. He played golf in the eighties. He was an outstanding wrestler, swimmer, dash man and tennis champion. Least likely of all, he became an expert at billiards and trap shooting.

Self-confidence oozed from him. Before a contest he was very likely to remark, "That fellow thinks he's a sure-fire winner because he's got two arms but I can beat him the best day he ever lived!" He came to be considered one of the most extraordinary athletes in the annals of intercollegiate sports.

That is what can happen to an apathetic, easy-going sort of chap when he suffers an insult to his body-ego.

Some men, deprived of their legs, will settle down complacently to being a basket case, supported by the government, the insurance company, or the family, never stirring a stump.

Not Sunny Osterberg.

During the first World War Sunny, losing both legs above the knee, wrote home: "Dear Mom, In time no one will ever know I've lost a limb or two." One of his first attempts to establish this fact came on Armistice Day, when, deciding that the occasion could be properly celebrated only in New York, he persuaded a sergeant to convey him there, knowing full well this was against Army regulations but arguing that a man with no legs was above such petty considerations.

He selected one of Fifth Avenue's swankiest hotels for his night on the town and entered the ballroom pickaback on the sergeant's shoulders. Seeing which, every man and woman present rose and stood until Sunny was seated!

Thereafter Sunny learned to drive a car with his artificial legs, then went into the automobile agency business and eventually headed the agency. In time no one knew he'd lost a limb or two.

I once heard a young man who, during the war, had lost one leg and almost all use of the other, end a public address with these words, "Thanks to Dr. Rusk, I am not a cripple."

Thanks to Dr. Rusk—

Dr. Howard Rusk, in charge of rehabilitation at New York–Bellevue Medical Center, takes the crippling out of men's minds.

"A man who has lost a limb or even two can still lead a normal life," says Dr. Rusk. "He can still be self-supporting and well-adjusted to his environment. For all practical purposes, *he is not a cripple*. The average person uses only 25 per cent of his physical ability. What society pays for is the strength in his hands and the brains in his head, not for a superb physique, the ability to run or the strength to put the shot. Economically, a man who has lost an arm or a leg is not handicapped at all. Some disabilities are actually an advantage in some jobs. A blind person in a dark room turns out one-third more work than a sighted person. Here it is the sighted person who is handicapped. The amputee who develops strength in his arms is at no disadvantage in static jobs. Here the man who *can't* move about freely has the advantage over the man who can and who therefore resents immobility.

"Our trouble is that we still carry the subconscious body image, the idea that physical qualities and abilities are synonymous with beauty and strength. That is not true. They are matters of the spirit. A man can be truly crippled only in his mind."

When a man loses a part of his body he invariably goes through a phase known as "the psychology of the crippled." This may last all his life—or it may last only a few weeks.

With a chap named Alfred Gerald Caplin it lasted for years. And yet, if he had not lost a leg in a streetcar accident, he would probably have remained the anonymous Mr. Caplin to the end of his days. As it was, being barred from any active work, he settled down in a chair, began drawing cartoons and soon became known to the civilized world, and large areas of the uncivilized, as Al Capp, creator of Li'l Abner. It took him years to realize that that accident was the best thing that ever happened to him, that if he forgot he was a uniped, other people would, too, and that work, love, and marriage were still to be considered matters of course. Certainly in his biped state, the $200,000 gross annual income he eventually achieved, never would have been a matter of course— or even probability.

This "psychology of the crippled" stage some men can cut to a minimum.

During World War I a pilot in the Russian Imperial Naval Aviation, Alexander de Seversky, was shot down over the Baltic. As he clambered out of the water onto a wing of his wrecked plane, he saw that his right leg was missing. He realized in that moment that life was over for him.

His whole life had been one long sporting event—running, boxing, swimming, fencing, skiing, motor racing, airplane stunting, gymnastics, the war. He had been a champion in every event he entered. With one leg gone—!

But de Seversky was no sooner off the operating table than he began to reconsider, and during his convalescence a new personality began to emerge.

"I owe my entire career to the loss of my leg," he now

says. "With two legs, I'd certainly have broken my neck in a short time since I went in for all the more lethal sports. Thanks to a natural exuberance and self-confidence, I skipped the 'psychology of the crippled' phase entirely. I started on my new life emotionally well-adjusted to the fact that nothing could ever give me back my leg."

He did not give up flying and stunting—he became the top naval ace of Russia, with the rank of commander.

He did not give up skating, diving, riding, dancing, golf—he learned these things all over again.

He gave up nothing—he merely added new interests— inventing, military strategy, writing, the science of strategic air power. He invented, to make flying possible for a one-legged man, hydraulic brakes, spin chutes, and balanced rudders which led to balanced ailerons and flight controls. He adapted skis for flying boats, conceived a bombsight which was the model for the first fully automatic bombsight. He invented the prototype of the P-47 Thunderbolt, one of the decisive factors in winning the war. He wrote a book, *Victory Through Air Power*, which caused President Truman, when awarding him the Harmon Trophy *for six consecutive years*, to say:

"As a result of Major de Seversky's outstanding contributions to aviation and his advocacy of strategic air power, our country was psychologically prepared to apply those principles against the enemy at the crucial moment, thereby winning control of the air and guaranteeing victory."

"I have never thought of myself as a cripple," says de Seversky. "I don't believe anyone else ever has either. If you overlook your disability, so will others. I have always thought of my wooden leg as a military decoration."

A sense of inferiority for a specific handicap has a

tendency to spread until it involves the whole personality.
A man with one leg becomes psychologically a cripple
as well as physically. A cripple is an inferior human being.
No use trying to keep up with the human race. Count
me out.

But let him ask himself to whom, as a human being,
he is inferior. To everyone? Always? In all respects?
In all circumstances? From every point of view? Only
a man seriously ill mentally would answer these questions
in the affirmative. Most men would find themselves still
on the credit side of the ledger. With one leg gone, most
of their assets still remain. It is what is left that counts.

When the sense of inadequacy invades the entire personality and a missing hand becomes a generalized feeling
of inferiority, the individual tends to withdraw from
society. He avoids superiors, he will not compete or
co-operate, he shuns social contacts. He is convinced in
advance that he will fail in whatever he undertakes. He
feels continually frustrated. The sense of inferiority
spreads and becomes habitual—the psychology of the
crippled.

But let him substitute an ability for his disability and
he becomes a different human being. This idea was never
better expressed than by Artemus Ward. "I knew a man,"
he once said, "who didn't have a tooth in his head, not
a tooth in his head—and yet that man could play the bass
drum better'n any man I ever heard."

A one-legged man is not handicapped as a lawyer; a
one-armed man is not handicapped as a professor of
Greek; a man with two useless legs is not handicapped as
President of the United States. A blind man can learn to
play golf—Charley Boswell, a blinded war veteran did,
shooting around 80. A blind girl can learn to ski—Thelma
Keitlen did, guided down the slopes by an instructor who

preceded her carrying an alarm clock with a very loud tick. Such people localize their sense of inferiority—and then eliminate it.

It is all relative. To some people anyone who can't speak French is an uncultured lout. To an artist anyone who can't see beauty in the scum of a pond might as well be blind. To the world traveler the stay-at-home is a benighted being. According to other people's points of view there isn't one of us who isn't terribly handicapped in some respects.

The person who fails because of a physical handicap is a defeatist from the start. He sits on the side lines, his alibi all prepared. "*If* I had tried I could have been a success." Never having made an effort, he never suffers any humiliating failure. Yet the fear that he might have been vanquished in the struggle festers in his heart, severe tensions develop out of his difficult attempts to conceal the truth from himself, and his whole life becomes an evasion of action in order to avoid a sense of defeat. Never defeated, he is the supreme defeatist.

So much for the deformed and crippled.

To most people it might not seem the greatest tragedy in the world to be somewhat under the average height and not to be able to lick his weight in wildcats. To the boy who is puny or a runt, it is the supreme tragedy. There is almost nothing he wouldn't do to be six feet tall or as strong as Samson.

It may not be a law that you have to be born a weakling in order to become a famous strong man, but it certainly helps. Take the three most famous strong men in recent history.

As I mentioned earlier, young Charles Atlas was "a 97-pound runt, pale, nervous and a prey to bullies." After seeing an exhibition of statues of Greek gods in the Brooklyn Museum of Art and learning that they were actually statues of Greek athletes, he decided to make himself over in their likeness. He wound up, not only a famous strong man, capable at forty-eight of pulling the seventy-two tons of the Broadway Limited along its tracks, but "the world's most perfectly developed man . . . the possessor of the true classic physique, a blend of Hercules and Apollo."

Sandow was quite as puny a specimen, quite as humiliated, quite as determined to be a Hercules. By sheer will power he built a pitiable physique into one bulging with levators and flexors until in his heyday he could support a load of thirty-three people on his back.

Bernarr MacFadden's case was even more remarkable. Inheriting from a consumptive mother and an alcoholic father a constitution that was not expected to last him through childhood, he built it into a physique that carried him through eighty-seven strenuous years and was liberally displayed in the press of the world to the envy of all males and the admiration of all females. To its durable quality he bore witness at sixty-five when he took up flying; at eighty-one when he celebrated his birthday by making his first parachute jump; at eighty-three when he parachuted into the Hudson River; and at eighty-four when he hit the silk over the Seine, wearing on that memorable occasion a suit of red flannel underwear.

MacFadden went further. He not only became one of the strongest men in the country, he became one of the richest, running hotels, publishing magazines, establishing military schools, sanitariums, physical-culture gyms, and so forth. He was taking no chances. He killed that inferiority complex in every way known to psychiatry.

The shame of being a weakling has driven many a boy to great things. One such boy, who adored nothing so much as a gun-totin', hard-ridin', quick-ropin' cowboy, painfully built a scrawny body into great cords and knots of brawn. Then at the earliest opportunity he broke away from the practice of law and headed West, bought a ranch, became a practicing cowboy and a violently active sheriff, organized the Rough Riders and led them in the war in Cuba. He became known as "T. R., the Strenuous," and was usually depicted in cartoons wearing an athletic grin and a cowboy hat, leading his men up San Juan Hill. After which it was comparatively easy for the athletic hero to get himself elected Governor of New York and President of the United States.

Theodore Roosevelt had his followers, among them Anthony Drexel Biddle, of the Philadelphia Biddles. A Biddle might easily become effete, especially one born, like Anthony, puny and asthmatic. But modeling himself on his idol, T. R., Anthony grew up a dedicated athlete and a howling militarist. Whatever he was, he was belligerently. He founded a religion called Athletic Christianity, about equal parts religion and pugilism, and wrote a number of books in a sort of half-nelson style. Being too old for military service when the recent glorious war broke out—he was sixty—he thrust himself into it by murderously teaching jujitsu to the Marine Corps.

Such are the compensations of weaklings. Now for another category.

In 1835, Richard Lawrence made an attack on the life of Andrew Jackson, President of the United States.

In 1865, John Wilkes Booth shot and killed Abraham Lincoln, President of the United States.

In 1881, Charles Guiteau assassinated James Garfield, President of the United States.

In 1901, Leon Czolgosz fatally shot William McKinley, President of the United States.

In 1912, John Schrank made an attempt on the life of Theodore Roosevelt, President of the United States.

In 1933, Joseph Zangara, assaulted with intent to kill,
Franklin Roosevelt, President of the United States.

In 1950, Oscar Collazo shot at Harry Truman, President
of the United States.

Seven attempts to assassinate presidents of the United
States, three of them successful.

The seven assassins had one thing in common. They
were all little men attempting to be big men.

To the masculine ego it is almost as galling to be an
inch or two shorter than the average of his countrymen
as it is to be crippled or deformed. A man lies as automatically about his height as a woman does about her age.
There are no men 5 feet, 11 inches tall—they are all 6 feet.
There is a definite psychology of "the little man" as there
is of the crippled or the deaf. You know the type—cocky,
aggressive, belligerent, pompous, or exactly the opposite—
pathologically self-conscious and shy.

Barely 5 feet, 1 inch in height, James Barrie was all
his life tortured with shyness. He dreaded entering the
adult world. He would always, he knew, appear a child
to other men—let him remain a child. It is this longing
he expresses in *Peter Pan*. So intense was his shame over
his tiny stature that he appeared in public as little as
possible, would never make a public address, and was
never at ease with strangers. On one occasion when he
and the equally shy A. E. Housman met for luncheon, not
one word was spoken throughout the entire meal. A
midget in size, Barrie became a giant in literature.

From the day a boy realizes that he is not going to be
as tall as his fellows, a sense of inferiority invades him.
He tries to elevate himself to the height of other men on
elevator shoes or psychological stilts. He may turn braggart or show-off. He may struggle for leadership, for conquest in war or in love, for power over other men. But no

matter what compensations he makes, he will probably never rid himself of a sense of inferiority until he also achieves a philosophy that I have never heard better expressed than by Brigadier General Carlos Romulo.

Romulo became a general, yes. He also became president of the United Nations General Assembly, President of the Philippines, and Philippine Ambassador to the United States. But all this would not have wiped out his sense of inferiority at being a very little man had he not, early in life, learned that his very littleness could be an advantage to him. On the Columbia University debating team, his short stature made him appear a high-school boy rather than a college student, and the audience, feeling he was the underdog, always rooted for him. It was the same in 1945 when, at the opening session of the United Nations in San Francisco, he made the famous speech beginning, "Let us make this floor the last battlefield," his head scarcely visible above the speaker's stand. The extraordinary ovation he received then was, he swears, chiefly due to the smallness of himself and his country.

"I'm glad I'm a little fellow," says Romulo. "Many little fellows feel a sense of inferiority because of their stature. I once experimented with wearing elevated shoes. They weakened one of my great natural advantages, which is this: the little fellow is generally underrated in the beginning. Then when he does something well, people are surprised and impressed. . . . It has been that way all my life. What little I do has often seemed extraordinary because people were expecting so little of me.

"One day at a United Nations session in Paris, Mr. Vishinsky turned all his gifts for contempt directly upon me. 'You are just a little man,' he said, 'from a little country.'

"For him, that answered the argument. My country,

compared with his, is just a dot on the map. And I stand
only 5 feet, 4 inches in my shoes.

"In my lifetime I have given much thought to the problems of littleness. And I want to say that I'm glad I'm
a little fellow!"

He has this advice for the little man:

Don't inflate yourself into a stuffed shirt. In a big man
this may appear as dignity. In a little man it is just
cockiness.

Don't blow your top. The big fellow in a towering rage
may be impressive; the little fellow is just spluttering.

Your smallness is a great advantage in making friends.
People feel the little man is more approachable; they feel
protective toward him and find it easier to be confidential
with him.

Don't throw away these assets. Friendliness is as great
a force as physical prowess.

With such an attitude, the sense of inferiority as nearly
disappears as it ever can. The other day a friend said to
me:

"At thirteen I knew I was going to be a 'little' man.
I made up my mind then to develop a personality to out-
weigh this disadvantage. I would not be a show-off or
a clown, I would not be pompous or cocky. I would always
let the big man talk first, listen attentively, then try to
answer in a way to gain his interest. A man is more willing
to listen to you if you have listened to him. I wouldn't
endeavor to be glib or clever. I would develop my best
qualities and let others judge of my value. I have found
it pays off."

Fancy the state of mind of a man who must be stretched
to get a job! Men have been stretched to get into the
army; men have been stretched to get onto the police
force. Five feet seven and one-half inches is the minimum

for the police force and there are physical culture salons which specialize in assisting undersized men to achieve that height. Strapped to a contraption with a couple of wheels and a handle which is turned till they turn red and gurgle, they are stretched an inch or two, grab a cab to police headquarters and take their physical.

No, it's no fun being a little man in a nation of tall men, not unless one cultivates the philosophy of a Romulo.

With women littleness is no handicap—it's tallness that hurts. Beyond a certain height, a woman feels herself a freak. It cuts down alarmingly on the number of beaux and of men who are willing to walk up the aisle with a woman who looks as if she could take them over her knee and spank them. Such a girl must try to think of herself as a willowy Burne-Jones, as one of the exquisite, long-stemmed American beauties "Lucille" (Lady Duff-Gordon) and Ziegfeld glamorized. She must learn to walk like a procession and never, never attempt to be cute.

Eleanor Roosevelt managed very well. Her height, placing her head and shoulders above most women, even many men, put her extraordinary plainness on permanent exhibition. Yet not only did she marry one of the outstanding men of our generation, but she became a distinguished person in her own right. . . . Many a tall girl grows up with nothing to show for it but a stoop.

It is plainness, not littleness, that women agonize over. The day that an adolescent girl looks into her mirror and realizes that she is never going to be a beauty, that, in fact, she is going to be downright plain, something in her dies. Many girls thereafter just wither into old maids or grab the first man they can lay hands on and take their bitterness out on him or remain forever sickeningly grateful to him for having married them.

Agnes de Mille spoke for all plain girls when she wrote in her autobiography:

"Ugly ducklings sometimes change into swans. The reverse is equally possible . . . I had been a pretty child. I found myself suddenly imprisoned in someone else's body, heavy, deep-bosomed, large-hipped. I was built like a mustang, stocky, sturdy. My skin went muddy and on my face there developed seemingly overnight, a large, hooked nose, my father's nose. 'Full of character,' people have told me since. But it would fool no girl. It was ugly. And it was mine for life. From that unmarked day when as a narcissistic youngster I looked in a mirror and realized I was not going to be a beautiful woman, I gave up caring how I looked—or thought I did."

From childhood she had wanted one thing—to be a dancer.

Her father told her, "Stop dancing. Look at yourself in the mirror."

Archie Selwyn poked a finger into her thigh and announced, "You're too fat."

Her partner remarked, "You're too fat, too slow and too timid."

Her uncle, Cecil de Mille, pronounced, "You can't be photographed—teeth and nose, you know."

But if something died something was also born in Agnes de Mille the day she realized she would never be a beauty. All the physical attributes of the dancer were forever denied her; the spiritual qualities could never be. Against impossible odds she kept working with her unsuitable body until eventually she became a leading ballerina and one of our greatest choreographers.

The beauty of many of the great enchantresses of the past has been questioned—Theodora, Cleopatra, Ninon de Lenclos, Mary Stuart, Pompadour, Marie Antoinette, right down to the Duchess of Windsor. But no one has ever doubted their charm. They all possessed, like the ugly Germaine de Staël, Napoleon's eternal enemy, an inner vitality that made them vibrate before your very eyes, an incandescence of spirit that can be felt if not actually seen. While there may be no substitute for victory, there certainly is for beauty. It is charm.

"She isn't pretty," said a Frenchman of a famous courtesan. "She's worse."

Charm is what all these enchantresses of the past possessed, most of whom deliberately cultivated it when they realized they were never going to be beauties.

"As a child I was told and convinced," wrote the daughter of a small German princeling in her memoirs, "that I was a regular ugly duckling and so I tried to acquire other virtues."

She succeeded extraordinarily well. She was able, before she was the age of Juliet, to charm a young Russian Grand Duke and at fourteen to snare him in marriage. Then she waited for Peter to die, which, with a little assistance from two of her lovers, he eventually did—and she became Catherine, Empress of Russia. From then on, she not only grew in stature as a ruler but in charm as a woman.

Her vitality was such that she habitually rose at 5 A.M., made her own fire, worked twelve to fifteen hours and still had energy left for a ball and for love. She crammed fifty-six love affairs into a lifetime of sixty-seven years. When she had grown stout and gray, she still had lovers, not because she was an empress, but because she was a woman able to delight and to be delighted.

A brilliant mind was no less a part of her charm than a vibrating personality. Light reading for her was Buffon's *Histoire Naturelle*. She wrote a history of Russia, comedies, proverbs, tales. She made a digest of Blackstone's *Commentaries*. She was an excellent artist. And she was a great ruler, extending the boundaries of Russia in all directions through war, diplomacy, and just plain robbery.

The Prince de Ligne christened her Catherine the Great.

Voltaire named her the "Semiramis of the North." And many men called her desirable. She had indeed acquired other virtues to take the place of beauty.

We have seen such a duckling-into-swan transformation in our own day. The former Mrs. Simpson is scrawny, with a square jaw, a large nose, and not even the saving grace of beautiful eyes, but she will go down in history with the great charmers, few of whom ever married their kings and for none of whom that I recall did a king ever give up his throne. Whatever else may be said of her, her charm cannot be denied—nor her chic, another substitute for beauty. By her own confession, she became one of the ten best-dressed women in the world in order to compensate for her plainness. At forty, when a beauty is bankrupt, such women are just coming into their own.

The psychiatrists' offices are filled with women who have missed beauty, perhaps only by a mole or a birthmark, by a long nose or the wrong color hair—which is any color the owner happens not to fancy—and who have made no effort to develop a mind, a heart, a character, or a personality to compensate for their deficiency. They have chosen the way of neurosis instead of compensation.

The more one thinks of it, the more likely does it seem that almost all of us have some feeling of inferiority concerning a physical inadequacy or disability, be it only a sprinkling of freckles across our dear little nose or a heavy outcropping of hair on our manly chest. It is up to us whether to let it rankle as a complex or to compensate for it by developing other assets.

As for the complexes that arise from being born on "the wrong side of the tracks" (that being a state of mind rather than a physical location) few of us escape those, as we shall now see.

CHAPTER VI

The Wrong Side of the Tracks

HE WAS BORN, this Schicklgruber, in the wrong country and on the wrong side of the tracks. He wanted to be a German—he was an Austrian. The son of an illegitimate, illiterate shoemaker and a servant girl, he was left a half-orphan at thirteen, a full orphan at fifteen, dependent upon the charity of relatives.

Even as a boy he was liked by no one and disliked by many. This did not disturb him, since he disliked everyone and hated many. As he grew older he came to hate more and more people, in particular trade unionists, Marxists, democrats, Masons, but most of all Jews. Every act of his life was motivated by these hates. Hatred became his religion.

His education was negligible—he did not even finish secondary school. He tried art and failed, architecture and failed. He was reduced to being a house painter. To the end of his days, in whatever splendid uniform, he still looked like a house painter. He longed for wealth, power, culture. He was poor, insignificant, and illiterate. For all this the Jews were to blame.

He was convinced that he was uniquely gifted—certainly a genius, perhaps a god. In time a whole nation came to agree with him.

Goering said of him: "We are all the creatures of Der Führer. His faith makes us the most powerful of men. If he removes his confidence, we are nothing, we are plunged into darkness and lost to the memory of man."

Hans Franck, speaking for all Germany, said, "Hitler is lonely. So is God. Hitler is like God."

This man is unique in history. Never before has any man, starting from scratch, created a national revolution, a world war, and a great empire. Caesar and Napoleon used the revolutions of others as stepping stones to power. Philip, King of Macedonia started his son, Alexander the Great, on his conquest of a world empire. Lenin made a revolution, but Stalin built the empire. This man, single-handed, did both.

Plans which appeared fantastic to everyone else, he carried out quite simply and easily. If they seemed the dreams of a madman, they were—but he made them come true. Even when his revolution aborted and his empire came crashing about his ears, even when he had brought ruin, disaster and near annihilation to his people and was living underground in a bomb shelter, even then he was unhesitatingly obeyed. His genius was to arouse and organize hate. Thus he compensated for his neurotic inferiority complexes, the inner insecurities and anxieties caused by hating and being hated, the frustrations of his youth, the degradation of his childhood. Finally he rose so high that he dared "to spit into the eye of God."

Gertrud Klasen was born within sound of Bow Bells, a cockney from her first yell. Her father was a drunkard and a singer in low music halls. At thirteen Gertie went to live with him and his mistress in one room divided by a curtain. He was "in the theater" and that's where Gertie wanted to be. Playing bit parts, she was soon being told she looked almost like a lady. Thereupon she decided to learn to act like a lady—drink her tea out of the cup, crook a little finger, kick a train about, and speak in a voice suggesting the need of an adenoidectomy.

She went to see Miss Italia Conti, a well-known coach. Miss Conti assured her that, though she might learn to look and act like a lady, with her raucous voice and cockney accent she'd never fool anyone.

That was all Gertie needed. From being wistful, she became determined. She haunted the premises until finally Miss Conti consented to take her on.

You may have seen this same Gertie in Shaw's *Pygmalion* on Broadway, in the role of Eliza Doolittle, the flower girl who bawls out a lady for the rude behavior of her son in a flood of cockney. That was Gertie, uttering her native woodnotes wild. What Professor Higgins does for Eliza in the play is exactly what Miss Conti did for Gertrud Klasen, transforming her by the simple process of phonetics into Gertrude Lawrence, as perfect a lady as ever graced the British stage. From thence she rose to become a dashing figure in international society, the friend of nobility and royalty, indistinguishable from them except by the sparkle royalty so notoriously lacks. To this did a cockney girl attain.

She did more.

With no education, she read herself into a full-fledged professorship at Columbia University. For poverty, she substituted wealth. For commonness, good breeding. For cockney speech, exquisite diction. For social ignominy, a brilliant social position. For neglect, adoration. For emotional insecurity, the stability of marriage to a devoted husband.

Gertrude Lawrence herself recognized that her whole

life was motivated by a "wrong-side-of-the-tracks" complex. In her early years in the theater she dreamed constantly of the day when, dripping with furs, flashing paste
jewels, "the star of the London stage" would return to
the neighborhood where she had kicked up her heels to a
barrel organ and, "descending from her chariot" (a taxi),
would demand of her assembled relatives, "What about
my cousin Ruby now?" (Her cousin Ruby, she of the
golden curls, the pert nose, and the elegant manners, was
the paragon held up to her for emulation all through her
childhood.)

"Does this sound trivial and selfish?" asks Gertrude
Lawrence in her autobiography, A Star Danced. "Most
of us, I believe, have indulged, or do still indulge, in
some such fantasy as this which compensates for a lot
of hard knocks and heartaches."

What is there on the wrong side of the tracks that produces such violent reactions—that drives a Schicklgruber
to become a Hitler, a Gertrud Klasen to become a Gertrude Lawrence?

On the wrong side of the tracks there is everything
that breeds shame—poverty, squalor, social stigma, lack
of security, lack of education, common birth, vulgar
speech, sordid surroundings, ugliness, filth.

One need not actually be born there to experience a
sense of social inferiority. The slightest social inequality
will do it, a mere difference in income, parents of foreign
birth, a mother who works, a father who is not white-
collar, parents who are divorced, common speech, or just
no mink coats in the family.

We have only to glance about us to see the symptoms
of these social inferiority complexes everywhere.

The check grabber, the too lavish tipper, the inveterate
Cadillac owner. (Early poverty.) The name-dropper, the
lion-hunter, the title-lover. (Lowly birth.) The individual

whose conversation drips with four-syllable words, French phrases, and literary references. (Lack of education.) The person who is tongue-tied or who, fearing silence, indulges in a stream-of-consciousness monologue. (Lack of social breeding.) People of narrow interests, marked verbal rigidity, a limited vocabulary bolstered by bromides, slang, clichés, profanity, without which linguistic props they wouldn't last ten minutes. (Lack of culture.)

From the day laborer to the millionaire, practically no one is free from a sense of social inferiority on some count, whether it be insufficient education or lowly birth or poverty—to which practically no one but St. Francis of Assisi is devoted. Even royalty does not escape. It is so traditionally ill at ease on occasion that there is a definite syndrome known as " royal shyness," which H.R.H. Edward, Prince of Wales, at his most beautiful and most popular, used to exhibit in the nervous fingering of his tie.

Each class has a complex as regards some other social class. The commoner loves a lord; the aristocrat is flattered to be invited with celebrities; the intellectual is honored to be welcomed among the nobility; the American is gratified to be accepted into international society; the European is delighted to meet American millionaires and cowboys; movie stars are tickled pink to be received at Buckingham Palace—and Buckingham Palace loves being invited to Drury Lane.

We are constantly taking our social temperature. Are we being invited to as many cocktail parties this season as last? Have the Joneses dropped us? Why did the Cavendishes refuse two invitations to dinner? Why were the Bellamys asked to the Bradshaws' opera party and not we? In some milieus it takes a while to know just where we stand. In others—Hollywood, for example—one is never for a moment in doubt. As Joan Blondell put it, "People out here either greet you with a wild hello and a wallop on the back or they completely ignore you."

Any new situation is likely to bring our lurking sense of social inferiority to the surface. The GI joining the army, the young man visiting his fiancé's family for the first time, the new professor entering his classroom, the new boarder, the latest comer to a community, all will feel a sense of inferiority until they are accepted.

Being patronized, even by a friend—especially by a friend—frequently kindles the latent sense of inferiority. By a simple gesture of good will the friend puts himself in a position of superiority and makes an enemy. One can forgive being exploited, not being patronized.

If we are forced to do work we consider beneath us we experience an acute sense of inferiority. Some men would die and let their families die of starvation before they would accept work they feel is degrading. Not hard work. Not dangerous work. Just *inferior* work.

A corroding inferiority invades all who, in modern industry, are mere cogs in a manufacturing process. No one can long tolerate such standardization, taking from him all sense of individuality and human dignity. Eventually a million or so little egos, like a million or so little atoms, just explode. Without the safety valves of strikes, greater leisure in which to be a human being, an independent attitude toward management, and so forth, an industrial nation like our own would blow up and burst.

Each of us reacts most forcefully to that factor in our early social environment from which we suffered most. For one child it may be neglect, for another class distinctions, for a third poverty, and so on.

Say it is neglect that cut deepest into the child's heart.

John Frances Roche was such a child. An alcoholic father died when the boy was seven. An alcoholic mother turned him over to institutions and foster homes. His probation report read, "Basically and repeatedly rejected and materially and emotionally deprived, he began early to accept a virtually anarchic and jungle-like adaptation to his social climate."

At twenty-seven, having, in the course of his short career, killed five persons, for loot or for lust, he was sentenced to die in the electric chair. He had no objection. "I want to die," was all he said . . . He had had enough of neglect and his own terrifying reaction to it.

On the other hand—

There was the girl named Norma Jean Baker.

All her life this girl has thought of herself as "nobody's little girl." Her father was killed in an automobile accident; her mother was too ill to care for her. She can't begin to remember the places where she lived, the families she briefly joined, the orphanages, the foster homes. All she remembers is that she was so starved for mother love that she still cherishes, as a once-in-a-lifetime memory, the day the director of an orphanage stooped and dusted a little powder on her nose. Her only parent was Los Angeles County.

Whatever it is that some people have and others don't, this girl had it. Like many another girl, she dreamed of becoming a motion picture star, beautiful, glamorous, but above all, adored. The difference was that she organized her whole life around this dream. She worked only to earn the money for singing, dancing, acting lessons. No one told her then, few have told her since, that she had talent. Even that didn't matter. She would succeed without it.

Today Norma Jean Baker is known wherever the celluloid strip has penetrated as Marilyn Monroe. The child starved for love receives the adulation of millions. An inferiority complex is worth whatever you make of it.

Say it is the lack of education which hurt most in childhood.

It wouldn't be difficult to prove that many of the best educations on record have been acqired by those with little or no formal education. Most of the great literature of the world has been produced by "uneducated" writers. Chaucer was the son of a vintner, Marlowe of a shoemaker, Spenser of a linen draper, Donne of an ironmonger, Milton of a scrivener, Shakespeare of a man variously credited with being a glover, a butcher and, at odd times, a dealer in barley, timber, and wool.

As to their education, among some two dozen playwrights writing at the same time as Shakespeare, only three or four had a university education. The "learned" Ben Jonson was a bricklayer, soldier, and actor in his youth, when he acquired his vast learning. Chapman translated Homer and Drayton wrote poetry in every form from sonnet to epic with only a homemade education. The world's greatest dramatic poet, Shakespeare, attended his small-town grammar school only until the age of thirteen, when he seems to have been apprenticed to a local tradesman. It is not the rich, the aristocratic, the university-bred who write the world's great books, compose its great music, paint its great pictures.

Even today, when a good education is practically inescapable, we find that many of the best educations anywhere around belong to those who have educated themselves.

We know Samuel Chotzinoff as a famous pianist, music critic, and the musical director of N.B.C. He is also the author of an autobiography which he calls *A Lost Paradise*. And where do you suppose his lost paradise was? The slums of the lower East Side of New York and the ghetto of Vitebsk in Czarist Russia.

"Life was rich and wonderful there," he says, and his nostalgic reminiscences somehow convince us. It was not poverty, nor lowly birth, nor the stigma of living in the ghetto that ate into the soul of young Samuel. No, what he longed for, what he would have died without, was learning. To be able to read and study he needed privacy, which does not exist in the slums. But Sam created it in a tiny storeroom of the railroad flat which he transformed into his "library" with two-cent copies of Horatio Alger, *The Liberty Boys*, and free pamphlets from the Department of Agriculture. Here he retreated from hunger, insult, gang warfare, bedbugs and family quarrels into the world of learning. With hoarded pennies he began to take music lessons. On stolen and borrowed time he read and studied until finally he became the master of two arts—music and literature. That is the kind of education that sticks to your ribs.

The higher a man rises in the world the more does he feel the lack of an education. A day-laborer suffers no pangs of inferiority from knowing nothing of languages or literature but the self-made millionaire does. I have heard presidents of banks and large industries say, "As far as business is concerned, I didn't need a college education. But I regret it now because of its cultural value."

Such men are apt to overrate the value of formal education and to underrate self-education. I once heard Herman Shumlin, producer of *Inherit the Wind*, and many other Broadway successes, admit that he had a terrific inferiority complex regarding his lack of education. (He finished only two years of high school.) So great is his veneration for education (by which he means what you get in a college, with part of the alphabet attached) that he believes that Hemingway and Bernard Shaw (don't turn over in your grave, G. B. S.) would have been better writers if they'd had a college education! Mr. Shumlin is so obviously a man with an IQ which must hover in the vicinity of genius that it's pretty silly of him to worry over a lack of formal education. Such a mind picks up its own education.

Perhaps it was the shame of foreign birth or of foreign parents that most deeply wounded the childish ego. There is no worse agony for a child than to be pursued with derisive cries of "Dago," "Dutchy," "Chink." Chiefly in America, with its large immigrant population, do we find among children this shame of their foreign-born parents with their unreconstructed love of the old country and their clinging to its manners, religion, folkways, languages. The new generation becomes belligerently American, makes a clean break with the past and sees red at the word "Wop," "Spik" or "Harp."

One after the other as they immigrated to our shores, we looked down upon the Germans, the Irish, the Russians, the Poles, the Puerto Ricans, and always upon the Jews. The Statue of Liberty welcomes them with these gracious words:

> Give me your tired, your poor,
> Your huddled masses yearning to breathe free,
> The wretched refuse of your teeming shore . . .

Wretched refuse—is that a nice way to greet the newcomers to our country?

To some children this scorn for the foreigner is a tremendous stimulus. They set out to prove that they are better Americans than *born* Americans.

A "Dutchy" named Bok, arriving here penniless, with only a few words of English and outlandish clothes, was treated at school like an early Christian martyr. Schoolboys know pity as the tiger knows it.

He could have hated them back. He didn't. Instead he resolved to become an American that America would be proud of.

He learned to speak and write English as none of those boys ever did. In *The Americanization of Edward Bok,* which he wrote after thirty years as editor of *The Ladies' Home Journal,* he made us understand what it means, not to *be,* but to *become* an American. It received the Pulitzer Prize and the gold medal of the Academy of Political and Social Science.

Suppose it was poverty that ground into the child's soul. In America as in no other country on earth it is possible to compensate directly for this particular complex by becoming wealthy. It is the American credo that it is a man's *duty* to rise from rags to riches, a doctrine preached from pulpits from the time of Cotton Mather, taught to babes in their McGuffey readers, to boys in the Horatio Alger books, and to adults in *Poor Richard's Almanac.* On moral as well as on economic grounds, the American male has failed if he does not accomplish this. He feels properly inferior.

It is this complex that has led to our being the most prosperous country in the world, with the highest standard of living in history. All our little individual inferiority complexes about poverty, working together, have produced a compensation on a national scale.

Poverty is so usual a cause of inferiority feelings and its compensation by acquiring wealth is so commonplace in America that it is unnecessary to mention examples. But there was a Swedish girl—

Greta Gustafsson's earliest memories are of waiting for hours with a sick father in a free clinic for a handout of medicine and of seeing him suffer and die without medical care. It was then that the love of money entered her soul. On his death, when she was fourteen, she went to work as a soap-lather girl in a barber shop.

As she rose from this lowly position to enter the movies and then to go on to Hollywood and become a star, it was clear that money was to be her chief incentive. She seems never to have felt very much her lack of education. Exposed to every sort of cultural influence, her incredibly bad taste in literature, art, and music remained intact. Her favorite bedtime reading was *Peter Rabbit* and other children's books. She was incapable of sustaining a conversation, not so much because she was shy as because she had nothing to say.

"I am one of those people who do not think," was one of the few autobiographical remarks she ever made.

This is the woman who became the most famous motion-picture actress in the world, the greatest actress of our day, about whom more has been written than about any other performer of stage or screen who has ever lived—Greta Garbo.

While still young (in her thirties), still beautiful, talented and popular, she retired. She had all the money she could ever use. That seemed to her reason enough.

Perhaps it was a sense of class distinction, that others were superior to us because of birth or social position, that caused the keenest suffering in childhood. That is the complex that produces the social climber and the professional party-giver.

I know of no better example of how this particular complex works than that of George Bryan Brummell.

George was the grandson of a valet—lower than that no Englishman can fall. In spite of which his father got him into Eton where he was immediately made to feel the full ignominy of his lot. Fortunately George had a sharp wit and he used it ruthlessly, drawing many a spurt of blue blood. He also had a nice taste in haberdashery and soon began to outdress, outswank, and outsnoot his aristocratic schoolmates.

Out of school and in the army, he quickly won the reputation of being the best-dressed captain in the regiment, then the best-dressed captain in the army, the best-dressed man at court, the best-dressed man in England, finally the best-dressed man in the world. He still ranks as the best-dressed man of all time.

This he accomplished through his impeccable taste. The Beau would enter a ballroom where all the males flaunted satins, laces, ribbons, and jewels, dressed in a suit of somber black that was an exclamation point of simplicity, distinction, and cut. With it he wore a fluted shirt, gloves and shoes of a quiet elegance that no one could imitate. His grooming, having occupied him half the day, was faultless. He changed the dress of an entire nation. Since his day the British male has been the best-dressed man on earth.

Thus he achieved a social position that compensated for all the snubs of his youth. He became the idol of the Prince Regent, fat, slow of wit, and with no more taste in dress than an organ-grinder's monkey. He remained his idol until the day when, in a fit of pique, the Beau, looking directly, at the Prince, inquired loudly and publicly of a courtier, "Who is your fat friend?"

The wit that had made him was finally his undoing.

Everyone feels this sense of social inferiority—some of us all of the time, all of us some of the time. Properly compensated for, like an old wound it hurts only on occasion. Uncompensated, it remains an open wound, always bleeding a little.

When you find a man like Sinclair Lewis, who compensated so magnificently for many early deficiencies, still, at the height of his fame, terribly concerned about whether he'll be invited by Somerset Maugham, fearful that he might be patronized by Hugh Walpole, that Arnold Bennett might think him uncouth, that H. G. Wells might not introduce him to John Galsworthy, that he might be thought less important than Fitzgerald or

Hemingway, and when you hear him comment after a party that everyone there seemed to enjoy "being superior to funny me," you realize that he has never been able to wipe out the sense of social inferiority due to being born of ordinary people in a small, simple Middle Western town.

The uncompensated social inferiority complex was never better illustrated than in the case of a former mayor of New York, Hylan by name. Hylan was so indisputably from the wrong side of the tracks that he seems never to have made any effort to disguise it. He just ducked any involvement with top-drawer personalities. When in 1924 the then Prince of Wales invited him to lunch aboard H.M.S. Renown, anchored in the North River, "Hizzoner" declined with a gracious, "Everybody here will tell you I never eat lunch."

Hylan's panic about greeting distinguished visitors was of pathological proportions. Faced with even a minor celebrity, he died a thousand deaths. Finally he delegated the task of welcoming celebrities to his secretary, a young man from the Lower East Side who had no such inhibitions. Grover Whalen's antecedents were no more fashionable than Hylan's, but unlike the Mayor he had surmounted any complexes about being born on the wrong side of the tracks. With perfect aplomb he could escort the King and Queen of England on a tour of New York's World Fair; he could drive with the Prince of Wales along Broadway under the first paper shower ever accorded a visiting celebrity (which he initiated), making pleasant small talk all the way; he could, and he did, meet every man, high or low, on his own level without obsequiousness and without swagger. He knew he was as good as the next man, no better, no worse.

Hylan or Whalen—which is the best way to handle a complex?

It is the firm conviction of many people, particularly the English, that a gentleman is born, not made. It is the equally firm conviction of many other people, particularly Americans, that a gentleman can be made. One American set out to prove it.

Over twenty years ago an American athlete, a champion sculler, Kelly by name, was barred from Britain's Henley Regatta on the grounds that, having worked with his hands as a bricklayer, he was not a gentleman.

Something entered that boy's soul that was to change his whole life. From being a bricklayer, he became a brick manufacturer and eventually the millionaire head of the largest brick-construction company in the country. But there was something he wanted more.

He had a son whom he named for himself, John B. Kelly, Jr. He trained him from childhood as a sculler and never permitted him to work with his hands. Then, in 1947, he went with him to Britain, saw him entered in the Henley Regatta—*and saw him win it!*

Kelly also had a daughter who had the good fortune to be born beautiful. He brought her up like a lady according to the British definition. In 1956 that girl became Her Serene Highness, Princess Gracia Patricia of Monaco, the wife of Prince Rainier of the 140 titles.

Thus did the former bricklayer compensate for not being born a gentleman.

But even the best-bred, most sophisticated people may occasionally feel a twinge of social inferiority. The trick then is to pick ourselves up, brush off our knees, and go right on as if nothing had happened.

An American playing polo with the Duke of Edinburgh, after the game, was invited to Windsor Castle for a drink. Entering a living room, he found himself face to face with the entire royal family—Queen Elizabeth, the Queen

Mother, and Princess Margaret. Considerably jolted, he endeavored to recall anything he might have read concerning the protocol for such occasions. It appeared he had read nothing. While trying to decide whether to bow from the waist, kneel, kiss the ladies' hands or back toward the door, and whether to say "Your Majesty," "Your Serene Highness," or perhaps use the third person, he was rescued by the Duke with the simple dukely remark, "I presume you know all these people. What will you have to drink?"

After that he was perfectly all right.

The social stigma that cuts deepest is illegitimacy for it can never be reversed and never eliminated by the acquisition of any amount of wealth, education, or social position. Only honor can fill the hole dug by dishonor.

A boy named Lawrence—Thomas Edward—who had always believed himself to be the legitimate son of an Irish baronet, one day discovered that he was the bastard child of the family nursemaid. Thereafter he swung pathologically from the pursuit of glory to retreat into obscurity. Shame drove him forward and shame dragged him back.

In the First World War he organized the Arabs and led them to victory against the Turks and Germans to become Lawrence of Arabia. For this Britain and France proffered him honors and decorations. He made one of his famous retreats by refusing them all.

He was one of the important figures at the Peace Conference, he was called to the Colonial Office as adviser on Arab affairs by Winston Churchill, he helped to make Faisal King of Iraq—and then, without warning, he suddenly retreated into anonymity as "Private Shaw," a mechanic in the Royal Air Force.

From this self-imposed obscurity he emerged in 1926 with a book which, had he done nothing else, would have

handed him down to posterity—*Seven Pillars of Wisdom,*
which later, in a shorter form, known as *Revolt in the
Desert,* became a best seller.

Once again he withdrew into anonymity by legally
changing his name to T. E. Shaw. Why Shaw? Because,
it is said, he had on one occasion been mistaken for the
legitimate son of George Bernard Shaw!

So it went all his life. He achieved fame and honor,
sometimes wildly exaggerating his exploits, only to retreat
hastily from the notoriety he had attracted.

Whatever else in his controversial career and his contradictory personality his biographers may differ about,
they are at one in this: that his obsession regarding his
illegitimacy molded his mind, his character, and his whole
career. No accomplishments (and he was a brilliant
archeologist and linguist as well as soldier, military strate-
gist, and writer), no fame, no praise (not even Churchill's,
"I deem him one of the greatest beings alive in our time")
could wipe out for him the shame of his birth. No compensation was ever enough.

It is on such distinctions as these—birth, economic
status, education, and so forth—that the class system is
built. There is no such things as a classless society. Social
barriers may not be so well defined nor so insurmountable
today as under feudalism; they still exist and are exploited
by those from the right side of the tracks and resented
by those from the wrong side. Where they tend to disap-
pear, someone always rushes to restore them. West German Defense Minister Strauss was reported to be making
a big hit with the rank-conscious Germans by restoring
the army boots of the Third Reich, Hitlerian-type parachute caps, and insignia of rank down to and including
red pencils for use by officers of field grade only. So small
a thing as a red pencil can give a man a feeling of
superiority! Actually, no two lords feel themselves to be

on exactly the same social level, nor do any two Bowery bums.

There are many ways to face up to the situation of having been born on the wrong side of the tracks.

One can move over to the right side—as Ben Franklin did.

One can act as though there were no right and wrong side—as Lincoln did.

One can straddle the fence—as Lawrence did.

One can exploit the situation—as Elsa Maxwell did.

One can compensate through the next generation—as John Kelly did.

One can invent a past, disguise it, or drop it into a well of oblivion—as Ann Crowell did.

Ann, a beautiful young woman, married to a man of excellent social position, lives in a lovely home on Long Island. They own a string of race horses, one of them the most famous horse of its day, Nashua. They belong to all the right clubs, know all the best people, go to all the smart parties, associate with royalty when it's around. She seems completely at home in her environment. Only a keen observer would remark that she never mentions her childhood, never refers to events in her past life, never produces a relative.

Then one day her picture is in all the papers. By accident, she has shot and killed her husband. The reporters unearth her father, living in Detroit. They show him a picture of the young woman.

"Yes, that is my daughter," he says. "I saw a picture of her the other day in the newspaper but I didn't recognize her. It's twenty years since I've heard from her."

Why?

The father was a street-car conductor, not a proper background for a woman of Ann Crowell Woodward's position. She herself had been a model, not a past to boast about. She dropped the whole thing into a well of oblivion.

Most Americans are snobs in reverse. The self-made man actually brags about his lowly beginnings, figuring that the lower he started, the more extraordinary he is. It is not so much the positions they hold as the distance they have come that makes these men seem astonishing to themselves.

Benjamin Fairless, called the most powerful single figure in the country's basic industry, president and later chairman of the board of the United States Steel Corporation, writes in an article in *Life:*

"What has happened to me could not have happened in a good many countries of the world where a boy is stamped from birth with his father's occupation. It could not even have happened in the America of a hundred years ago, in the days of the family-owned business when you had to be a member of the clan. [Here] a boy from the wrong side of the tracks can go just as far as a rich man's son.

"I began life in the most modest circumstances. I was born in Pigeon Run, Ohio. Most of the men were, like my father, coal miners. In the summer . . . they would work as hired hands on the surrounding farms . . .

"I [disagree with] men who say they have been retarded in their careers because of humble origins. My experience has been just the opposite. It has always seemed to me that people went out of their way to help me when they learned of my modest beginnings."

In the case of most self-made men like Fairless, a youthful sense of inferiority later becomes a sense of pride in their accomplishment.

The social position he has attained often becomes a man's most prized possession. At the Nuremberg trials, when the Nazi generals were condemned to death, they still contended for the manner of their death. Hanging was for the common criminal. They demanded a general's death by shooting. One of them went so far as to offer to testify against the others in exchange for this boon. Goering escaped the noose by taking poison. Their honor —the honor of a Nazi criminal!—was at stake.

Anyone who would like to learn in one easy lesson how to turn a social inferiority complex into a brilliant career, could do no better than to study the case of Joseph Duveen.

When, at the turn of the century, young Duveen first came to this country from England, he made several observations which were to become the basis of a fabulous career.

He remarked that America had a bumper crop of millionaires and that all of them—the Altmans, Morgans, Kresses, Huntington's, Fricks, Wideners, Baches, Carnegies—were men of humble birth with little education and few cultural or social advantages. They were self-made men who had risen from farm boys, office boys, factory workers, storekeepers, butchers and grocers. They were also lonely men with no interests outside their business.

He next observed that, having made their millions, they hadn't the faintest notion how to spend them.

He discovered that, if they were not actually ashamed of their humble origin, they (or their wives) yearned to rise in the social scale and to acquire a cultural background. They felt keenly their exclusion from "society." The people upon whom their money made no impression were the very people they longed to associate with. The men also craved a kind of prestige that money alone could not give them—fame of some sort, recognition by posterity.

Finally he remarked that, while America had money,

Europe had culture and that that culture existed in tangible and exportable form, to wit, in paintings, sculptors, antiques, castles, and so on.

Putting two and two together, he came up, not with four, but with four trailing seven or eight ciphers behind it. He would, he decided, sell these men not art, in which they had no interest whatsoever, but a cultural past and a glorious future. He would sell them social acceptance and, yes, even immortality. He would supply them with an aristocratic past by selling them the treasures of the palaces of Europe—paintings by the great masters, centuries-old family portraits, masterpieces of the goldsmith's art, antique furniture, thrones, suits of armor, brocades and tapestries from castle walls, yes, even the walls themselves.

On these simple observations Duveen built the most fabulous career and fortune that any art dealer, back to the Medicis, had ever achieved.

It was not on the basis of enthusiasm that he was able to sell paintings for several million dollars apiece. That had been tried before and no one had grown extravagantly rich by it. Duveen decided to appeal to more universal motives.

Take, as an example of his method in practice, the case of the H. E. Huntingtons. Arabella, wife of H. E., had money, but money was as dirt to her. What Arabella yearned for was to be "in society." She built multimillion-dollar houses and invited the best people, but the best people stayed away, all four hundred of them.

Duveen convinced her that he could change all that. He persuaded the Huntingtons that once they had established their claims to culture through the possession of a unique collection of paintings by the great English masters, all doors would be open to them.

He began by throwing out all the ugly furniture in their

houses and replacing it with expensive English antiques.
Then he added paintings. Gradually the Huntington mansion in California became a museum, boasting the famous
"Blue Boy and "Cottage Door" by Gainsborough, "Sarah
Siddons as the Tragic Muse," and others. Soon the Huntingtons were numbered among the foremost patrons of
art in America. There could be no question of their culture
now. Many doors were opened to them.

Not all. Arabella's social success was still somewhat less
than she had hoped. Whereupon Duveen drew her attention to the fact that after all American society was not
English society. He escorted them to England, taking them
into many a fine old castle and introducing them to many
a fine old peer. If it usually transpired that the fine old
peer had whole galleries of portraits of his ancestors,
some of which he could be induced to part with, they
were still delighted to associate with a duke on any terms.

Not all American millionaires, however, were willing to
settle for social success. To them Duveen presented the
simple, unworldly philosophy that no price was too high
to pay for the priceless, that a collection of great works
of art would give them prestige here and abroad and that
their devoted adherence to this simple creed would hand
their names down to posterity. Also it had its mundane
rewards. A man brought up on cheap chromos could not
but be flattered to sit down to dinner with a Rembrandt,
glance over his newspaper at a Titian, entertain his friends
in a room with a ceiling by Watteau and go to bed with
a Fra Filippo Lippi hanging over his head. In life he
would be associating with the immortal artists themselves,
a kind of immortality in itself.

Kress, Mellon, and Frick became so imbued with this
philosophy of Duveen's, a philosophy which gave their
lives a significance it had never had before, that they practically gave up business to devote all their time to becom-

ing immortal in the Duveen sense of the word. Without this sense of buying immortality, it is doubtful if Mellon would have made his unrivaled collection, given it to the nation and erected the National Gallery to house it, with a bequest of five million dollars for upkeep.

Then Duveen moved in on Kress.

"You're not going to let Mellon have the whole National Gallery to himself, are you, Mr. Kress?"

Kress, sensing at once that Mellon was his rival for immortality, decided to co-operate with Duveen . . . Duveen did not let him down.

This system of Duveen's appears so simple and obvious that it seems odd no one ever thought of it before. Actually there were special reasons why it was Duveen who invented it. He held this key to the psychology of others because it was the key to his own.

Duveen was a Jew, in itself enough to give anyone an inferiority complex. But in addition, one of his grandfathers had been a blacksmith, another a pawnbroker, and his father had been successively a lard salesman and proprietor of a shop selling delft and furniture. Joseph's education was sketchy, and until he was a grown man his mind was a complete blank as far as painting was concerned.

Once, however, he had had his revelation concerning millionaires, art, and immortality, he began his lifelong study of art, sitting at the feet of such connoisseurs as Bernard Berenson, acquiring their knowledge, their taste, their intuition, their enthusiasm and finally becoming an authority himself. It was not money primarily that motivated him, since by the time he was ready to go into business, his family was already well to do. What then?

At a birthday dinner given by Duveen for Prime Minister Ramsay MacDonald, in Duveen's magnificent house in New York, MacDonald remarked to a friend, "I think

I know what Duveen's ambition is—and I'm going to get it for him."

It took some doing, Duveen being what he was—a Jew, the offspring of blacksmiths, pawnbrokers and lard salesmen—but MacDonald personally canvassed for a petition to the King asking for this favor. And in 1933 he was able to announce to Duveen that he was to be made a peer of the Empire—Lord Duveen of Millbank.

It was because this desire for social recognition was the driving force in his own life that Duveen was able to understand it in others and, instead of trying to sell paintings as art, to sell them as social acceptance and immortality.

A social inferiority complex can be as strong an incentive to success as one due to a physical defect or inadequacy. Great careers have been motivated by it; whole lives have been built around it. Earth-shaking failures such as Hitler's, immortal successes such as Abraham Lincoln's, have resulted from a sense of inferiority due to having been born on the wrong side of the tracks. It is up to the individual whether he will be destroyed by these complexes or spurred to high achievement.

Unlikely as it may seem at first glance, it is nonetheless true that being "born to the purple" may be almost as fertile a source of inferiority feelings as being born on the wrong side of the tracks. Suppose we see how.

CHAPTER VII

Born to the Purple

ALEXANDER THE GREAT was born to a throne, to wealth and to power. He was even, according to his mother, born a demigod. What could he aspire to? What was there to drive him to make any great effort?

An inferiority complex born of his very advantages.

His father, Philip, was a king—he would be a greater king.

His father was a famous warrior—he would be a more famous warrior.

His father was the ruler of a small kingdom—he would make himself ruler of the world.

He and his father and Macedonia were despised by the Greeks—he would conquer and humiliate the Greeks.

At eighteen Alexander dreamed of conquering the whole civilized world of his day. At thirty he had accomplished it.   · ·

The Greek complex was crucial in his psychology. The Greeks of that day, the fourth century B.C., were the most civilized people the world has yet produced. To them Macedonia was a hinterland, populated by barbarians. Demosthenes had called Philip "a barbarian pest from Macedonia, that country which cannot provide even a

decent slave." Alexander, brilliant, cultured, educated by
Aristotle, the greatest teacher of all time, raged beneath
their contempt. Historians recognize his resentment of the
Greeks' assumption of superiority as a prime motivation
in his life. Sir Harold Nicolson speaks of his relentless
determination "to surmount this sense of cultural inferiority" and to be accepted in Athens as an equal.

Thus goaded, Alexander embarked on a career of conquest such as the world has never witnessed before or
since. Once, offered all of the Persian Empire west of the
Euphrates, he refused—he would take *all* by conquest.
Always outnumbered, he was always victorious.

His goal of Greek acceptance never wavered. Held up
once by a flood in the Punjab, he revealed his lifelong
sense of inferiority in the cry, "Oh, Athens, if you only
knew what dangers I undergo to win glory in your eyes!"

In the end, the haughty "pure bred" Hellenes bowed
beneath the yoke of this semibarbarian colonial. He was
not their equal—he was their superior.

To those born to poverty it may seem downright per-
verse to harbor a sense of inferiority because of wealth
or social position. "They should worry!" is the comment
from the other side of the tracks.

They should indeed. To live in the shadow of the wealth,
position, fame of one's forebears can be as crushing as
to live in the shadow of poverty and ignominy. The poor
boy has no place to go but up, the rich boy, no place but
down. In addition, he is deprived of the normal incentives
to effort. He has everything, why struggle? The proportion
of those from the wrong side of the tracks who make good
is far greater than of those born to the purple.

Of all the types of privilege to which one may be born,
wealth is generally considered the most desirable. To
inherit millions seems to most people the ultimate in
good fortune. Yet the moral dangers of wealth are greater

than the moral dangers of poverty. It takes higher quantities of mind and soul to fight it. The temptation to sink back and enjoy one's privileges is well-nigh irresistible. Why fight when one already possesses what everyone else is fighting for? The very qualities that are born of struggle, that build moral fibre, atrophy and die in an atmosphere of wealth.

"Well, now that I've got it, what am I going to do with it?" a man asks himself.

Be a playboy, Tommy Manville, heir to the Johns Manville millions, seems to say. So Tommy becomes the husband of his country, marrying and divorcing, ten wives in all. His idea of a helluva time is giving a party for five of his nine previous wives—or running home when the court rules the furniture is to be divided on a fifty-fifty basis between divorced husband and wife, to saw it all in half.

Micky Jelke, heir to a $3,000,000 oleomargarine fortune, sought sensation in sex and crime and got himself sentenced to two to three years in Sing Sing for compulsory prostitution.

Bobby Schlesinger tried to outsmart the Wall Street boys. The son of Mrs. Harrison Williams, now Countess Mona Bismarck, inveigled several of them into investing $170,000 in a phony Louisiana Oil Syndicate, and was sentenced to five to ten years in jail.

Barbara Hutton, heiress to the Woolworth millions, tried marriage six times, always with a notable lack of judgment. A neglected child—"I never knew a real father or mother," she once told a friend. "I was brought up in tearooms by governesses or sent away to school"—she longed for devotion. A plain girl, she wanted to marry glamour—all six husbands, from Prince Mdivani to Baron von Cramm, were glamorous. She hoped to be married for love, not for money. It's amazing the things money won't buy.

Live madly, says Diana Barrymore, intolerably inferiorized by a brilliant and dominating mother (the poet Michael Strange), and handsome and talented father (John Barrymore) and a fortune—and proceeds to become our foremost Cinderella-in-reverse. In her no-holds-barred autobiography, *Too Much, Too Soon,* she describes the whole sordid debacle. From glamorous debutante she became a social outcast. From Hollywood star she fell to playing bit parts. She became an alcoholic ("Take that drunken woman out of my house," stormed Alfred Hitchcock, venomously insulted by her). She married several times—disgracefully—once a professional tennis player, later jailed on a white-slavery charge; another time Robert Wilcox, with whom she was locked out of a cheap Hollywood room for non-payment of rent and with whom she went to a supermarket to steal food. She attempted suicide. Why did she publicly regurgitate all these sordid details. "To make a fast buck," she is said to have answered a reporter.

Some of the heirs of great wealth finally realize that it is a handicap and do something about it.

Alfred Gwynne Vanderbilt, heir to $20,000,000 and once classified as our No. 1 playboy, when in his forties suddenly sold thirty-seven of the forty-two thoroughbred race horses from his famous Sagamore Stables and began devoting his time and his money to social causes—the World Veteran Fund, the National Urban League for the advancement of the Negro, the United World Federalist Movement, and the Wiltwyck School for Boys.

Sometimes the founder of a great fortune realizes that while making millions may be an exciting adventure, spending it can be an awful bore. And sometimes he trains his heirs to spend it as a great fortune deserves to be spent.

John D. Rockefeller, Jr., the son of the richest man in the world, was trained from childhood for the responsibilities of great wealth. His biography in *Who's Who* starts right off with "President of the Board of the Rockefeller Institute for Medical Research" and winds up with "Trustee of the Rockefeller Foundation." He spent his life, his money, his heart, and his imagination on his unparalleled contributions to everything from education to the restoration of the Palace of Versailles. He considered that very little of his wealth belonged to him personally.

It would be almost impossible for a man or woman to inherit great wealth without harboring a sense of guilt as being the almost unlawful possessor of this wealth, as well as for the ruthless methods by which, quite often, it has been acquired. A sense of moral uneasiness as he faces a world in which other men must slave and sweat for a living invades him.

Averell Harriman grew up in a mansion in Manhattan and a twenty-thousand-acre estate on the Hudson, with his own polo field, his private race track in which to exercise his trotters, his own hunting preserves. It was not until, through no fault of his own, he became vice-president of his father's Union Pacific Railroad that he began to be aware of several uncomfortable facts:

That it was his father's wealth, not his own abilities, that had put him where he was.

That he would never be able to match his father's financial success and business genius.

That his father, E. H. Harriman, had been considered a public malefactor (Theodore Roosevelt had labeled him "an undesirable citizen" and a "malefactor of great wealth"), and that the 5 billion dollars' worth of railroads he dominated and the personal fortune of 100 million dollars he left were held by many to be "ill-gotten" wealth.

Young Harriman, having absorbed these facts, set out to prove two things: that *he* was not a malefactor of great wealth and that he could achieve a success in his own right.

To that end he went into politics and soon ran up a record of service in the federal government that few other men in public life today can match. Among the many important posts he has held are ambassador to Russia and to the Court of St. James, roving ECA ambassador, and Governor of New York State.

Given his extraordinary drive, the work of campaigning and of holding office never taxed him. What got him down was his inability, born of his aristocratic training, to be folksy. It was repellent to him to be chummy with people he'd never met.

"Please," begged a photographer during one campaign, "make one more effort to be friendly with the baby."

Throughout his career the younger Harriman, unlike the elder, has fought consistently for the underdog, has supported labor against capital, has warred on poverty, protected the civil liberties of all citizens, and defended the rights of all nations to freedom.

No doubt he has to a large extent wiped out the sense of guilt at being the heir of a "malefactor of great wealth" and the feeling of being inferior in ability to a successful father.

It takes some such misfortune as this to drive the sons of rich men to make their own place in the world. I once heard the poet, Robert Frost, say:

"A certain boy had many disadvantages. He came of a wealthy family. He went to Groton, then to Harvard, then into a plush law practice. One day God took a look at him and said, 'This fellow is not fighting. The trouble with him is, he hasn't enough disadvantages.' So God gave him polio—and that was it."

Could the career of Franklin Roosevelt be better described?

The man at the top has his social inferiority complexes just as does the man at the bottom. The greater a man's wealth and power, the greater his fear of being unable to hold on to them; the greater his authority, the greater his sense of responsibility—if he has a conscience; and the less he lives up to his responsibilities, the greater his feeling of guilt.

True, the will to power and the love of risk to some extent cancel out the factors making for a sense of inferiority. So do wealth, success, the opportunity for self-expression. Nevertheless the capitalist can scarcely escape a sense of guilt for his "exploitation" of labor, as well as the feeling that he is facing a powerful and dangerous enemy desirous of destroying him. All this does shake a little his self-esteem. The fierce competition of business today adds a final touch of insecurity. Between the two, capital and labor, a constant mutual struggle to inferiorize the other goes on.

During the present generation the relations between the two have improved enormously. Management has radically changed its attitude since the days of the sweatshop and child labor. Even if it hasn't always yielded these rights and privileges willingly, it still has fewer painful inferiority complexes on this score than in the days of the robber barons of big business.

Many heads of industry today go further. They hold themselves to be stewards of the wealth of their companies and of the welfare of their workers. A French investigator, visiting our great factories, was bowled over by this attitude on the part of management. Everywhere he was confronted by suggestion boxes, coffee breaks, piped-in music,

libraries, clubs, free entertainment, sports, free psychiatric
services, industrial research, and financial aid to workers
who wanted to attend night schools. And everywhere he
saw executives and workers going to picnics and office
parties together. Even when strikes were brewing, there
was a complete lack of class resentment and a sense of
equality, with boss and employees calling each other by
their first names—a situation unheard of in Europe.

Still most millionaires today harbor a vague sense of
unease in the face of their uncommon luck. The number
of men who have inherited or acquired vast wealth and are
no longer satisfied merely to go on piling it up or to
squander it on yachts, race horses, and big estates has
increased enormously since the turn of the century. No
longer do they consider that wealth is a right. It is a
responsibility, and if they shirk it they suffer from a sense
of inferiority. Increasingly they retire from the making
of money to devote themselves to public service, as in
the case of Benjamin Fairless, of Charles E. Wilson, Lewis
Douglas, Laurence A. Steinhardt, Thomas K. Finletter,
Eugene Meyer, Bernard Baruch.

To be born the child of famous parents may be as much
a handicap as to be born to wealth. How would you like
to bear the name of Einstein? Or Churchill? Or Eisenhower? Or Roosevelt? Yet there are men struggling against
the handicap of those names today. They cannot hope
to surpass them or even to equal them—they can only
hope not to disgrace them. To the child of a Smith or a
Jones it may seem the rarest of good fortune to be the
offspring of a Hoover, a MacArthur, a Toscanini. To the
child itself it may be the most frustrating fact in his whole
life. If there is one point on which Adler and Freud agree
it is that the son is impelled to outdo his father—Adler
on the basis that the boy must prove he is superior to his
father, Freud on the ground that he is his father's rival

for his mother's love. If the father is famous, the boy's lot is a tough one.

Fame is the most frustrating of all handicaps to overcome, for it depends upon factors beyond our control—a thing called genius. Rare are the sons whose talents equal their famous fathers'—a Dumas fils, a Johann Strauss, a Johann Bach—and who, instead of being crushed, are stimulated by that fame.

None know this frustration better than the sons of presidents.

Only one of Lincoln's sons lived to manhood. Robert Lincoln's whole life and character were predicated on his inevitable inferiority to his father and his determination to be as unlike him as possible in order to be *himself*. Lincoln did nothing to lessen the boy's sense of inferiority. He openly favored his second son, the adored Tad. He once referred to Robert as "one of the little rare-ripe sort that are smarter at about five than ever after." The only piece of advice he ever gave him was not to go to Harvard. To Harvard Robert went.

With a less famous father he might have amounted to something for he had a number of good qualities. But all his life he sweated under the sun of that fame and wilted in the glare of that publicity. Nicholas Murray Butler reported him as once saying:

"No one wanted me for Secretary of War; they wanted Abraham Lincoln's son. No one wanted me for Minister to England; they wanted Abraham Lincoln's son. No one wanted me for president of the Pullman Company; they wanted Abraham Lincoln's son."

Several men in our own time have lived under the same shadow—the Roosevelts, Robert Taft, Major Eisenhower, Herbert Hoover, Jr.—some of them men of real ability. But how can names like theirs be surpassed? The

best a man can do is to be a person in his own right—as
Hoover, Jr., is.

Before he was six, Hoover's father was already famous.
When he was graduated from Harvard he was offered big
jobs by big corporations at big salaries.

"My name is not for sale," he said.

Again and again he reset his course in life to escape
any benefits from his father's position. Cameron Hawley
says of him:

"He has shunned public life and avoided publicity,
always living in the shadows, grimly resolute that no
advantage be taken of reflected fame . . . He has gone
out of his way to steer clear of his father's path."

If referred to at all in the press it was inevitably as
"the son of the former President."

Newspapers kept no files on him. All that was publicly
known of him when he was fifty years old was that he was
an engineer living in California, who had been a private
consultant on petroleum problems to several foreign governments. His self-effacement was complete. He preferred
not to be known at all rather than to be known as his
father's son.

When he came at last, under President Eisenhower,
to be Undersecretary of State, he was one of the least
known men ever to occupy that important post. For the
first time he was spoken of, not as "the son of the former
President" but as Herbert Hoover, Jr., the man chiefly
responsible for the settlement of the British-Iranian oil
dispute, averting a Communist victory in Iran, and giving
wicked old Mossadegh, howling in prison, his come-
uppance.

While he can never equal the performance of his great
father, at least he is his own man, he is without bitterness,
he is his father's greatest admirer. He has done as well

as anyone can be expected to do bearing a name like
that. . . . Perhaps great men should not have sons.

However, if the name is not absolutely overwhelming,
it may act as a spur instead of a gag to the ambition of
an energetic youngster.

And here comes Agnes de Mille again, the girl with
all the complexes.

Agnes was born into a family where success was taken
for granted. Uncle Cecil was a one-man spectacular.
Father was a brilliant playwright. Mother was the daughter of Henry George, the famous single-taxer in whose
funeral cortège marched a hundred thousand mourners.
When Mother, herself a personage, entered banquet halls
and parliaments, the entire audience rose. The de Mille
home crawled with celebrities, everyone from Somerset
Maugham to Charlie Chaplin, from Rebecca West to
Rosa Ponselle. The career of Uncle Cecil alone made
failure unthinkable. From childhood Agnes was aware
of her rendezvous with fame.

After years of study she failed in her very first ballet
audition.

That, she comments in her autobiography, was the first
failure her family had ever known.

At thirty, an age at which most ballet dancers retire,
she was ballet's most faithful failure. She wore her sister's
castoff clothes and lived on small handouts from her
mother. Inferiority penetrated the very marrow of her
bones.

She never gave up, quit working, lost hope. If she
couldn't dance like Pavlova, she could—she felt it in every
muscle of her body, every cell in her brain, every drop
of her blood—create ballets for others to dance in.

And eventually she did. In rapid succession she produced her great American ballets. At long last the famous-
family complex paid off.

There can be worse complexes than those caused by the wealth or fame of one's forebears. There can be those caused by the wealth *and* fame of one's forebears. A chap named John Hay Whitney had *that* to contend with.

One of his grandfathers was John Hay, Lincoln's Secretary of State and later Ambassador to Britain.

Another grandfather was William C. Whitney, Cleveland's Secretary of the Navy. *And* he inherited an enormous fortune. When, as a prisoner of the Nazis, he was asked what his civilian occupation was, he answered automatically, to the utter incredulity of the Germans, "capitalist." He couldn't have been more right. One private portfolio of selected securities into which he put $20,-000,000 of his personal fortune, was reported some years later to be in the $60,000,000–$80,000,000 range. That's just *one* investment.

His 500-acre estate with its palatial residence might make even Buckingham Palace squirm a little. He attended Groton, Oxford, and Yale; later went in for quail hunting on his 15,000-acre preserve in Georgia, racing his own horses, playing national polo, collecting Seurats, Utrillos, and other costly paintings.

Altogether a pretty bad start.

But there were Grandfather Hay and Grandfather Whitney staring down on him from the walls of his mansions and causing him to curl up around the edges.

Finally he could stand it no longer.

Returning from the war, he set up a $10,000,000 John Hay Whitney Foundation to provide scholarships for the underprivileged, and finance a study of the causes of industrial peace, labor-management relations, and so forth. He appointed Dr. Charles Johnson, the distinguished Negro president of Fisk University, to be chief consultant to the foundation. He gave money, time, and thought to it himself, in the effort to broaden democratic horizons, defend freedom of thought and opportunity for all races and all nationalities, and to promote measures to make our capitalist system worthy of respect throughout the world.

In his personal life he had a creed—no, not a creed, an inner conviction—that no one was superior to anyone else and he could never help acting in accordance with that conviction. Dr. Johnson was always his house guest when he was in New York, and he always stayed with the Johnsons in the South, let the whites gabble as they would. He insisted on his name being dropped from the Social Register, which he considers a "travesty on democracy." Perfect strangers call him "Jock" on a few hours' acquaintance. He hadn't the slightest objection when his wife's daughter by a former marriage, adopted by him, married the talented son of a Seventeenth Street barber. He is just as amiable with the people of his own station in life as he is with those of any other station.

This is the man whom President Eisenhower, in 1957, appointed our Ambassador to the Court of St. James . . . He had at last caught up with his famous ancestors and his wealthy father. He had justified his existence and laid the ghost of inferiority.

To live in the shadow of a successful father after he is dead is bad. To live in it while he is alive is definitely worse. The old men today do not give up easily. They live longer and retire later. Living on to improbable ages, they maintain control of their interests and dominate their offspring. We are accustomed to reading such announcements as:

Thomas J. Watson, Sr., the man who built the International Business Machines Corporation into one of the largest concerns in this world, stepped down yesterday

as chief executive of the firm. He is succeeded by his
son, Thomas J. Watson, Jr., who becomes chief executive.
Mr. Watson, Sr., will continue as chairman of the board.

How old is Watson, Sr.? Eighty-three.
And Junior? Forty-two.
It is a rare case if the man who built the business doesn't
feel that he is better qualified to run it than any young
squirt still wet behind the ears—and who can tell a man
of eighty that forty or even fifty is not still juvenile? The
psychiatrists' files are filled with case histories of the sons
of business tycoons who refuse to make way for Junior.
There is Tom Fletcher.
Tom received the education his father had never had—
Groton, Harvard—where he acquired a faint distaste for
his old man's un-Harvard diction. On graduation he was
expected to go into his father's business and he did, though
there were things he'd rather have done, like going on the
stage. At first he didn't mind too much. He was used to
taking orders from the old man, he received a big salary,
he was learning the business, he advanced steadily in
position and salary.

Yet, at forty-five, with all the paraphernalia of success
about him—town house, country place, wife right out of
the Social Register, three beautiful children, Palm Beach
in the winter, Europe in the summer—he knew he was a
failure.

"My father is a self-made man," he told his psychoanalyst. "He is seventy-eight and no more ready to quit
than he was forty years ago. He directs the policy of the
company down to the last detail. No matter how much
I earn, I'm still the office boy. He doesn't think I know
enough, am smart enough, care enough, work hard enough
to run the company. I think I could have been a pretty

good actor or singer. But every time I mentioned quitting, he offered me more money." Then bitterly: "Once a kept man, always a kept man."

Tom was never willing to risk poverty and struggle in order to be his own man. They would have been less galling than the sense of inferiority he must live with the rest of his life.

Today, in America, the older generation is living longer (over twenty years longer than in 1900) and staying healthier than at any time in history. It is not going to relinquish its power, its prerogatives, and its money while still in command of its faculties. It is not going to abdicate to the younger generation—why should it? Age has its rights as well as youth. Yet their children are mature men and women, physically and psychologically ready for the responsibilities of life.

Too many parents treat their adult sons and daughters as though they were still children, rewarding and punishing them according to how well they play the role of childlike submissiveness. Too many adult sons and daughters submit to this domination. This is a new situation in the world. Never before have men lived long enough to dispute authority with the next generation. It is a situation conducive to inferiority feelings in the younger generation, especially those from families of wealth and position. Those in less privileged circumstances are earlier thrown on their own resources. The solution would seem to be for the younger generation to assume its own responsibilities and for the older generation to keep hands off.

It is these factors—wealth, fame, success—which have, in the course of time, built up an aristocracy. To be "born to the purple," in its most literal sense, means to be born into the aristocracy, perhaps the nobility, perhaps even royalty. When the caste system was the natural and normal way of life, when the nobility was really doing its

job of protecting its dependents and was actively applying
its creed of *noblesse oblige,* it had no qualms as to its
value. But today their jobs—and frequently they themselves—are being liquidated. A great name means only
what its present bearer makes of it, be that name Bourbon
or Windsor, Hapsburg or Bonaparte. Of two men of the
name of Churchill, one becomes the greatest individual
ever to bear that name; the other is arrested for being
drunk and disorderly and barking like a dog while his wife
mews like a cat.

In a world becoming swiftly democratic, there is even
a tendency on the part of the aristocracy to eliminate
itself. Count Leo Tolstoy was a pioneer in this movement
for a classless society. The heir to vast estates, innumerable
serfs, and a great fortune, he grew up with the traditional
peer-and-peasant point of view and led the gay social life
of a Russian nobleman.

Until he began to be disturbed by a vague feeling of
guilt. Why, he asked himself, should he have everything
while his peasants, in any real sense of the word as worthwhile human beings as himself, lived in misery? The caste
system, he decided, is built on a fictitious system of values
and the resulting social structure is necessarily artificial.
The rich have exploited and demoralized the poor, who
nevertheless have remained closer to what nature intended
man to be.

To achieve our goal, which is happiness, we must
abolish this caste system, private property, wealth, and
all man-made institutions including governments and
churches. All these social injustices and inequalities, built
up over the centuries, must be done away with, not by
war and rebellion, but by nonresistance, by faith, love,
and Christian brotherhood. In his day this new religion
(a sort of Christian communism) was known as Tol-
stoyism or primitivism. It spread throughout Europe and

lapped at the shores of China, making him the most ven-
erated man in the world. He himself endeavored to live
this religion, renouncing his wealth, his properties and
serfs, dressing, eating, and working like a peasant.

The classless society he advocated has not yet come to
pass. It could not be legislated into existence; it had to be
lived into existence. That is what is happening today.
Royalty and nobility are gradually passing, the aristocracy
of birth and wealth is losing importance, social barriers
are melting away. The caste system, source of so much
social inferiority feeling, is disappearing.

We come now to the complexes of age—not necessarily
old age, just any age. From infancy right through to
senility, there isn't a period in our lives that isn't calculated
to give us a raging inferiority complex. If this seems faintly
incredible to you, suppose we now look back into our
childhood and adolescence, into our present maturity, and
forward into what is euphemistically termed our "later
maturity."

CHAPTER VIII

Every Age Is the Dangerous Age

IT HAS ALWAYS been considered that the first-born holds a favored position in the family—the first, the oldest, for a long time perhaps the only child, made much of, ruler of the world, possibly of the sun, moon, and stars.

But it can also be a very dangerous position. One is no sooner established in a certain way of life, accustomed to being the only child in the world, treated like a king, than along comes a usurper. Who, may I ask, is this? Surely not another child! Throw him out! I had no idea such things could happen in a well-ordered world, run by the right kind of people. Surely you don't expect me to put up with this!

But gradually it develops that such things *can* happen and must be put up with. For the first-born the world will never again be the same—rose-colored, perfect, his oyster. Ever after he takes a faintly cynical, disillusioned view of it.

In childhood, says Adler, nothing is more crucial than our position in the family constellation. Each position— first-born, youngest, child-in-the-middle—has its special dangers and its special advantages. The child in each position can give each of the others a complex. This is known as sibling trouble. A sibling is that interloper into *your* family called by courtesy a brother or a sister.

Here we must again employ our classic example, Agnes de Mille, the girl who had *all* the inferiority complexes. Agnes was the older of two sisters. As they grew from childhood to adolescence, it became obvious that one of these girls was going to be a raving beauty—and it wasn't Agnes. Margaret's complexion was legendary even in her teens. She had suitors at eleven. Flowers, escorts, telephone calls, dates followed her as the tides follow the moon. Adolescents, enslaved by her beauty, her wit, her ready laughter, smoldered on her doorstep, beseeching her to go to the movies. Since it was Agnes' practice to challenge every boy on first sight to a test of skill on the tennis court and then to beat hell out of him, she naturally had no beaux. At fifteen she was her sister's chaperone.

In school and college, while Agnes consistently failed, "Mag" took honors. Later, while Agnes trudged from office to office in search of work in the theater, Margaret landed parts after a single reading with the Theatre Guild and thereafter had only to ask for work to get it.

Today anyone can see that such a situation can lead to but one thing—a colossal inferiority complex. But until Alfred Adler came along, looked over the family with a psychological eye, studied the relationships among the children and discovered the enormous difference a child's position in the family constellation can make in his attitude toward life, no one had ever realized this. Who, until Adler, had ever pointed out that the course of a whole life hangs on the accident of being a first-born, a youngest, a boy born after a girl? Once someone announces that the earth is round, it seems that we have always known it.

It was his own experience in childhood which first drew Adler's attention to the decisive effects of the relationships among siblings.

He had an older brother. Count one against him.

This brother was strong and healthy. Alfred was frail and had rickets. His most vivid memory was of sitting on a garden bench with his father watching the older boy running and playing games, lost in the wonders of loco-motion. Count two against him.

The brother was a brilliant scholar, Alfred a mediocre student, terrified of mathematics. Count three against him.

In every way he was outdone by the older boy, always bigger, always stronger, always smarter. When he was a mature man, Alfred said. "I was always overshadowed by the first-born, the model of all the virtues, who soared high above me. I have never gotten over it. He was always ahead of me—he *still is* ahead of me!"

But there was one thing Alfred had that the other boy did not. He could charm people. He bent his whole soul on that. He became the most popular boy in his neighbor-hood and at school. This represented a major triumph for him since his was a willful and passionate nature.

The older brother's reaction to Alfred was as typical as Alfred's to him. When he was an old man and Alfred was dead, he said, "When quite a little boy, Alfred was already terribly popular. I never understood why. We never got on together. I always found him quarrelsome and ambitious. I never liked him. I don't understand why other people did." . . . The dethroned king, still resentful of the usurper.

Adler traced his character and career back to this situa-tion in his childhood. As he sat there crippled on a bench and watched his brother leap about, his whole childish soul was possessed with the desire to emulate that god-like creature. As a man his greatest desire was to move freely, to be independent, and this led to "to see all psychic manifestations in terms of movement." His desire to emulate his brother implanted a burning ambition to excel.

Each position in the family, Adler pointed out, develops certain typical character traits. No human being, he held, can be completely understood until his position in the family constellation is known. The eldest child tends to be bossy, conservative, authoritarian, dependable, ambitious. All his life, unconsciously, he is endeavoring to regain that lost paradise when he was the only child or to maintain that position of authority and responsibility which was his when he was the eldest of the children.

But if this first-born child is somehow placed at a disadvantage in the family, he may develop quite different characteristics. Suppose he is threatened by a smarter, stronger, handsomer, or more popular second-born. Then he may become discouraged, and seeing he cannot hold his position by fair means, he may resort to foul, defy authority, and turn to crime in the manner of Cain.

If circumstances favor it, the eldest boy is likely to adopt a father-surrogate attitude, assuming responsibility for the others, confirming his sense of superiority by his protective attitude toward them, and dazzling them by his superior performance.

The younger child needs no excuse to be rebellious—he is born rebellious. He just naturally resents the authority of the older children. He fights authority; he refuses to conform; he starts projects of his own. Unthreatened by a successor and spurred by an intense desire to surpass his predecessors, he goes into high gear, becomes intensely restless, active, and ambitious. He often surges ahead to become the most successful member of the family. History as well as folklore and fairy tale is filled with the exploits of the daring, the adventurous

youngest son. The Francos of Spain illustrate the two
types, Francisco, the eldest, being a dyed-in-the-wool conservative, and Ramon, the youngest, an out-and-out
revolutionary.

Or, lacking courage, feeling himself licked before he
starts, the youngest may become the discouraged adolescent, indolent and apathetic. He cannot be expected to
surpass all—why try to surpass any?

In all his cases and in all his reading of history and
biography, Adler found that the youngest child closely
followed one of these two patterns. In the folklore of many
lands—German, Russia, Scandinavia, China—he found
these adventurous youngest sons. Even in the Old Testa-
ment it was the youngest who was usually the hero,
including Joseph, David, and Saul. Joseph, he pointed out,
was virtually the youngest, since he was seventeen years
older than Benjamin.

The position between oldest and youngest is the least
favorable of all. Attacked from both sides, these children
must fight on two fronts. Confronted with superior knowledge, authority, and strength on the one hand and with
superior spunk and ambition on the other, they develop
a two-way inferiority complex. Such a lad, with enemies
to right of him, enemies to left of him, fights a losing
struggle. Completely discouraged, he is usually the least
effectual, the least successful of the children.

The most dangerous position of all is that of the only
child. Overloved, overprotected, overpraised, this spoiled
child, flaunting a superiority complex, can scarcely escape
a gnawing sense of inferiority when confronted with more
self-reliant, aggressive children. Since he has always been
the center of attention, it remains his goal through life
to continue in that position.

His position in the family is the central fact in a child's
mind. It exercises the most profound effect upon his

character and determines his *style of life,* which closely approximates that of the great majority of similarly placed children.

On these basic patterns, there are many variations depending upon the sex of the children, the size of the family, the distance between their ages, in what circumstances each is brought up, how each reacts to his environment.

For example:

Ordinarily the role of the first-born boy is an enviable one. But say he is followed by a girl who has the temerity to ignore, not only her lowly status as to age but her infinitely lower status as a girl. And suppose she is a proud child who, realizing that boys are considered superior, puts on extra steam to surpass this young lordling; she has one tremendous advantage: nature is on her side. She matures faster than the boy, especially as she approaches puberty. The boy panics, seeing the fiction of masculine superiority torn to shreds before his very eyes. He loses faith not only in himself but in his sex. Confused, discouraged, he turns against the female of the species, perhaps for life.

Nor is the child caught in the middle necessarily doomed to failure. Feeling himself outstripped by the eldest, slighted on account of the youngest, he may develop the sturdiest character in the family. He learns how to get along with people, how to attract favorable attention by good behavior, how to be brave and modest and useful—if he can't build a space ship, at least he can weed the garden. Humble methods scorned by his more favored siblings.

We are in large measure the products of our sibling relationships. Say a woman walks, talks, dresses, plays games like a man. Say she is a rabid politician or reformer, a bespectacled intellectual or a star athlete. Why? The answer very likely is that she had a beautiful sister with whom she could not compete as a woman and so must prove her superiority in some other field.

Say a man is overly competitive in everything from business to golf. Why? He is probably still trying to knock the stuffing out of a big brother.

Or say a man hates women. He may marry, but if he does it will probably be either a weak woman to abuse or a strong woman to fight. He is a misogynist and a sadist. Why? He had a sister who shook his pride in his own sex and his trust in the opposite sex by outstripping him in everything.

Or say a man is inordinately ambitious. Since he is an only child, it can't be due to sibling rivalry. What then? A cousin will serve quite as well. "Why can't you get good marks like your cousin Joe? . . . Stand up straight like Joe . . . Joe always washes his hands before meals . . . If Joe can learn to play the violin, why can't you?" That sort of thing.

Gertrude Lawrence, you remember, had one ambition in life—to return to her home, dripping with furs and jewels, and remark haughtily to her mother, "What about Cousin Ruby now?"

"Beware the brilliant cousin," warns Adler.

We often carry these childhood wounds through life.

Prince Sadruddin, second son of the late Aga Khan, is a young man beset on every side. A non-white living in a white community, he can't but feel the color line. An inheritor of vast wealth associating with commoners, he can't but feel isolated. The son of a fabulous father, he can't but feel overshadowed. But most of all, as the younger brother of the dashing Aly, with his women and his horses, he feels he's up against impossible competition.

"It's tough being Aly's kid brother," he says. He feels that he can't lick Aly and he can't join him. Sometimes the press reports that he's not at all like his older brother, and at others, if he takes a girl to a night club, it comments that the two brothers are birds of a feather. Always the comparison.

"I wish I could rise above my family connections," sighs Sadri. "Why can't I be myself—not my father's son, not my brother's brother—just myself, Sadri Khan?"

The best way to rid ourselves of these early wounds is to recognize the cause and to realize that it is no longer valid, that we are far removed from it or can remove ourselves.

A child builds up a certain "style of life" within the family constellation. This is designed to get him the best deal possible, all things considered. It is adjusted to the hazards of his particular place in the family hierarchy. He works on it constantly, slowly perfects it—and then, suddenly, another child arrives or, almost equally catastrophic, a child dies. His whole style of life must be readjusted to meet this emergency. The death of one child may so alter sibling relationships that the whole character of the others often seems transformed.

Say the eldest son dies. The second-born, previously submerged, suddenly finds himself elevated to a position of importance. He may gravely assume his responsibilities, or he may start right in bullying the lesser fry and turn out to be a far greater tyrant than their former boss.

A child can't fight these hazards alone. The parents must be wise mediators and guardians. It's too late to help a first-born son after the interloper has arrived. On that very first day his heart can break. No one but a first-born can know this bitterness. He should have been prepared. He should be helped to understand that he has not lost a mother but has gained a companion.

A new world should be opened up to him at this time— school, friends, wider activities, added privileges. He should be made to feel that he is more important, more loved than ever. A sense of rejection at any age is cruel as nothing else in life is cruel, but never crueler than in childhood. Never is a sense of security, given only by love, so necessary as when we're building our world. Denied it, we grow up disillusioned, forever hurt children.

There is another count on which children are misunderstood and mishandled. If there is one phase of human relations where the idea of equality is more difficult to understand and more difficult to practice than any other, it is in the relationships between children and adults.

Most adults assume their superiority to children. Subconsciously they harbor as many prejudices against them as men do against women or the aristocrat against the common man. We have always unmercifully exploited children and there has always been an undercurrent of hostility between the generations. Only recently has it flared into open revolt.

Adults, it seems, simply cannot look upon children as equals. They love, pamper, spoil them—but treat them as equals? Never. Adults are bigger, stronger, more powerful—true. But more beautiful, more intelligent, more ethical? No. Adults are not more intelligent for their age than children are for theirs and God knows, morally, they're not fit to live in the same world. Beyond a doubt children have far more creative imagination.

Actually children, even the very young, have much more sense than their parents give them credit for. They want—and can take—much more responsibility, and at a very early age, than they are generally allowed. Most of them constantly outwit their parents.

Where they have a very definite superiority is in the field of morality—in their honesty, their innocence, their integrity, their greater sensitiveness, their ability to forget and to forgive. They are much readier to understand another point of view and more flexible in action. On every count it is completely unjustifiable to regard them as inferior to adults. They should be respected, not ordered about. They have a dignity of their own which should never be violated.

It is because they sense the natural superiority of children and feel themselves defeated by them, that adults inferiorize them. Children of whatever age are human beings who rebel against being assigned an inferior status. Out of this rebelliousness comes most of the conflict and bitterness of family life today, the social upheaval of the teen-agers and juvenile delinquency on a frightening scale.

Behold the poor parents of today, responsible for all this! Continuing to employ outmoded authoritarian methods, they are faced with the opposition of a whole generation. Their authority is questioned, their power defied, their rule overthrown. They cannot tolerate this defeat. They are terrified not to be able to enforce obedience. So they redouble their tyrannical efforts, persuaded they have the children's interests at heart. Actually they are chiefly interested in upholding their threatened superiority. The children sense this and step up the rebellion. In the end it is the children who win.

They leave home—they can't wait to leave home—and the broken and desolate parents find their vaunted superiority at last proved a sham. This happens in the best of families, often seemingly the most closely knit.

When the Dionne quintuplets were twenty-one, the world was shocked to learn that they were living away from home. Their brokenhearted father complained bitterly of their lack of filial love. A close friend of theirs explained it as considerately as possible.

"They want a little private life of their own. No, they're not even going home for New Year's. They have gifts for their parents and their brothers and sisters but their brother will take them home. For the first time in their lives they are enjoying a normal social life and making their own decisions." That this was no hasty decision was proved by the fact that succeeding Christmases were likewise spent away from home.

The child never for a moment ceases to contend for his standing as an equal. Quietly, in their own way, they wage a campaign for "children's rights." When they fail to get them, they rebel. Only when the rebellion flares up in some ugly orgy of juvenile delinquency do we blame the parents. And *then* we are wrong. It is not any particular parent's fault, it is *all* parents' fault. It is the result of the contempt in which children are unconsciously held.

Parents are easily the most confused people in the world today, and more so in America than anywhere else. Having for the most part abandoned the old autocratic system of bringing up children, still in force in Europe, they have found nothing to take its place. Those who have tried the laissez-faire system find it doesn't work. "Please, teacher, do I have to do whatever I want to do today?" is the way one small boy expressed his distaste for the whole thing.

Children want to be guided—but they also want to be consulted. They want to be led—but they also want a sense of equality. They want to respect their elders—but they also want to be respected. Quite a feat of tightrope walking for the adult.

One thing is sure—domination will no longer work. In the end you have a flattened-out personality or a terrific explosion on the day when at last the suppressed ego blows up. For years a son or daughter waits, resentful, smoldering, for the day of release from parental domination and when that day comes they turn on their tormentors, venting all their pent-up antagonism, even hatred, in the triumphant cry, "I don't need you any longer! I'm getting out!" . . . And the heartbroken parents have never suspected the fierce rebelliousness seething beneath the surface docility.

Strong natures as well as weak may be dominated by a parent, not through timidity or fear, but through pity or love or respect. Charles Darwin was such a man.

Darwin's father wanted him to be a doctor. Charles tried but couldn't make it. So papa settled for a clergyman, a profession even less suited to the future discoverer of the theory of evolution. Again, out of respect, Charles tried. This time he got his degree—and immediately went on that famous voyage to South America and Australasia which started him off on his scientific career. Even then, having formulated his theory of evolution at the age of thirty, he delayed over twenty years, out of deference to his father, before publishing it.

It is not too difficult to learn to treat a child as an equal. Anyone who makes the effort can learn to converse with children on their own level. They have only to consider their ideas with the same seriousness the children themselves do. They will soon find themselves respecting the integrity of these small human beings and will never, never demean them with blows and shouts, lies and hypocrisy.

Dr. Rudolf Dreikurs, founder of the Community Child Guidance Centers of Chicago and Professor of Psychiatry, Chicago Medical School, holds that it is a distinction of man of the twentieth century to have lost an ability which all other creatures on earth possess—knowing how to raise his brood. A whole new democratic technique for dealing with children, Dr. Dreikurs believes, must be learned by teachers, who are today too often the enemies of children, and by parents, who are their victims. Kurt Lewin, in his now famous Iowa experiments proved, with three groups of children, that those trained under a democratic system, turn out far better than those brought up under either an autocratic or a laissez-faire policy. The democratic system in education and in the family is far more difficult to administer than the old autocratic system, just as in government it is more difficult than dictatorship. But the technique, once acquired, will turn out better people than the old arbitrary methods.

So much for the inferiority complexes generated in childhood.

But finally we are through with childhood and have slipped all unconsciously into adolescence. What then? Will things be better now?

At first it would seem so. We are on our way to the coveted goal of maturity. We are passing from weakness to strength. We experience a surge of physical power. Our minds expand. True, but—

Agnes de Mille, we noted at the beginning of this chapter, had a gift for developing the complexes appropriate to each period as it came along. She describes the complexes of adolescence with clinical exactness.

"Anything can happen in adolescence," she says. "The best-brought-up child is taken over by powers as divorced from daily habits as earthquake. And the important point is that what happens now is definitive, physically speaking. Up to this moment there has been margin for correction. . . . After sixteen—this is it—for life. The chances are good you won't like it. I didn't . . . [At school] there were dances. There were sorority teas. I was not asked to a single rush party. I did not have one date that first year."

At a dance she was not just overlooked—she was deliberately shunned.

"I sat with that alert indifferent air of one who has too much on her mind of interest and charm to notice she is bleeding to death at the heart. I held my head very high and turned it vigorously with an exaggerated interest on every single thing that was in no way connected with the stag line. I told myself with somber pride that when I was a great dancer with all the capitals of Europe at my feet, they would be very surprised indeed to remember they had passed me up!"

That is not just *one* girl speaking—it is *most* girls speaking.

Well, that's adolescence. Enjoyable?

At its best it is a period highly conducive to feelings of inferiority. In childhood we contracted these symptoms without really knowing we had them. In adolescence we know. Brother, do we know! A word, a glance can shatter our fragile egos.

Dr. Smiley Blanton, author of *Love or Perish*, commenting on this painful period, said to me:

"We psychiatrists believe that the sense of inferiority is based on a feeling of lack of power or of virility or on a sense of guilt. These feelings of guilt and inadequacy are especially strong in young people, hence their heightened consciousness of inferiority. They don't know whether they are going to be able to grow to be men and women, make their way in the world, get married, have children. These doubts assail the adolescent and cause him to feel inferior. Sometimes he thinks he is ugly, that his body is inadequate in any number of ways, that he may be impotent. He can worry over a cowlick. We must look beyond these superficial feelings and try to discover their roots, if we are to help him."

Never before, never again, will self-consciousness inflict the torture it does then. Wherever he goes, whatever he does, the adolescent feels that all eyes are upon him. Gladly would he exchange places with an ostrich. Some individuals never outgrow this cringing state of self-consciousness. In spite of success, adulation, even fame, they carry it to the grave. Others recover from it only slowly and by great effort.

Kim Novak, never referred to in the press except as "the fluorescent blonde," "the blonde surprise," "the high blood pressure blonde," "wow girl," or "whistle bait," and such, after her success in *Picnic* and *The Eddy Duchin Story,* is almost as shy as when she was an unknown salesgirl.

"In small groups I get along fine," she recently confessed. "I try to avoid big parties. The shyness is still there but you learn how to hide it. I know how to bring myself out a little more."

Tennessee Williams, famous author of *A Streetcar Named Desire, Cat on a Hot Tin Roof, Baby Doll,* and other Broadway successes, still suffers from an abnormal shyness.

"A morbid shyness once prevented me from having much direct communication with people," he wrote when he was in his forties, "and possibly that is why I began to write them plays and stories. But even now when that tongue-locking, face-flushing, silent and crouching timidity has worn off with the troublesome youth that it sprang from, I still find it somehow easier to 'level with' crowds of strangers in the hushed twilight of orchestra and balcony sections of theaters than with individuals across a table from me. Their being strangers somehow makes them more familiar and more approachable, easier to talk to."

No, things are no better in adolescence—worse, actually. Few people recall their childhood as happy, fewer still their adolescence. The small boy was pretty well satisfied with himself, and what he lacked he could always make up for by boasting. But nothing about himself pleases the adolescent. He is tortured by the conviction that his body is awkward, his conversation unsophisticated, his personality colorless. He longs to shave but has no beard. His changing voice embarrasses him. He is neither child nor man. He is convinced that the only thing about him that anyone notices is his acne.

A girl is confronted with the double hazard of the frightening male and the necessity of pleasing him. She must also contend with the strange phenomenon of maturing. Both sexes are almost morbidly conscious of their bodies, sensitive to criticism, and easily embarrassed. They feel they should know everything—and are conscious that they know nothing. This would be enough to give Napoleon an inferiority complex. But there is worse.

Now is when sex rears its pretty, touseled head. It finds the adolescent all unprepared. Everything about sex is alluring—and frightening. No matter what he does about it, he's going to be wrong. If he does what he believes is right, he's a sissy. If he does what he supposes is wrong, he's a cad. He can't win.

The inferiority complexes arising from such painful situations as these—and in adolescence all situations are painful—make this the most vulnerable period of our lives. Like witches riding their broomsticks, they drive their victims to success or to failure.

The hatred or harshly treated child soon learns how to take care of itself by certain fixed responses, usually anti-social, which gradually form a mechanical pattern of behavior. Thereafter he meets all his problems by these stereotyped reactions. He becomes a juvenile delinquent.

The gang and the fanatical loyalty of its members are the result of the necessity for "belonging." These boys from broken homes, foreign families, squalid surroundings feel rejected and inferior. Only the gang gives them a sense of importance. The very names of the gangs betray their longing for identification and self-esteem—

Imperial Counts, Bladesmen, Noble Englishmen, Bishops, Bandit Queens, Dukes, Viceroys, Ambassadors, Enchanters. After one shooting by a lad with the significant nickname of "Dillinger" Ramirez, his gang saluted him and then separated, feeling, as one of them later put it, "somehow bigger, more important and secure because they had played the parts of men."

A seventeen-year-old boy, on trial for first-degree murder in the death of a man beaten up and pushed into the East River, said, "I like to beat up bums because it makes me feel big and strong. We use them like punching bags to see how hard we can hit."

During the Christmas holidays a teen-age girl entered a department store dressed in blue jeans and an old sweater. Two days later she emerged wearing a $25 cashmere sweater, Bermuda shorts, and a topcoat, and carrying a suitcase, an overnight bag, and a hatbox containing sweaters, blouses, skirts, hats, jewelry, and cosmetics to the value of $600. She had, she admitted to the police, spent a delightful week-end selected a bobbysoxer's dream wardrobe so she could make every girl of her acquaintance feel like a worm.

It is amazing how often the adolescent recognizes a sense of inferiority as the motivation for his crimes.

"Why did I join de gang? I don't belong nowheres. Nobody wants me aroun', 'cept the gang—dat's why."

"I stole dat car—yessir, I stole it awright. I wanted to show de guys I wuz a big shot."

"Sure I murdered him. I ain't chicken. I had to show de gang I wasn't yellow, like dey said I wuz."

No one could have better described a criminal in the making than a sixteen-year-old colored boy arrested for murder.

"When I eight years old I walk by two cops and I hear one say, 'There goes a cop killer.' I feel good about that . . . I start going to gangster movies all the time. I always like those pictures where some big guy is real mean, real tough . . . I met this kid Muggsy Mason, see? He was a real mean guy, real tough. And he was leader of a whole lot of gangs—not like me, I could never get to be a leader. I guess he was my ideal like. It makes me feel good to be with such a big shot, see? . . . One night Muggsy knocks me down, with everybody watching, and right then I think about killing him for shaming me in front of all those people. . . . We go down stairs into this basement. Then I walk up behind him in the dark, put the gun behind his head and pull the trigger . . . I stays there for a little while, looking at him and feeling real good. . . . Now they got me in prison for a long time. But I'll get out some day, and I'm only sixteen now. And already I'm a big shot, see?—the way I always wanted to be."

Frequently the adolescent not only recognizes the reasons for his antisocial conduct, he can even suggest the remedy. A seventeen-year-old boy explained juvenile delinquency thus: "The feeling of complete worthlessness we have is one cause. We need to be given a sense of community responsibility and to feel we are wanted by the community."

A reformed gang leader, looking back on his youth, remarked, "Seems like when you're seventeen, you're crying inside all the time."

The adolescent needs help. He needs to understand himself and to be understood. He is likely at this period to be introverted, confused, fearful of exposing his feelings to anyone, especially his parents, dreading they will discover the small boy in him and all his inadequacies. But with the right approach, a teacher, a friend, a clergyman, even a parent can get past his guard and help him through this difficult period.

Youth needs a legitimate sense of importance. There are many ways it can be helped to achieve this and not the least sensible is that suggested by Jacques André Istel, ex-Marine and third ranking parachutist in the United States.

Teach them parachuting, says Istel. We're a nation of sissies, Istel intimates, when it comes to parachuting. In Europe it rivals skiing as a sport. It takes a lot of guts and brings a lot of thrills. France and Russia have the most and best parachutists, Russia leading with 800,000. America had, at the time Istel spoke, a mere 200 professional jumpers. We deliberately discouraged parachuting, even going so far as to pass laws against it. Ridiculous, says Istel. Why have hundreds of thousands of juvenile delinquents when you could have that many parachutists instead? Nothing like it to give a youngster stamina, self-confidence, and a sense of responsibility. Kids would be so tired after jumping they wouldn't have the energy to do anything but crawl into bed. It would provide an outlet for the hot blood of youth, give them a feeling of importance and of belonging. It's the parents, not the youngsters, who must be won over. As it stands, most parents would prefer a live delinquent to a dead parachutist. The good ones, Istel adds, seldom die.

Youth! The most adorable period in life! Yet how many would live through it again?

And then comes maturity. Surely now things will be better. We're adult, we're independent, we're toughened up. Nothing can ever hurt us so much again.

Yes, certainly things are different. But better?

With independence we assume responsibilities. We've entered the most fiercely competitive period of our lives. For the first time we are faced with the three great problems of life—work, society, sex.

Since Freud announced his doctrine of pansexuality as

the prime motivation in human conduct, our society has shown an exaggerated interest in sex, particularly its sensual aspects. Adler looks at sex in a different way. To him sex presents a moral and a social problem, the solution of which demands a high degree of courage, of the ability to adjust and of a sense of responsibility. It is not the Cleopatras and the Don Juans, those most successful in enslaving the opposite sex, who have found the best solution. A lifetime of one-night stands and a trail of broken hearts, are not socially constructive, however delightful. They are rather a symptom of a deep-seated inferiority complex. The male who feels compelled to test his prowess of seduction on every female he meets is none too sure of his sex appeal. Nor is the female.

Those who feel incapable of finding a satisfactory solution to this problem usually seek ways to evade it. One way is simply to put sex out of their lives. The men and women who consider sex synonymous with sin, who hate the opposite sex, who have an abnormal dread of venereal disease, who fear disappointment in love, who claim never to have met their ideal—in short the prudish, the puritanical, the overly romantic, the mysogynist, the hypochondriac, the old maid, the old bachelor—all are dodging the problem because they are unable to solve it.

Others evade a solution through the fiction of an organ inadequacy, claiming they are impotent, frigid, incompatible with their mate, and so on.

Still a third group dodges a solution by an abnormal indulgence in sensuality until, finally, satiated, vicious or fearful, they lose all healthy passion and only some perversion, some abnormality in their sex relations—masochism, sadism, fetichism—can arouse their desire. The homosexual harbors a profound fear of the opposite sex, of the unknown and the untried, of the responsibilities of marriage, of pregnancy, of childbirth, even of children.

In spite of their claim to be "the perfect sex," superior to the other two, they suffer from a tragic feeling of inferiority.

In a final category are those who avoid a constructive solution by exaggerating the importance of sex to the neglect of its higher aspects—love, marriage, children, companionship, family solidarity. Though they may appear triumphant, these satyrs and nymphomaniacs are making as poor an adjustment as any pervert or celibate. Too great emphasis on the sexual aspects of love indicates an unsatisfactory solution. Even so great a human being as Victor Hugo, who mixed love with sensuality in such generous proportions, can scarcely be said to have found a satisfactory solution, since he never ceased seeking new experiences and new solutions.

Hugo not only knew how to make himself beloved, even by such connoisseurs as Sarah Bernhardt and Judith Gautier, he knew how to love.

He loved one woman passionately in his youth and married her. Ten years and five children later, they separated and Hugo, age thirty, spent the rest of his days, until his death at eighty-three, in amorous adventures.

Once loved, he was never *un*-loved. Juliette Drouet, with whom he set up housekeeping when he left his wife, loved him for fifty years. On all the anniversaries of their first night together she prayed, "Oh, God! So order it that he shall never be absent from any day of my life or from one single moment of my eternity."

To satisfy all his inamoratas, Hugo worked out an arrangement whereby he dined with his wife and children, went to Léonie Biard (a second mistress) in the evening, and actually lived with Juliette. At eighty-two he was still being unfaithful to her with younger women.

Taking all this in conjunction with Hugo's notorious egotism and vanity, it cannot be doubted that he harbored a flourishing inferiority complex, and considering that love and marriage are social as well as personal problems, his can scarcely be called a satisfactory solution.

The men and women in all these categories are evading a solution of the sex-and-marriage problem because of an inferiority complex. But suppose, attempting no evasions, one really tackles the problem courageously—falls in love, marries, raises a family, fulfills all one's responsibilities to them—then will one be free from feelings of inferiority?

Probably not. In any union, however, perfect, there is always some lurking sense of inferiority. . . . I'm not good enough for her. . . . He's so much better looking than I am. . . . I don't love him as much as he loves me. . . . Her family is far superior to mine. . . . He is so much cleverer than I am.

No need to be morbid about it. Lacking one virtue, one can make up for it by another. And in any event, the sense of inferiority accompanying a good solution of the problem is not so painful as that accompanying failure.

The sex problem is the only one of the three with which we are confronted in maturity that we can safely leave unsolved. By safely we mean that a man won't perish or be completely isolated as he would be if he failed to solve the work or social problem. He will merely be a poor, miserable, ingrowing old curmudgeon or a dissolute old roué. He'll lead a wretched life and deserve every minute of it.

The second of the three big problems with which we must wrestle in maturity is work—and here it is survive or perish. The average youth enters the arena all unprepared, unsure, or rather as nearly sure as he ever was of anything, that he's a foregone failure. Either that, or he's so cocksure of himself that at the first setback he's shocked and disillusioned. The quietly optimistic, modest type is rare indeed.

Little by little success gives a man confidence but not before he's acquired a nice crop of complexes. And even when he's on top of the heap, he often has a sneaking suspicion that he doesn't really belong there. On the top or at the bottom, all the way up and all the way down, we constantly face situations which make us feel inferior. All you can say is that with success such feelings are fewer and less painful than with failure.

A man who does not achieve the recognition he feels he deserves is sometimes driven to desperate measures.

A chap named Stringfellow received an award from the United States Junior Chamber of Commerce as one of the outstanding young men of 1953. Soon after he began campaigning for the nomination for Congressman from Utah. In his campaign speeches he frequently recounted his wartime experiences, in particular his assignment to a daring parachute mission into Germany to capture a key scientist and thus halt the development of the Nazi's atomic bomb.

It took a little time for the facts to catch up with him but eventually it developed that, not only had there never been such a mission, but that his only overseas service was as an Army private who never saw combat.

Why did Stringfellow risk a promising career by such a hoax?

Because he never rose above a private; because, due to a mine explosion, he was a paraplegic; because he hadn't won any sort of recognition, not a single medal or honor—and he yearned for glory.

Then there was the fellow in Canada, named George DuPre, confidential assistant to the Minister of Mines, Minister of Lands and Forests in one of the provinces, and later branch manager of a chemical firm—a good, solid man, respected by all who knew him.

Mr. DuPre's sole interests outside his work were his

family, the church, and the Boy Scouts. He was a devoutly religious man who spent much time spreading the message that "no man can survive without faith in God, and that with faith a man can do anything." To illustrate his thesis he recounted his experiences as a spy during the second World War and later, to earn money for the Boy Scouts of Canada, he inspired a book called *The Man Who Wouldn't Talk*. It was an account of his training by the British Intelligence to play the role of a half-witted Frenchman who was parachuted into France to join the Resistance and help R. A. F. pilots shot down behind the German lines to escape; of his capture by the Nazis; of his torture and crippling by the Gestapo; of his escape with a broken body but an unbroken spirit because of his trust in God. The book turned to be one of the most thrilling spy stories ever written.

"Compared to him," wrote the New York *Herald Tribune*, "all other spies whom we have read about were amateurs."

Good! Then what was wrong?

All that was wrong was that there wasn't a word of truth in it. DuPre had never worked for British Intelligence, he had never been in France, he had never been captured—none of it was true. Why, then, had he invented it?

To carry the message of faith throughout the world, was DuPre's explanation.

The truth is somewhat less flattering.

DuPre had won fame by telling of his exploits up and down the land before military groups, churches, and business organizations. Put between covers, the story would hand him down to posterity, make an international hero of him, justify him in his high opinion of himself. It was his bid for the recognition he felt should be his.

This is no different from what all of us do on a smaller

scale. Being in our own eyes incomparable creatures, it is only natural we should want others to see us in the same light. There is scarcely an hour of the day that we are not boosting our own stock, exaggerating here, inventing there, just plain lying at other times. If it is not ourselves that we are extolling, it is our children, our ancestors, our servants, or anything that is ours.

The way of a Stringfellow or a DuPre, the way of the braggart and the boaster, brings no permanent satisfaction. Sooner or later the bubble bursts, the balloon is pricked, and the ego shrinks to its normal dimensions, feeling much smaller than if it had never blown itself up to an unnatural size.

The third problem we face in maturity is our relation to society and here the penalty for not finding a satisfactory solution is isolation. This is so important a problem that it will be discussed in a separate chapter, "No Man Is An Island."

So now we're right up against the fourth period of life, discouragingly referred to as "old age."

Suddenly the battle is over, we wipe the blood and sweat from our faces and look about us. We find ourselves on a darkening shore—and we don't like it. Terrible as it was, the fight was better than this.

But at least we are out of danger. Our enemies have departed. There will be no new threats to our self-esteem.

We couldn't be more wrong. Now come humiliations that engender such a sense of rejection and inferiority as we have never known. To begin with, no one is interested in us. We are finished, *kaput*, and we should have the good taste to move on. We're taking up valuable space. We have no function in society and we certainly add nothing to the gaiety of nations. Even if we have managed to achieve financial security, we are still excrescences. Merely being able to pay our way does not give us any feeling of belonging, of being needed, of being important. Besides, our heirs feel they could be making better use of the money.

This is the time of life when men retire, women see their families melt away, incomes shrink, social life dwindles to a trickle, husbands and wives die, and monotony and idleness stretch endlessly before us. Our only value is as a babysitter—and some of us weren't cut out for babysitters. It is obviously impossible for men and women who have been active, useful, and of some consequence all their lives to settle for a life of lolling on a beach, fishing, or puttering in a garden and still retain their self-respect.

Today there is no need to submit to such a fate. During the past fifty years, over twenty years have been added to human life—not feeble, senile years, but vigorous, active ones. In 1900, our arteries, if not our employers, made retirement compulsory at an early age. Today with sixty-eight the average life expectancy for men and seventy for women, to consider retirement at sixty-five or even seventy-five is slightly soft-headed. Even heads of organizations are beginning to realize that. For years they have been talking about new blood, young ideas, bright, fresh, young faces. Now they are delighted to see some tired, beat-up old professionals around.

Lloyd's of London, the insurance company with a leer (it has insured such sly items as Mistinguette's legs, Pearl White's dimples, and Monty Woolley's beard) kept records over a ten-year period on men who retired. It found that those who retired at sixty were dead at sixty-three, whereas those who continued to work after sixty lived to be over seventy. Lloyd's, the insurance company with a sense of humor, commented: "They retire. They sit down for a while. Then they lie down. And then someone carries them out."

At sixty you may easily have ten to thirty years ahead of you. Loll on a beach for ten years soaking up the sunshine? Live in trailer camps for fifteen years? Putter around a garden for twenty years? The mind reels at the prospect.

What then?

One of three things:

Don't retire.

Semiretire.

Retire *to* something, not *from* something.

The first is, when possible, probably the best solution.

Isidor Wasservogel did not retire as a justice of the New York Supreme Court until he was seventy. Three years later he was back on the bench looking as though he had merely adjourned court until 2 A.M. Summoned back after retiring at the statutory age limit, he was the first man in the history of New York State ever to be so honored. At seventy-six he arrived at another constitutional age limit but this time he knew better than to pay any attention to it. He continued to serve without pay for the sheer fun of it and to escape the boredom (with pension) that was the alternative.

Who would not prefer to die like Senator Barkley at the age of seventy-eight in the midst of a quotation from the Bible while addressing a large audience than in a wheelchair at Atlantic City?

The second solution, semiretirement—working part time, running a small business in a suburban community, taking more and longer vacations, stepping down to a less arduous position, or something of that sort, is not a bad one. But sometimes neither of these two solutions is possible. The third always is.

Doubtless there is something you have wanted to do all your life but never had the time for. *Now* is the time. Approaching his later years a man is apt to think, "Well,

I married, raised a family, did my job—now what? Is that all? Is there nothing more?"

There *is* something more. This need not be a wasted period of life, a mere waiting in the antechamber to eternity. Dr. Martin Gumpert, geriatrician and specialist on old age, author of *You Are Younger Than You Think,* yearned for an old age he never attained. Once, for six weeks, he almost achieved it. After a heart attack he was confined to his bed and forbidden to wriggle a toe.

"But I was happy," he later wrote. "At last I was an old man."

To all who complained of old age he said, "The choice is this: Are we going to convert ourselves into a gigantic old-age asylum—or are we going to have fun?"

In 1916, at the age of forty-two Winston Churchill took up painting. He's been at it ever since.

"I hope to spend my first million years in heaven painting," he once said. He recommends it especially for three types of people—those who toil to death, those who worry to death, and those who are bored to death.

"If it wasn't for painting I couldn't live," he has said during many crises in his life and the life of the British Empire.

Nothing can prevent your painting except your belief that you can't. According to the laws of aerostatics, a bee can't fly. Only thing is, it doesn't know it.

Perhaps you've always wanted to write. Now is the time to try. A lot of men sixty and over have tackled it and not done badly.

William de Morgan retired from the manufacture of pottery at sixty-five and immediately started his career as a writer, producing such masterpieces as *Joseph Vane, Alice-for-Short,* and *Somehow Good* at the rate of one best-seller a year.

George Du Maurier, an artist by profession, suddenly,

at the age of sixty, decided he'd rather be a writer and without further ado produced such famous novels as *Trilby* and *Peter Ibbetson.*

Lloyd Douglas, after a long career as a minister, never giving his age or lack of training a thought, started right in and wrote a series of best-selling novels, including *The Robe* and *The Big Fisherman,* which not only sold in the millions but were made into "colossal spectaculars."

If you are absolutely convinced you haven't a shred of talent and nothing can shake your complete lack of confidence in yourself, then consider one of the handicrafts which have claimed such celebrated practitioners as Andre Kostelanetz (metal work), Mary Martin and Queen Mary of England (needlepoint), Lotte Lehmann (china painting), Mrs. Theodore Roosevelt, Jr. (embroidery), and Dean Acheson (cabinet work).

A lot of middle-aged and elderly Americans have recently discovered that they need, want, and can get a great deal more education than they have. Adult education is the biggest thing in education that has come along since Froebel and his kindergartens. From Canada to Florida and from Maine to California hundreds of schools of adult education have sprung up, with curriculums including everything from French to Sanskrit, from interior decorating to public speaking, from painting to psychology. Millions of men and women in the United States who thanked God that they had long ago finished with school are going back to study the things they've always wanted to know and never had the time for*

Finally there's the fellow less fortunate than yourself. Many older men and women devote as much time to civic welfare, community service, juvenile delinquency, politics

---

* For a survey of activities for adults consult *The Best Years of Your Life* by Marie Beynon Ray, published by Little, Brown & Co., Boston, 1952.

or government as they once did to their jobs. When a man is through with work he isn't necessarily through with life. He can retire from the making of money to the making of a better world. Once more he can be a person needed, wanted, depended upon, a person of some importance.

If old age is not to be a period of futility and frustration, of loneliness and boredom, of inferiority complex piled on inferiority complex, we must fill it with activities and interests. Properly prepared for, confidently faced, it can be what Browning meant when he wrote:

> Grow old along with me!
> The best is yet to be,
> The last of life for which the first was made.

And now we come to what Freud considered the most important of all the complexes, but what Adler referred to as "not my favorite complex"—sex.

CHAPTER IX

The War of the Sexes

A SLENDER FIGURE erect in the middle of the arena, sword poised beneath the crimson muleta. A sudden furious onrush of the bull—death in the afternoon awaits one or the other.

The bull is within feet—within inches. The matador rises on tiptoe, leans between the horns, sinks the sword into the powerful neck, swings aside. The bull drops to its knees, rolls to its death.

A roar goes up, not because the matador has killed the bull—that is expected—but because that afternoon this matador has been knocked six times to the ground and, although forcibly restrained by the attendants, has each time fought them off to re-enter the ring. Therefore the rare prize of the bull's ears and tail is awarded.

This is elemental male courage, courage of a variety, one would say, that only men display, and among men, only Spaniards.

Yet this matador is a woman, Patricia Hayes, of San Angelo, Texas, who for years has had spectacular success in the bullring. Nor is she the sole female bullfighter. There is also Pat McCormick, likewise of Texas, who, in four years, has killed some 200 bulls; there is Bette Ford from Pennsylvania, formerly a model but now a wildly acclaimed matador; and there is Bertha Trujillo whom they call "Brave Bertha." Bertha is always being gored and tossed—she is not as skilful as she is brave. During one *corrida* she was knocked down seven times in fifteen minutes, was impaled on the bull's horns against the barrier, and finally was pursued by a bull she had failed to kill. The crowd screamed to stop the fight and Bertha, pinioned by the attendants, wept.

"Everybody expects a girl to quit," she sobbed. "I cannot quit. I get sick to my stomach when I am hit so many times. I can't see. I can't walk straight. But I *must* kill the bull."

Why? Why must these women fight bulls?

They are not so much fighting bulls as they are fighting men. They are reacting to the most colossal inferiority complex ever foisted on any segment of humanity. All human beings are born inferior but women are born more inferior than anyone else. From the beginning of time, deliberately and with malice aforethought, one sex set out to inferiorize the other.

The very first woman was born inferior. On the authority of the Bible (written by men) woman was created as an afterthought of the Almighty solely to relieve Adam's ennui. She immediately proved her inferiority by bringing sin and death into the world through her congenital frailty. Not from that day to this has the masculine sex let up in its derogation of women.

As Adler was the first to point out that the child's position in the family constellation is a fertile source of inferiority feelings, so he was the first to analyze that deep sense of inferiority foisted upon one-half the human race by the other half. To this reaction on the part of women he gave the name "the Masculine Protest."

"When a woman's resentment against masculine assumption of authority and superiority is so great that it is expressed in her refusing to accept her sex and striving to be as much like a man as possible, we have the Masculine Protest," he writes.

In almost all women today we detect symptoms of this protest, if in no more than the smoking of cigarettes. From this small prerogative, which they took over in the Jazz Age, they have gone right on to bullfighting. Today the business world bristles with females who have elected to fight it out on the man's own ground with his own weapons.

No woman, however beautiful, however rich or brilliant or highly placed, can escape a feeling of inferiority on the score of sex. It begins in childhood with the privileged position of boys. (If a boy had been born to the Prince of Monaco he would have received a 101-gun salute; since it was only a girl she received a mere 21.) It is continued in maturity under the law, in business, in the professions, in government, in society. Born, in every age and every country, into a world where from birth she is less welcome than a boy, relegated to menial tasks unworthy a man, her self-confidence undermined from childhood, what is a girl to think of herself? How will she react?

Many will passively submit. Some will actually believe themselves inferior and revel in it—the "less than the dust beneath thy chariot wheels" type. More will carry on the sex war *sub rosa* as a strictly private affair. A few will glory in their feminine role. Only the strongest natures will, on the unfairest possible terms, with all the rules made by the enemy, fight men on their own ground and openly contend for the equality of the sexes. All—well, almost all—will, in their inmost hearts, wish they were men.

How typical of a male!

Are they equipped to enter masculine fields and to compete with men? Judging by past performance, no.

In no field of endeavor do they hold first place—with a few brilliant exceptions, in the arts, in religion, in philosophy, in statesmanship, in business, in the professions and, God knows, not in war. All the explanations in the world cannot change the record. Lack of opportunity? Semi-servitude for centuries? Being physically weaker and therefore unable to compete in a world largely controlled by physical force? Being so long deprived of education, training, experience? Being tied down by childbirth, motherhood, household duties? Having their creative energy drained off by the creating of the race?

These are merely explanations of failure, not proofs of ability.

The record, however, isn't what worries most women. What worries them is, not how history and the encyclopedias regard them, but how their husbands and their employers regard them. How society regards them. How their children regard them. *How they regard themselves.*

Women simply cannot feel that their role in life is as important as that of men. Childbirth is no great achievement. Any female, human or subhuman, can give birth. It requires no special gifts or abilities. It is, in fact, harder to avoid than to accomplish. Thus a woman's chief claim to glory is written off.

The pressures exerted upon women to inferiorize them, the frustrations and injustices to which they submit, even today, even in America, are not to be borne by any human being. The whole history of civilization proves that they always have and always will arouse rebelliousness.

It is not in human nature to accept forever the stigma of inferiority. In the past individual women have risen up to proclaim their equality. Today the whole sex has risen in protest against this unfair discrimination. The War of the Sexes is on.

Even in the Orient women are, coming out of purdah.

In the Western world, particularly in America, they are
more and more assuming masculine prerogatives. They no
longer feel that motherhood is a sufficiently creative and
interesting activity to consume their whole time and their
whole energies. They crave the broader experience of life
that is open to men. About a hundred years ago they
launched a concerted effort to share this experience.

They had four rights to fight for: political, economic,
social, sexual. Considering their lack of experience, they
have worked in considerable harmony—or what passes for
harmony among women—to achieve political equality.
They have won the right to vote and, in theory, the right
to be elected to office, but a woman President is still as
unthinkable as a Negro President, and a Congress equally
divided between the sexes is far less probable than a two-
headed calf.

Economically? Formerly a husband not only owned his
wife, he owned whatever she owned. No longer. In America today women own a majority of the private wealth,
between 60 and 70 percent or better. But it is still the
men who control this wealth. As for equal pay for equal
work and equality of opportunity, only sixteen states and
Alaska, at last reports, had equal pay and equal work
laws—and a law is not a custom.

Socially? Men are still much freer than women. Many
social situations affect women more adversely than they
do men—being divorced or being single, for example. They
are not as free to go where they want, when they want,
and to do what they want as are men.

Sexually their initial attack was on the double standard.
To the ladies equality meant that they should enjoy the
same sexual privileges as men. The shocked male, faced
with this distasteful situation, began muttering that it
could also mean that men might accept the same standard
they had always demanded of women, to wit, chastity and

fidelity—within reason, of course. Following up this lead, prostitution was outlawed, the social stigma attached to the unwed mother diminished, divorce became less disgraceful, and monogamy was conceded to be a natural, perhaps even an acceptable, arrangement. But even so, extramarital relations are still regarded as more reprehensible for women than for men. Certainly men object to them more on the part of their mates than women do.

In all four categories women have made considerable headway but they are still a long way from equality. There are plenty of women working for a living, with their husbands applauding from the side lines, but the female top executives in big business are still as rare as the whooping crane. To win recognition in any of the fields which men have always preëmpted demands greater ability from the woman than from the man.

If Soviet government statistics are to be believed (and I suppose they're not) they seem to be doing better there than we are here in America. According to the statistics, 52 percent of all students in the universities and higher institutes of learning are girls; three out of every four doctors are women; one-fourth of all the members of their parliament are women; half of all the "people's judges" and two out of every three students of law and economics in state universities are women. Of course Soviet women are also granted the privileges of shoveling snow, laying railroad tracks, pouring steel, and mixing cement.

One of the big difficulties in the way of achieving equality is the still very large segment of unreconstructed males among us. Sir Thomas Beecham spoke for many a Neanderthal man when, on discovering some females in an orchestra he was to conduct, he commented: "Women are like vultures on the battlefield; they appear after everyone else is dead. . . . The sooner they are allowed to run their course, the sooner the present era will blow

up in ineptitude, inefficiency, and incompetence. There
will be five years of no music, and at the end people will
say, 'Now we'll start over.' "

Sir Thomas is obviously a gentleman of the old *Kinder,
Küchen,* and *Kirche* school.

If it is difficult in America for a woman to make good
in a man's world, it is well-nigh impossible in a country
like India. The inferiorization of women did not drop
from these women with the veil. Consider even so highly
placed and brilliant a woman as Vijaiya Lakshmi Pandit,
sister of Nehru and High Commissioner for India in the
United Kingdom.

When her husband died, writes Mme. Pandit, there
came "the humiliating realization that, in the eyes of
Indian law, I had no individual existence. . . . In law
we women were still recognized only through our relationship to men. Now as a widow without a son, I was not
entitled to any share of the family property, nor were
my two daughters. I resented this galling position. I was
bitter towards those members of my family who supported
this antiquated law."

Deprived of all rights as an individual, solely on the
ground of sex, Mme. Pandit fought for the rights of all
Indian women and in so doing became one of the great
women of our day, achieving a magnificent compensation
for her sense of inferiority.

The fight on the economic and political fronts might
be called the cold war. But when it moves into the home
front, then you really have the hot war, atomic weapons,
guided missiles, and such. The war of the sexes is tre-
mendously stepped up after marriage with each partner
struggling to establish his or her superiority. Yet the realization that monogamy is not an alien doctrine imposed by
society but that it is a natural relationship between the
sexes, an expression of the desire of a man and a woman

to be a unit, spiritually as well as physically, has made it imperative that they be equals.

No such relationship had ever existed before and our remarkable lack of success to date in making it work, with more unhappy marriages, broken homes, and divorces than ever before, leads us to wonder if perhaps the whole idea is not unsound and untenable.

Give it time. The doctrine of equality as between classes, the generations, the sexes, is still so new as to be completely incomprehensible to most people. Certainly in that closest of all relationships, marriage, it is too early to expect any spectacular success. The desire to "belong," which is at the very center of every human being, can find fulfillment only in this dream of every individual to be half of a spiritual whole. Those who are sufficiently mature to make it work, find it the most satisfactory relationship possible between a man and a woman.

It is small wonder if most women still fight the age-old war with outmoded weapons—subterfuge, chicanery, hypocrisy, flattery, lies, deceit, camouflage, sex appeal, whatever strategy has served them in the past. Intellectually they haven't grasped the fact that they are living in a new era, an age in which on every front, equality is being fought for, and that the sex war is only one phase of a great revolutionary movement toward democracy that no prejudices, no traditions, and no laws can halt. Emotionally neither men nor women are as yet sufficiently mature to handle this problem rationally and good-naturedly. The more women gain, the more intractable they become. The home is a battlefield, where the woman, having married the most superior male she can lay hands on, must now establish her superiority to him and he must at all costs maintain his.

Hy Gardner, columnist of the *Herald-Tribune*, explains

how the ideal marriage of equal partners operates. A friend, celebrating his tenth wedding anniversary at the Stork Club, made the whole thing perfectly clear to him.

"Before we got married my wife and I made a deal," he said. "She'd make all the minor decisions in our family, I'd make all the major decisions."

"Such as what?"

"Well, the minor decisions include where to live, how much rent to pay, how to bring the children up, what kind of car to buy, how much insurance to take out, how to budget our income, how to invest our savings, if any, et cetera."

"And the major decisions?"

"Well, I'm responsible for such matters as the Suez Canal, the Israeli-Arab war, whom to elect President, segregation, the H-bomb, you know, stuff like that."

Having won the right to a career, should women now meekly retreat to the stove, the dishpan, and the washtub? Having won the right to vote, to sue for divorce, to own property, to receive as high an education as a man, to consent to her own downfall and to wear pants in public, is a woman now to settle for the same old *Kinder-und-Kirche* life she had before the conquest? Faced with a choice between a career and marriage, most women will plump for marriage. But why should they be forced to choose?

One evening on his interview program Mike Wallace asked Sylvia Porter, financial editor of the New York *Post,* "Deep down, Sylvia—*deep* down—which would you choose if you had to, your career or your life as a wife and mother?"

"Suppose," said Sylvia, "I said to you, 'Mike, which would you choose: to be Mike Wallace, doing what you're doing now on TV or to be, as you also are, a husband and father?' "

For a long moment Mike said nothing. Then: "That was a pretty silly question, wasn't it? I withdraw it."

Why should a woman, any more than a man, be forced to choose. Both are possible—and millions of women are proving it. Quite as much as a man, some women *need* a career. They should not have to choose between a career and a family—the whole trend of social evolution is against it.

Actually, women have always worked, and at the most menial, hardest, dirtiest kind of work with the lowest pay and the longest hours, and men have never (it was damned decent of them!) objected. It was only when the "Woman in the Gray Flannel Suit" appeared on the horizon and proceeded to take over the paneled office with the wall-to-wall carpeting and the cove lighting and to take home the $30,000 pay checks that the men began muttering. Even then, it wasn't so much their pocketbooks as it was their pride that was hurt.

Even men whose intellectual equipment is of the mid-Rutherford B. Hayes era are now willing to admit that it's all right for some women to have careers—unmarried women, married women who have no children or whose children are grown up, plus a few women geniuses. But *not* women with young families—definitely not.

Yet even for some of these women a career is the only completely satisfying compensation for their inferiority complexes. Only by successfully competing with men on their own ground can a proud and ambitious girl who has been suppressed by an authoritarian father or forced to perform menial tasks unfit for the boys of the family, overcome a burning sense of inferiority. And yet, having won the victory, women are not pushing their advantage. By and large they are passing up the office for the home.

more have changed society
innovation

But *if* they're going to stick to the home, why don't more of them make a better job of it? Why, even in the field that is traditionally theirs, do they still, as in the past, continue to prove themselves inferior to men? There is no department of homemaking in which men have not outclassed women. Cooking? Where are the Escoffiers, the Béchamels, the Vatels, the Carèmes among women? There are no *cordons bleu* in our homes; few ever attend cooking schools.

Decorating? We will look in vain for the Wrens, Adams, Inigo Joneses among women. All the great periods of decoration have been created by men; all the great furniture has been designed by them—Boulle, Oben, Riesener, Chippendale, Hepplewhite, Ince, Meissonier, Biedermeier, Gibbon, Duncan Phyfe—not a woman among them. Is it too much to expect a woman to attend a school of interior decoration so that she may at least decorate her own home?

All the great movements in education have been initiated by men. There are no feminine Erasmuses, Melanchthons, Rousseaus, Rabelais, Pestalozzis, Froebels.

In short, everywhere where they should have been leaders, women have been outclassed by men. There is no phase of their job that men haven't done better.

Many types of personality are produced by the Masculine Protest. When we first began fighting for votes for women, we had the fanatical feminist who looked and dressed and acted as much like a man as possible, who shot her cuffs and smoked cigars while balancing a whisky and soda on one knee. Today this type survives in the woman who is antagonistic to men on general principles, who goes in for politics, leads movements, and refuses to bear children or to do housework.

Other types who fail to make a satisfactory compensation are: The unconscious homosexual who refuses to play a feminine role, fearing intercourse, childbirth, babies, men.

The Lesbian who plays the masculine role to the hilt.

The odalisque who makes a cult of sex, demands all the privileges, but accepts none of the responsibilities of her sex.

The siren who uses sex to enslave men, and establish her power over them.

The sacred cow who elevates motherhood to a sacrament to lessen the importance of the male.

The promiscuous woman who takes revenge for her inferior status by infidelity to her husband.

Nothing is plainer than that women have always harbored a sense of inferiority toward men. What is by no means plain is that men experience a sense of inferiority as regards women. Adler, pointing this out, used the same term, the Masculine Protest, to cover both of these conditions.

.At bottom men are afraid of women, a state of mind perfectly apparent in adolescence. In the presence of girls of their own age, who seem so much more mature, boys feel inadequate, shy, self-conscious, fearful of not acting the part of men, of making fools of themselves. Only an understanding woman, usually an older one, can help them to overcome this fear, which is one of the most ineradicable of the complexes. Some men never recover from their adolescent fear of women. Some, like Schopenhauer, carry it to a pathological extreme, not daring to yield one iota of their masculine prestige for fear of losing all.

Two types of men result from this state of pathological fear: the brute and the homosexual.

Nietzsche spoke for the first when he said, "When you go to women, take your whip with you."

Such men remain incomplete human beings all their lives, never knowing the joy of responding fully to womanly charm and continuing to feel inferior because they have never entered this charmed realm.

Byron was such a man. Dominated in childhood by a mother who taunted him with his lameness and alternately bullied and spoiled him, terrorized by a fiendishly cruel nurse, he revenged himself in manhood by torturing the woman he married, and by subjugating and tormenting every female, from contessa to concubine, from adventuress to prostitute who came within striking distance of his beauty and brilliance, compelled to prove over and over that women no longer had any power over him.

André Gide is an example of the second type, the homosexual whose way of life is dictated by his fear of women. All his life Gide was dominated by strong-minded females, chief among them his mother. At twenty he was not permitted to go out at night without an escort to protect him from the bad women of Paris. On one occasion, in Morocco, he was about to make his debut as a lover when his mother arrived unexpectedly from France, having had a premonition that, away from her, he might find a woman to replace her—from which dire fate she saved him. In the background of many homosexuals lurks a dominating female, usually a fanatically possessive mother.

The great American cult of momism is built up on this childlike submissiveness to Mom. Moms give their sons a little-boy complex, spoiling them and instilling in them the belief that no woman can ever love and protect them as Mom can. Liberace has made a career of momism, annexing 200 sponsors, pay checks 400 percent larger than those of Marlene Dietrich or Noel Coward, and millions of misty-eyed middle-aged moms. Tousled curls, redundant dimples, wreathed smiles, cute sayings, and if not an actual lisp, something just as adorable in his speech, there is Liberace before us on the TV screen with Mom in the background to encourage and approve as he toots his horn.

The reactions to the Masculine Protest are as many and varied in the case of men as of women. One man will marry a much younger woman to whom his age, position, and experience make him seem important and to whom he will be a father-substitute. Another will marry an older woman, who will be a mother-substitute and will have no children but him. Another, fearing rivals, will resent his wife's pregnancy, and use it as an excuse for infidelity and debauchery. One man married to a woman who is culturally his superior will endeavor to lift himself to her level; a second will leave her for a woman on his own level; a third will identify himself with a son and achieve equality with his wife by the cultural advantages he gives him.

Even a man who isn't actually afraid of women is likely to find them baffling, mysterious, and unmanageable. He feels that he is up against a combination of forces he can't possibly understand and which he has variously termed the Eternal Feminine, the Sphinx, the Mona Lisa, the *femme fatale*. A great body of mystery, superstition, prejudice and just plain fear blocks his understanding of women and his acceptance of her as an equal.

Yet marriage is the final test of spiritual growth. Until society and the individual accept the equality of the sexes, there can be no real mutual understanding between them and no peace. Of all the fronts on which the war for equality is being fought today, none is more hotly contested than this of the sexes. The difficulty in getting a clear-cut decision is that there is just too much fraternizing with the enemy.

How is it that one-half of the human race has, since the beginning of time, been held inferior to the other half?

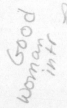

Good woman intr

Is it because women really are inferior? Until recently
this was pretty generally accepted as the answer. What
other answer could there be? There it was, on the record,
for all to see—the superior performance of man in all fields
of human endeavor.

But a short time ago, when psychology and psychiatry
began to delve deep into the unconscious and to re-exam-
ine many hitherto baffling problems, they came up with
a different answer. Might it not be, psychiatrists asked,
that women have been made by men to feel inferior
because in reality they are superior?

Scientists in various fields, given this clue, went to work.
Ashley Montagu, anthropologist of Princeton University,
has presented this proof in a book, *The Natural Superiority of Women*. First, he says, let us define *superiority*.

"Superiority in any trait, whether biological or social,
is measured by the extent to which that trait confers survival benefits upon the person or group," says Montagu.
"If you function in such a way as to live longer, be more
resistant, healthier, and behave in a manner generally
calculated to enable you and your progeny to survive more
efficiently than others who do not function as efficiently,
then by the measure of our definition of superiority you
are superior to the others."

Men, runs Montagu's first argument, show a higher rate
of achievement, not because they are naturally superior
but because "they are overcompensating for a natural inferiority, the inferiority of not being able to have babies."

I hear guffaws. "And a d—— good thing!" is the unani-
mous masculine retort to that one. But wait.

Women, Montagu goes on, possess an astonishing array
of natural superiorities. They are biologically superior to
men, not in physical strength but in constitutional strength
—and that is the real test. Muscularly less powerful,
woman nevertheless lives longer (and always has) because

she endures better. Starvation, exposure, fatigue, shock, illness, and other such calamities, do not undermine her as they do men. Within every age bracket, the death rate for men is higher than for women. Even the foetal female is more durable than the male. Not only in the Western world, but everywhere in the world, not only among humans but throughout the animal kingdom, the life expectancy of the female at birth is higher than of the male. Among white Americans, women have a clear advantage of six years over men. Not only are women more resistant to germs but they recover more quickly from illnesses.

Men are notoriously more fragile, falling victim to many disabilities from which women are immune. There are over thirty disorders which are much more common among men than among women, ranging through color-blindness, shortsightedness, hemophilia, baldness, ulcers of the stomach (four times as common among men), gout, and so on. The reason for this is that nature, because of the greater importance of women in preserving the race, has weighted the dice in their favor, giving them two complete x-chromosomes to a man's one.

Women, any amount of masculine propaganda to the contrary, are emotionally far more stable than men. The proportion of men in mental institutions in much higher. There are many more male alcoholics and deaths from alcoholism. More men have nervous breakdowns and more often develop physical and functional disabilities due to emotional disturbances. It is a mistake to assume that because women are more emotional than men, they are emotionally less stable. On the contrary, they get rid of an oversupply of emotion by expressing it instead of damming it up. They also absorb emotional shock much better. Dr. R. D. Gillespie reported that during World War II, 70 percent more men than women broke down and became psychiatric casualties under the strain of siege and bombardment. There are eight male stutterers to every female stutterer, and stuttering is a nervous "sex-factor" disorder.

Louis Dublin of the Metropolitan Life Insurance Company, in his famous study, *To Be or Not to Be*, reported that the suicide rate of men to women is ten to one. Thirty-two other governments gave figures from two to five times as many male suicides as female—and this has always been true everywhere. The darn things are just not very stable.

Biologically and constitutionally then, to start life as a male is to start life with a handicap.

Now what about the superior intellect of the Magnificent Male?

As to the much-vaunted greater size of the male brain, women's brains do average four ounces less—but what is four ounces in a total weight of over three pounds? Moreover, size has nothing to do with intelligence. One idiot's brain weighed 2,850 grams. Anatole France's brain weighed 1,100 grams. Also the ancient superstition that credited men with a larger amount of nervous tissue has been abandoned for the *proved* fact that this superiority— if it is one—lies with the women.

When it comes to mental abilities, if you omit arithmetic, mathematics, mechanics, and mazes, females achieve consistently and significantly higher ratings than do males in intelligence tests. Their superiority in some fields is uncanny. Language, for example. They talk sooner, better, more, and longer than men. They possess larger vocabularies and have a greater gift for foreign languages. They also have better memories. Naturally, not all the intellectual advantages are on the woman's side, but the evidence of most of the tests made so far indicates that if both sexes received the same kind and amount of stimulus and encouragement from their environment, they would do equally well. According to tests of boys and girls made to date, girls outrank boys. Later in life, in the comparatively few fields where both have been tested, men have slightly outdistanced women but chiefly because women have not continued their efforts in these fields.

The explanation of their lack of success in creative fields seems to lie here. They have transferred their interests and their efforts to other spheres. Child bearing and rearing drain off their creative energy. It takes time to be a genius. Moreover most fields have been closed to them and they have been discouraged rather than encouraged to develop their abilities. Finally, let it be admitted, they have never been and probably never will be, as much interested as men in the kind of achievement that attracts men. But humanly, socially (in its best sense), women, being more interested in people than in things or even in ideas, have in this respect a slight edge over men.

Biologically, constitutionally, and emotionally, Montagu concludes, women are superior to men. Intellectually call it a draw. But there is still another argument, not Montagu's this time, that really clinches the case for the superiority of women—and this one is going to hit the men where they live. It is presented by Sofie Lazarsfeld, psychologist, and it runs like this:

A man's sexual power is inferior to a woman's. It is unreliable, dependent upon circumstances, subject to limitations, whereas a woman can have intercourse at any time and repeatedly. The man's pride in his sexual prowess and his craving of recognition of it by his female partner indicate his insecurity in this respect. Placing so high a value on it betrays a lack of self-confidence. Assurance breathes more easily.

This inferiority alone is enough to make the male desire to humiliate the female and yearn to dominate her. But there is still another cause for humiliation—a feminine superiority so immense and so forever beyond his grasp that he can never hope to close the gap.

This is his uncertain fatherhood as compared to the woman's certain motherhood. This is more than a mere social and economic superiority—it is a spiritual superiority, for children are considered a kind of immortality. To know beyond any shadow of a doubt that his children are his is given to no man. This "beyond a doubt" belongs only to the woman.

Because of this undubitable fact and this indisputable disadvantage, men have sought, by every means they could devise, from the chastity belt to purdah, by the written and the unwritten law, by appeals to sentiment and resort to violence, by guess and by God, to insure the chastity of women and their own fatherhood. Whole sects have denied that the woman is even one of the parents of the child, claiming that she is merely the vessel that safeguards the germ of life for the male, who is the sole parent. In some primitive tribes the men even put on an act simulating childbirth on the day of the blessed event.

These two sexual handicaps produce in the male a much deeper sense of inferiority than do menstruation and pregnancy in the female. More handicapped sexually than women, men have made heroic efforts at compensation. Their natural inferiority has thus become the basis of their supremacy. Beaten in the sexual arena, they sought compensation in other fields, from which they were able to exclude women because of her preocccupation with pregnancy and child care. In these fields they overcompensated to such a degree that they were able to establish themselves as definitely superior. By keeping the woman barefoot and pregnant the male was able to make such strides that she could never hope to overtake him.

His supreme effort at domination was in making war,

a thing women would never undertake. In *Of Men and Women,* Pearl Buck calls war man's final and most formidable effort at compensation in a field where he need never fear woman's competition and so can be sure of his supremacy.

This, then, is the argument for the natural superiority of women. Granting its validity, it would appear that it is actually men who have the greater inferiority complex. In the effort to compensate, they have made this a man's world, constituted themselves the lords of creation and actually created God in their own image. Thus the natural superiority of women has brought about the unnatural superiority of men.

Whatever the truth of the matter, this contest as to which is superior should be shelved. Actually it is as pointless to ask which is superior as to ask which is the more beautiful, the female or the male body. Is the Hermes of Praxiteles more or less beautiful than the Venus de Milo?

Different but equal is the only answer. Women, having at last openly engaged in the War of the Sexes, are determined to fight it out until they have firmly established their equality even in the Cro-Magnan mentality of some segments of the male population.

The war for equality has spread to include not only women and children but the races, religions, and nations into which humanity is divided. As with the war of the sexes, resentment over these inequalities have always smoldered beneath the surface. Today, everywhere, it is out in the open. No longer will the blackest man or the smallest national admit that they are inferior to the whitest man or the biggest nation. So now for "the complexes that are contagious."

CHAPTER X

Complexes Are Contagious

> *You see that man over there?*
> *Yes.*
> *Well, I hate him.*
> *But you don't know him!*
> *That's why I hate him.*

THERE IS THE beginning of the racial, religious, national, class prejudices that divide humanity into warring groups. We fear—and we hate—the stranger. This person is different from me, we think, different in color, in religion, in nationality, in language, in customs. But *I* represent what is right and proper. Therefore this chap is an inferior article.

And always, everywhere, it has been accepted that these differences were valid and important. The whole social order is built on them. Everyone attempts to inferiorize everyone else on the basis of these differences.

Today a new wind sweeps through the world. Not one of the distinctions which in the past made a man feel superior or inferior remains unchallenged. Every inferiorized group—women, children, labor, Negroes, Orientals, Jews, Germans—is clamoring for equality. We are witnessing a titanic effort on the part of mankind to make democracy a reality in all human relationships. Never before in the history of man has anything like this happened. It started in the eighteenth century when it was found impossible to confine the idea of democracy to government.

"All men are created equal."

No one really believes it, no one actually practices it. The idea has always lurked in the backs of men's minds, but inequality came much more naturally. The Greeks conceived democracy as a philosophy and as a form of government. The Stoics outlined it two thousand years ago. Rome made it into law. Judaism and early Christianity proclaimed the equality of all men before God. Rousseau and the French Revolution announced it as an integral factor of the new social order. America swore allegiance to it in its Constitution. But no people has ever consistently lived it and few can even imagine a social order in which some people are not more equal than others. As a result, the people of every race, religion, nation, class have developed mass inferiority complexes.

A young girl cowers inside a university building while two thousand students riot outside, demanding her expulsion. Later five hundred students in a hundred-car cavalcade storm through the streets, state highway patrolmen are called out to curb the demonstration, the governor of the state is petitioned to send National Guardsmen to restore order, and the house of the president of the university is stormed by one thousand students who hurl eggs and insults at him and his wife. In the end the girl is surreptitiously spirited away to another city to save her from threatened death.

Why? What had this girl done to be so despitefully

used? Had she committed a murder? Thrown a bomb? Impaired the morals of the community?

None of these things. She had been born with a black skin.

She had been born with a black skin and had attempted to enter a white man's school. "Kill the nigger!" they yelled, and "Nigger lover!" they screamed at those who tried to protect her.

Complexes are contagious. We all harbor these group complexes; we all communicate them to others. Each individual, feeling himself threatened, communicates his fear to others of his group. Thus a collective inferiority complex is built up. We may think we are free from such prejudices, we may rationalize them—we still believe that somehow a white man is superior to a Negro, a Protestant to a Catholic, an American to a Greek, a Republican to a Democrat.

Today the inferiority complex of the American Negro is stronger than it ever was. In the days of slavery he took his inferiority for granted. The closer he comes to equality, political, economic, social, the worse he feels. The psychological law that small differences are more bitterly resented than big ones explains why the Negro of the North feels more intensely the color barrier than does the Negro of the South, the half-caste more than the full-blooded Negro (he has missed white supremacy by so little!), the cultured Negro more than the uneducated. I once heard an Englishman say of Paul Robeson, "I know of no one I'd rather sit next to at a dinner party. He is one of the most brilliant, cultured and charming gentlemen I have ever met." Yet Robeson was so galled by the contempt in which his race is held in this country that he became a Communist and, seduced by the Soviet claim to a classless society, sent his son to Russia to be educated.

That this sense of inferiority of the Negro in a white civilization is a dominating factor in their psychology is proved by the waves of emotion that sweep through Harlem when a Negro triumphs in an athletic contest, as when Joe Louis defeats Jack Sharkey or Sugar Ray Robinson gains a victory over a white contender. The rejoicing on such occasions engulfs the entire colored population, resulting in demonstrations that sometimes leave dead and wounded in their wake and that overflow into British Honduras. But let Joe Louis be beaten by Schmeling and the entire black population is plunged into deepest gloom. The white population is indifferent as to whether the victor is black or white, Catholic or Jew—but he'd darned well better be an American!

The prejudice against the Negro has barred him from normal compensations. Deprived of freedom, of education, of the rewards of equal pay, position, and prestige, he could not compete in a white man's world. The fiction was maintained that the Negro was of a lower order of intelligence, a theory long ago demolished by the psychologists and social scientists, just as was the master racialism of the Nazis, with its claim to German intellectual superiority. The Negro's intellectual potential is equal to the white man's. It needs only equal opportunity.

There are those among them who have proved this, Booker T. Washington, for one. Born a slave, he fought his way up the educational ladder until he became the head of Tuskegee Institute and a famous writer. Dr. Mary McLeod Bethune, who barely escaped being born a slave, says of herself:

"I was a 'cotton-pickin' chile,' and I might have remained there picking cotton all my life if one day a white child hadn't taunted me with, 'You can't read like me!' There and then I knew I must get an education."

She obtained so good an education that she became a great educator, founder and president of Bethune-Cookman College, Director of the National Council for Negro Women, Director of the Division of Negro Affairs in the National Youth Administration under President Franklin D. Roosevelt, and special adviser to him on minority affairs.

Is the social barrier between the two races any more necesssary than was the political barrier?

When Jackie Robinson, Dodger player, bought a twelve-room house with large acreage in an exclusive all-white residential section near Stamford, Connecticut, all hell broke loose. The smallest catastrophe prophesied was the rapid deterioration of real estate values in the neighborhood. After that anything might happen, up to and including intermarriage.

It so happened that in that vicinity were white clergymen who believed that the equality of all men before God was to be taken literally. They labored with their congregations to such good effect that when the Robinsons came to church they were made welcome. When they sent their children to white schools, they were well received—none of the black rubbed off on the white children. In time Jackie, Jr., was made a member of Cub Scout Den I, and when his dad laid out a baseball diamond on their grounds and began instructing the sons of his white neighbors in the national sport, their popularity knew no bounds. The white ladies began dropping in for tea and discovered a charming hostess, a graduate of the University of California, who was not at all self-conscious about her position.

"We are proud of our race," she said. "We feel that our children, as they grow up, will have chiefly Negro friends. We moved here solely to have a large playground for them. We have no interest in intermarriage but we do feel that the two races should learn to live together on a friendly basis."

Is that too much to ask? If it could be accomplished, the deep-seated inferiority complex of a whole race would be assuaged.

When the Gold Coast of Africa became Ghana with tremendous fanfare, the Duchess of Kent, Queen Elizabeth's representative to the new republic, resplendent in court dress and diadem, led off the independence ball by dancing with Ghana's strong man, Nkrumah, black as the ace of spades, wearing his tribal robes. If royalty can thus fraternize, why not the rest of us?

The attempt to hold the black-skinned race in subjection operates everywhere in the world. For centuries the white man has exploited the African, colonizing him, sending him into slavery, inferiorizing him in every possible way. All at once the black man would have no more of it. A collective inferiority complex can generate a tremendous head of steam. Today, throughout the world, these racial inferiority complexes have reached the point of explosion. What is occurring in the south of this country is a mere husking bee compared to what is taking place in Africa, where the whites still dominate the vast area from the Belgian Congo, Uganda, and Kenya southward to Cape Town. French, British, Dutch still hold out for their ancient sovereignty although outnumbered four to one in the Union of South Africa and 90 to 1 outside it. This handful of the master race expects not only to control the black tide of native life but to go right on disdaining it. In the South African Transvaal the Afrikanders, far more contemptuous of the natives than the British ever were in Egypt or the French in Algeria, tear from their family Bibles the names of those who have even so much as touched a native woman. They even, in raids at dawn, arrest any white men who have dared to side with the blacks, charging them with high treason, though they be ministers of God or members of parliament. They fail to see the writing on the wall warning them that they must either establish a friendly relationship with the black natives and yield control gracefully to them or be driven out within a generation or two. The African is secure in Africa. It is his continent. He will tolerate contempt no longer.

And yet, such is the cussedness of human nature, what they resent the white man doing, is exactly what, given the chance, they do themselves.

Look at Liberia, an African republic founded over one hundred years ago by freed American slaves. Believe it or not, they, like ourselves are going through the throes of integration—integrating, if you please, the native blacks. It is perfectly obvious to these descendants of American slaves, full-blooded blacks themselves, that they are a superior race to the native born Africans. They call themselves Americo-Liberians and refer to themselves as "the civilized peoples" and to the natives as "the uncivilized peoples," from whom they hold haughtily aloof. They send their children to private schools or abroad to be educated and refuse to intermarry with the tribal natives, making it abundantly clear that no government regulations, no franchise can ever make them their equals.

The white man's prejudice is not confined to the color black. Any shade slightly darker than our own breeds in us a faint distaste. We feel almost the same contempt for the yellow Chinese, the brown Arab, the red American Indian that we do for the Negro. Right here in America— specifically in South Carolina—is a twilight race of brown-skinned Turks whose ancestors were brought to this country shortly after the Revolutionary War and who, generation after generation, have lived on the dim borderland between black and white, despising one, despised by the other.

A large part of the trouble in Egypt, in India, in China, is due to the contempt we feel for any shade of skin but our own. Intellectually these people are our equals. They were civilized when Europeans were still living in caves. The whole Suez Canal episode has been described as the result of a "domination complex" on the part of Colonel Nasser and his countrymen, driving them to throw off the last vestiges of British influence. Nasser himself has said that the most important point for the West to grasp in dealing with the Arab countries is the Arab personality.

"We have complexes," he says, "complexes born of our long period of foreign domination."

Because of these complexes, Arabs are intensely suspicious of every Western move, fanatical in their determination to control their own destiny, and nationalistic to the point of xenophobia. That is what a festering inferiority complex can do to a people.

These color complexes have suddenly become dangerous. The Soviets constantly foment a Moslem revolution with the objective of establishing an Arab world dominated by Egypt—and Nasser. Nasser, like Hitler, has written a book in which he openly announces his objective and plan of operations. "The duty of Egypt," he writes, "is the creation of an immense power which will be able to drive these countries [of Africa] into revolutions" against their white overlords.

It was the arrogant attitude of Englishmen toward the natives rather than political bungling or economic oppression that brought about their downfall in India. The late Aga Khan, as quoted by Somerset Maugham, commented on this issue:

"What happened to the Englishman has been to me all my life a source of wonder and astonishment. Suddenly it seemed that his prestige as a member of an imperial, governing race would be lost if he accepted those of a different color as fundamentally his equals. The pernicious theory spread that all Asiatics were a second-class race and 'white men' possessed some intrinsic and unchallengeable superiority."

The root of the Britishers' white-supremacy attitude was, added the late Aga Khan, their own inferiority complex and lack of self-confidence.

To this explanation of the cause of the Englishman's loss of face in India, Maugham adds a satiric comment.

The Crown Prince in Hyderabad once remarked to him, "Do you know the difference between the Club at Bombay and the Club at Calcutta? . . . In one they don't allow either dogs or Indians; in the other they allow dogs."

Today whole continents have risen up against this shibboleth of white supremacy. In 1955, the Prime Ministers of the twenty-nine independent Asian and African nations, the so-called Bandung powers, held a conference to discuss their common problems, chief among them their relations with the white West, which was deliberately excluded from the council. One common thought and feeling hung over their discussions—resentment of the West's assumption of superiority, based solely on a difference in color. Their domination, their colonization, their exploitation by the European powers, welded them, in spite of all their differences of nationality and interest, into one solid anti-West bloc. The strongest bond they had was the fact that the white race had once ruled over them. Worse to the Indians than their material exploitation by the British was their spiritual humiliation by the Englishman's assumption of superiority. Free, they still burn with the shame of it. More closely than any other American issue, they watch our progress in raising the Negro to social equality.

At that conference the white West had one defender, Carlos P. Romulo, formerly President of a nonwhite country, the Philippines.

"The people of the West," said Romulo, "have yet to learn how deeply this [racial] issue cuts and how profoundly it unites the non-Western peoples. . . . [But] is there a single society or culture represented at this conference which does not in some degree have its counterpart of this kind of prejudice and ignorance? Where is the society in which men have not in some manner divided themselves for political, social and economic purposes by wholly irrational and indefensible categories?"

Two-thirds of the population of the globe is some other color than white. Their civilizations may be older, their past achievements greater, their cultures higher, the white-skinned minority still regards them as inferior.

It may be natural to hold these prejudices; it is no longer healthy. It is today a question of actual survival. We cannot continue to despise two-thirds of the human race and not be run off the earth ourselves. The despised race builds up a resentment, an energy and ambition far surpassing those of its self-styled superiors. In Asia, in Africa we see this resentment coming to the boil. This is the most important fact in the world today. It may destroy civilization. An inferiority complex could blow up the world.

No people resent white supremacy more than do the Japanese. This has been particularly true ever since, as once psychiatrist put it, "the American bombardment of 1864 caused a collective inferiority complex of such magnitude that history has not seen its like." The war laid bare this long-smoldering hatred in their torture of American prisoners. And it revealed a complex we had not suspected, a particular hatred for tall men. Themselves a small people, they bitterly resented the easy nonchalance of the tall Anglo-Saxons, for whom they reserved special tortures.

But it was the question of white supremacy that primarily inspired their hatred. When the war with Japan broke out, we had among us, concentrated largely in California, many of these little yellow men, called the issei and the nisei, the issei being those born in Japan, the nisei their children born in America. We put 72,000 of these native-born American citizens behind barbed wire in detention camps, not only, nor even chiefly, because we feared them as an enemy but because we despised them as a race. Even when the Japanese first began coming to this country, back in 1885, we started giving them the treatment we accorded all colored peoples. We called them the "Yellow Peril," refused them citizenship, boycotted Japanese businesses, prohibited their buying land. On the outbreak of war we immediately stigmatized all their American-born children as potential spies and declared the West Coast out of bounds for all persons of Japanese ancestry. We refused them the right of military service. In spite of which—

In spite of which their fathers and mothers, whom we had subjected to every conceivable indignity, wanted their children to be Americans. They had slaved, stoop-backed, in the fields and worked impossible hours in hole-in-the-wall shops to send them to American schools and colleges. *In one generation* they could claim the highest percentage of college graduates of any racial group in the country.

We weren't fooled. We still knew we were superior. So we refused these niesi university graduates the jobs to which they were entitled. We let engineers work as auto mechanics, girls with Ph.D.'s as housemaids, scientists as fruit and vegetable vendors.

They weren't discouraged. Even in detention camps they burned with patriotic fervor. In 1942 they begged to be allowed to harvest a bumper crop of sugar beets, rotting for lack of pickers. They gathered a million tons of beets, enough for a full year's supply of sugar for 11 million people.

We began to weaken. Gradually we admitted them into industry, permitted them to live on the same streets with us, finally to fight for us. They had, they claimed, as good a right to fight for democracy as any white man.

And how they fought! The 442nd Regimental Combat Team, 100 percent yellow-skinned Americans, fought through Italy and France and, with a Hawaiian nisei battalion won 3,600 Purple Hearts, 500 Oak Leaf Clusters, 342 Silver Stars, 810 Bronze Stars, 123 Divisional and Army citations, 47 Distinguished Service Crosses, 17 Legion of Merit Awards, 7 Presidential distinguished-unit citations, and 1 Congressional Medal of Honor—"the most decorated unit in the military history of the United States."

Before the war ended these little yellow men from the U.S.A. had a larger percentage of men in the armed forces than any other racial group.

We still knew we were superior, of course. But gradually we gave up confining them in Little Tokyos, the Supreme Court outlawed the alien land laws, Congress authorized the payment of millions of dollars of compensation for their financial losses while in detention camps, and finally passed an imigration law giving Japan a quota and permitting the issei to become in fact the Americans they had always been at heart.

We continue to feel superior, naturally, but the present generation is not quite so sure as their parents were. They see these full-blooded Orientals, born with yellow skins but with *America* written on their hearts, holding high positions in industry and the professions, winning honors and medals in the sciences, graduating from West Point and Annapolis, making track and field records, joining some of the best clubs—and they begin to wonder. . . . At least we're making progress.

The record of these Japanese-Americans demonstrates group compensation for an inferiority complex. The individual, sharing the inferiorization of the group, also compensates.

As, for example, Han Suyin.

Han Suyin you will remember as the author of those two remarkable books, *A Many Splendored Thing* and . . . *And the Rain My Drink*. Han Suyin writes English as few English writers can, yet she is not even partly English. She is half Chinese, half Flemish—a Eurasian. And if there is one thing worse, in a white man's eyes, than being all yellow, it is being half-yellow.

Having a choice, Han Suyin chose to be Chinese. She could be, to all the world, Mrs. Leonard Coomber, the wife of an Englishman; she prefers to be Han Suyin, Chinese patriot.

She is a woman with an understanding heart, but she cannot understand the Western scorn of the Oriental. It makes her very bitter. That she is angry against Western colonialism is apparent in . . . *And the Rain My Drink*, in which all the white officials are without exception arrogant, stupid, and cruel and not a single white woman is even slightly endurable. Like many other Asian intellectuals, so long humiliated by the white race, she overlooks no ugly characteristic in her white tormentors and finds practically all Orientals charming and admirable.

Han Suyin is a great woman, not only in the East (she is the most celebrated woman in all Southeast Asia) but in the world. Already at thirty-six she had achieved many compensations for her sense of inferiority—marrying an Englishman, writing and lecturing in the cause of a free China, becoming a famous physician. To her clinic in Johore Bahru, near Singapore, of which she is the head, she gives half of her time and a quarter of her income. With the rest of her time and energy, she is a wife, a mother, a housekeeper, a writer, a lecturer—and good at all of them.

Someday all this will no doubt succeed in wiping out the hurt that the white race has inflicted upon her and her people, and the white half of herself on the yellow half.

It is among scientists that we find the nearest approach on earth to a complete lack of color consciousness. Scientists are the implacable enemies of racism—black, yellow, brown. Let a Liberian or a Malayan do a good piece of scientific work and he'll receive as much credit as a Caucasian, probably more. If he rose from the ghetto of Warsaw he'll be as highly honored as though his ancestors were on the Mayflower. Scientists are notoriously colorblind.

In 1928, a young man received a letter from his father, postmarked *Berlin*.

"I had cards engraved for you in Paris with the name Felix M. Bartholdy since you were about to enter the world and make a name for yourself. . . . You must call yourself Bartholdy, because every name is a garment and this garment must be appropriate for the time, need and position, lest it be a hindrance or an object of ridicule. If you call yourself Mendelssohn, then you are *ipso facto* a Jew, and this is no use to you, simply because it is not true."

The young man did not change his name. Otherwise Bartholdy would be one of the greatest names in the history of music. Instead it is the name of Felix Mendelssohn that is famous.

Such is the pressure put upon even the greatest of their race to deny their birthright. It may be argued whether Jewishness is a race or a religion, but race *or* religion, its members are everywhere held to be socially inferior to Aryans and gentiles. Intolerance is never more fanatical than in the place of all others where it should not exist at all—religion. Men have hated each other more violently, fought more bitter wars and persecuted their fellowmen more ruthlessly over religion than over almost any other issue, generating more inferiority complexes in the process. It is doubtful if there ever was a religion most of whose practitioners didn't look down upon those of other religions. In any community where a religious group is a minority, it is inferiorized—the Catholics in a Protestant country, the Protestants in a Catholic country, the Presbyterians in a Baptist community, the Episcopalians in a Methodist.

A Negro boy, asked by a Catholic priest if he was a Catholic, hastily replied, "Oh, no, sir! It's bad enough being colored without being one of those things."

As for those of less familiar religions—Moslem, Buddhist, Confucian—we all know what we think of *them*. A man of any religion but Protestant would have no more chance of becoming President than a Negro, a Chinese, or a woman.

Never has there been a more remarkable example of a collective inferiority complex and the way it works to catapult a people to success than in the case of the Jews. No people have been longer, more consistently and more bitterly persecuted than the Jews. Confined in ghettos, deprived of the rights of citizens, robbed of property and money, barred from the professions, exiled from every land, spat upon and scorned, they have developed a stubborn resistance to inferiorization and a will to power that is characteristic of them everywhere. The Jewish complex is universal, felt as much by a Baron Rothschild as by a Polish refugee—more perhaps, for no one feels this discrimination more than the aristocratic Jew who is almost but never completely accepted into gentile society.

Individually and collectively, the Jew must get ahead of everyone, everywhere, all the time. . . . It is perhaps not a likeable trait—at least gentiles don't like it. They are not more gifted than others to begin with but it is a question if, by developing every resource, they do not in time become more gifted. Even gentiles admit that, in the past two centuries, Jews have played a disproportionately large role in our society and have proportionately produced a larger number of great men than any other people. They possess great natural gifts as musicians, artists, scientists, lawyers, doctors, actors, designers, managers, boxers. If a woman has to be twice as good as a man to get the same job, a Jew has to be ten times as good as a gentile. If he were Einstein, Baruch, and Governor Lehman all rolled into one, he couldn't get to be President.

Over the centuries the Jews have worked out many compensations. One is the ability to make money. The only trait they possess in common, after generations of living separated in many lands, is this desire and ability to make money. This, with their talent for getting ahead, is a great consolation to them. Their preoccupation with money is due primarily to their feeling of insecurity. Always in iminent danger of expulsion from any country, insecure in every way, they seek the security of money. Subconsciously even the wealthiest Jew, with assets in many countries, feels insecure. Their psychology at its deepest level remains that of the hunted.

But they have achieved higher compensations than

financial success. They have given as bountifully of their wealth as they have taken. They are among our greatest humanitarians and philanthropists, perhaps for no better reason than that it is a tremendous satisfaction to patronize those who consider themselves our superiors. Christianity itself, said Nietzsche, was the direct result of the Jewish complex. Given sufficient wealth, a Jew asks nothing better than to devote it to the public welfare.

Robert Moses is one of our outstanding public servants. You can't walk a dozen blocks in New York City without crossing a bridge, entering a park, encountering a slum clearance engineered by one of the most persistent philanthropists of our day. What Baron Haussmann was to Paris, this man is to New York. He it was who drove through such spectacular projects as the Triborough Bridge complex, the incomparable parkways that dash upstate and through Long Island, the outdoor playgrounds and indoor recreation centers, the seaside resorts like no others in the world (Jones Beach, for one), the public country clubs (the Bethpage Golf Course), the great monuments everywhere, the magnificent drives along the Hudson and East Rivers, a rejuvenated Central Park, the music center and Coliseum at Columbus Circle. He has not made himself loved in the process. He is a tough man to tangle with (you have to be to fight New York politicians) but he is one of a handful of practical visionaries who have made New York a city of daring and imagination, breathtakingly unlike any other city on earth.

In the course of his Thirty Years' War on the ugliness and inefficiency of New York, Robert Moses has dissipated a large private fortune. Of the dozens of posts with high-sounding titles he has held—New York City Park Commissioner, New York City Construction Co-ordinator, Chairman of the State Council of Parks—only one had a salary attached. The Park Commissioner in his corporate personality drags down $25,000 a year, insufficient to pay his income tax. His reward is not financial. While he is not a character to turn the other cheek, he has achieved a magnificent compensation by doing good to those who have despitefully used him and his race.

"Certainly there are no material rewards comparable to those which can be expected from similar devotion to private work," he said once in an after-dinner speech. "I made up my mind long ago to get my reward from tangible accomplishments, from the dogwood, the tulip, the chrysanthemum, the curving parkway, the spiderwork of suspension bridges, the reclaimed waterfront, the demolition of slums, the crack of a baseball bat and the shouting of children in the playgrounds."

What the Jew cannot achieve for himself, he counts on achieving through his children—they shall be his compensation. A gentile is usually satisfied if his son does as well as himself—he may even be outraged if he outstrips him. It is the rare Jew who doesn't want his son to surpass him and for that he will make any sacrifice.

Still another compensation, especially of educated Jews, is their extraordinary ability to identify themselves with the culture of the country in which they live. Until recently having no country of their own, they yearn for a sense of belonging. They can even, in a country which persecuted them relentlessly, feel themselves to be more German than Jew.

For the Jews as a race, assimilation is the solution and for this, too, they have a special gift. They have always been able to accept the government, the customs, and the culture of their adopted country. In certain European countries, notably France, England and Germany, where they were not too numerous, they would today be completely assimilated if it were not for fresh immigrations. The anti-Jewish investigations in Hungary and Germany before the last war, revealed many a Jewish ancestor in supposedly pure-blooded gentile families. In Spain, where, for four centuries, Jews have intermarried with gentiles, there is little trace of Jewish blood and no discrimination.

In the case of the individual, intermarriage can be cruel for both parties. A Jew of my acquaintance, wealthy and cultured, before he would propose to the gentile girl he loved, wrote her a letter explaining "what it means to be a Jew." It meant that she would lose her position in society. She could no longer associate with many people whose company she had always taken for granted. Her Jewish name would automatically close many doors to her. She would be dropped from clubs probably and the Social Register. Certain hotels would refuse her, others would give her inferior accommodations. Hard as this would be for her, it would be even harder for her children. They would not be accepted in certain schools, camps, fraternities, clubs. Half-Jew, half-gentile, they would deeply resent this unfair treatment.

This is the situation for the first generation but it becomes progressively easier with each generation as the two blood strains intermingle.

Just as races and religions engender inferiority complexes, so do nations.

"Just as a baby expresses by its very movements the feeling of its own insufficiency, its constant desire to perfect itself and to solve the problems of life," writes Adler, "so the march of human history must be interpreted as the history of the inferiority feeling and the attempt to work free of it."

It is no more difficult to recognize the mechanism of the inferiority complex at work in nations than in individuals. In the case of Germany, we have twice in one generation seen this complex lead to world wars. Probably no nation has ever burned with so deep a sense of inferiority and has reacted so violently as Germany. Living for centuries in such close proximity to that most illuminated, gifted, and cultured of nations, France, the German could not but feel uncouth. While France and England were at the height of their power, Germany was a fifth-rate nation. After the exhausting Thirty Years' War (1618-1648), the German economy, the German physique, German intellectual and spiritual qualities deteriorated. Then came 1870 and the resurgence of the German military spirit, nationalism, and the master-race philosophy. First under the physically deformed Kaiser, then under the psychologically deformed Hitler, the Germans, swollen with the *Deutschland über Alles* complex, almost wrecked the world. The Nazi assault on humanity is the most extraordinary example of a mass inferiority complex at work in the whole history of mankind.

In 1918 Germany was brought to its knees by a "degenerate" France, backed by a few other "inferior" nations. Then in the 1930's came the rise to power of a psychopath whose character, personality, and behavior were in the highest degree neurotic and whose speeches, gestures, facial expression and walk all betrayed his unstable nature. This man's whole life was an overcompensation for violent inferiority complexes. None knew better than he how to use them to his own advantage.

At Hitler's right hand stood Goebbels, a small man and lame, who, racked by inferiority complexes, used every device to conceal his crippled leg and passed off his wife's children by a former marriage as his own.

At Hitler's left hand stood Goering, whose vanity and pomposity were notorious. His hundreds of dashing uniforms, the medals, decorations and titles he constantly awarded himself, the loot he sent home from conquered countries were all neurotic compensations for a complex as big as his ego.

These three ego-maniacs, ably assisted by other neurotics of the inner circle of the Nazi party, such as Himmler, administered a powerful drug to the German people. Recognizing that the whole nation, like themselves, was suffering from a corroding inferiority complex, they decided to exploit it. Using modern psychological methods, they persuaded every thick-skulled lout that he was a superman, a pure Aryan, who today would rule Germany, tomorrow the world. To this *Deutschland über Alles* shot in the arm, they added large doses of old stale Nietzscheism and the pseudoscientific philosophy of the "nordification of the spirit," till finally the most insignificant of these people, who had been crawling around on their bellies, were clanking about in uniforms and helmets proclaiming themselves members of the master race.

Thus did Hitler, skillfully manipulating the inferiority complex of eighty million people, raise the Germans to a fanatical pitch of nationalism and lead them to assault the world. It is not a superabundant vitality that produces excessive nationalism but a low national morale—a national inferiority complex.

The Spanish, of course, have an inferiority complex of long standing. Having, in the sixteenth century, reached a position of world domination, they later fell to their present lowly estate. They reacted, however, in quite a different way from the Germans. They had a great past to bolster their morale. They are still the proudest people on earth. The very beggars among them are as haughty as hidalgos. One of their writers has called them "a nation of twenty million kings." Whatever may be behind the façade, the façade must be worthy. They spend a disproportionate amount of their income on clothes; the poorest hut is always freshly whitewashed. They are even proud of their shortcomings. Singly and collectively they boast of them.

"We Spanish are no good at—" is a phrase constantly on their lips.

"We Spaniards are too individualistic to organize and to co-operate like you Americans."

"We Spaniards are not technically gifted like the Germans."

The entire nation goes in for this sort of self-derogation. They recognize that they are plagued by inferiority complexes. They also recognize that their excessive pride is the mark of the superiority complex by which they seek to compensate. An unparalleled arrogance is the cloak for their feeling of inadequacy. Their literature, dating from their defeat in the Philippines and Cuba, abounds in references to this attitude. They adore a bullfighter because he is the embodiment of arrogance, the symbol of their own inordinate pride. José Ortega y Gasset refers to this arrogance as the national passion, the besetting sin, the ethic vice of the Spanish.

As to Russia—

Unexpectedly and surprisingly entering world politics as one of the Big Four after centuries of being a tenth-rate power, Russia feels compelled to foist its system of government (invented by a German) upon the rest of the world. It attempts this national compensation while imbuing the individual Russian with the most crushing sense of inferiority to which an entire population has ever been subjected. No man owns anything, not his own soul, not his night's sleep, not the right to speak or even think as he pleases. The nothingness of the individual is carried on occasion to the point of denying his very existence. Radio Free Europe reported an exchange of telegrams between a Pole living in West Berlin and the Embassy of the Polish People's Republic by which the Pole sought a visa to visit his birthplace in Breslau, Poland. The Embassy telegraphed him that Breslau was unknown in the People's Poland and that he probably meant Wroclaw. He then requested permission to visit Wroclaw, to which the Embassy replied:

"Wroclaw is old Russo-Polish city. If you assert you were born in Wroclaw, that is false. If you assert you were born in Breslau, then that's also wrong since Breslau not exists. If Breslau not exists you not born and not need visa."

Broad humor to us but deadly earnest to a Communist.

As for ourselves—

America has always had, and still has, an embarrassingly obvious inferiority complex. We have always felt—and with good reason—culturally inferior to Europe, with particular reference to Great Britain. We have had, toward England, the kind of inferiority feelings that a child has toward its parents, the feeling that any colony has toward the mother country. We still don't feel mature and can scarcely be prodded into taking over the world leadership that is being thrust upon us. We show our lack of self-confidence in our national propensity to worry about what others think of us. If some move, as in the Suez Canal crises, makes us unpopular in France or England, we get terribly upset and nervous and begin wondering if we did the right thing and why everybody doesn't love us.

Socially also we feel inferior. We are of humble birth, made up of the outcasts of Europe, the refugees from the poverty and oppression of every country in the world. Those who are successful at home stay there. Dukes don't emigrate.

The American who stays at home and comes into contact only with the emigrants from the ghetto, the potato fields of Ireland, and the rice paddies of China, the wetbacks from Mexico and the half-castes from Puerto Rico, does not feel inferior to foreigners—on the contrary. But those who travel, who meet the European on his own ground, recognize the superiority of a culture thousands of years older than our own.

America has made many compensations for this adolescent feeling of inferiority. Like a rebellious child it early threw off parental authority and announced its independence of the mother country. Unable to compete on a cultural level with Europe, it concentrated on industry, science, technology, medicine, above all on the making of money, and in most of these fields, notably the making of money, where no country in the world has ever equalled us, it quickly surpassed other nations. So that today England treats us almost as an equal, and Europe looks down its nose at us with envy.

The poor and oppressed of every nation adore us. They look with love and longing at our freedom—and our prosperity. No country has the power to make good citizens of foreigners in so short a time as America.

Some years ago in the Los Angeles Bureau of Naturalization, they were making citizens in the usual droning, humdrum fashion. Suddenly a young Ukranian began to recite the Pledge of Allegiance. It was as though it were the first time it had ever been spoken, as though he were thinking and feeling his way toward understanding of his new freedom. When he came to the words, "one nation indivisible, with liberty and justice for all," the whole room came alive. Applause rang out and the judge seized the young's man and said, "Thank you for giving the beauty of that pledge back to me, Igor Gorin!"

The love of our foreign-born citizens for America is perhaps our best compensation for our inferiority feelings.

A state, a city, a borough can acquire an inferiority complex. What does Texas do to California, California to Florida, or Northern California to Southern California? As for cities, their inferiority feelings come out constantly in their sensitiveness to criticism.

When, on a visit to Canada, Field Marshal Viscount Montgomery was asked whether he believed enemy aircraft could reach Buffalo, he asked crisply, "Where's Buffalo?" To which the citizens of that city replied indignantly, "Who's Montgomery?"

New York, of course, wouldn't have turned a hair.

But now suppose we take people of the same race, the same religion, the same nation—will they count themselves as equals?

Certainly not. There remain the distinctions of class. India, a country which rails against the Englishman's assumption of superiority and castigates America's treatment of the Negro, brands tens of millions of human beings Untouchable. So low is the Untouchable, so high the Brahman that the shadow of an Untouchable is believed to render the food of the high-caste Hindu inedible. An Indian can no more change his caste than a leopard his spots, be he Untouchable, Unapproachable or Unlookable.

England is a white, Protestant, democratic country, yet class distinctions there amount to a caste system. Art Buchwald, columnist, tells of entering a London shop to buy a shirt. A man in a tail coat snaps his fingers to summon a lowly salesman who stands respectfully by with his thumbs at the seams of his trousers. Art asks for a shirt with a button-down collar. The poor chap seems terribly embarrassed. Art asks what's wrong.

"Well, to be frank, sir, in England we don't think too much of the button-down collar. It's just not the sort of thing you would wear except to a very bad cricket match. Of course, if you want a button-down shirt—"

"Heavens, no! What is the proper shirt to wear?"

"Ah, the proper thing! *This* is the style now. You'll notice the Duke of Norfolk wears only this type of shirt. It is worn by gentlemen of distinction of every profession."

Art is shamed into buying a dozen non-button-down-collar shirts. Such is the force of the caste-system in a democratic state!

Even royalty may be more or less royal. The full version of the national anthem was until recently played only for Queen Elizabeth II of England and the former Queen, now Queen Mother Elizabeth. But now Prince Philip, for whom formerly only six bars were played, gets the full treatment. By decree of his wife, "the full version of the national anthem will in future be played whenever a royal salute is given for His Highness Prince Philip."

We recognize the equality of all human beings on the political and economic levels, not on the social level. We argue, very logically, that no one actually *is* equal to anyone else. One person is more intelligent, better bred, better educated, more beautiful, stronger, more virtuous, more useful than another—in a word, superior.

True. But none of these things implies a higher *social* status. Class distinctions are the result of putting undue emphasis on a single quality such as birth, wealth, education, which is not the true measure of the value of a human being.

The democratic idea of social equality is gaining ground. The class system is gradually breaking down. Kings, czars and emperors have disappeared overnight. Titles were abolished in one country after the other. Even the aristocracy of wealth, what with income and inheritance taxes, can last but a generation or so longer—and there can never be another. But the idea of class distinction is so deeply ingrained in human nature that it may well be the last barrier to equality to give way. Families which once had titles still cling to them, though their countries have become republican or even communist. Solemnly the English press announces that there are only two little princesses in the whole world who can

be considered as possible future consorts for the most
eligible bachelor of 1971, little Prince Charles. America
loses its head over the marriage of one of its girls to the
ruler of a 375-acre principality.

We pay lip service to the idea of a classless society
but nowhere in the world does it exist. Soviet Russia,
abolishing capitalism and inherited wealth, set out to
create such a society. But soon it was discovered (as if
it had never been discovered before!) that the incentives
human beings most readily respond to are money, position,
property, privilege. Any superiority in ability, education,
intelligence, energy demands recognition of this sort.
So in Russia today a general, a famous artist, writer, musician, ballerina, government official, factory manager demands and gets more money and better living quarters
than a factory hand. Having liquidated one aristocracy,
they are now in process of building up another. The old
round starts all over again.

Today in Russia the daughters of generals marry the
sons of generals. Marshal Zhukov's daughters married the
sons of Marshals Vasilevsky and Voroshilov. The sons of
rich men, refusing to work, sometimes outdo even American playboys in their dissipations. While the average
worker lives with his entire family in one medium-sized
room, the successful writers and artists live like millionaires. Aram Khachaturian, composer of *Gayne,* lives in
an eight-room duplex. Ilya Ehrenburg, whose novels have
made him one of the wealthiest of the new Russian aristocracy, occupies a luxurious five-room apartment and
owns an art collection that any millionaire in the world
would envy—Picassos, Matisses, Chagalls. The children of
this new aristocracy, well-educated and with good manners, speak of the "masses" with disdain, even a brutality,
which is unheard of in America or the rest of Europe.

To show the extent to which, in this "classless" society,

snobbery can go, there is the authentic report of an Austrian ambassador who applied through the Foreign Office for a proper mate for his cocker spaniel bitch. Inquiring weeks later as to the cause for the delay, he was informed that a cocker spaniel belonging to a Soviet citizen of equal rank with an ambassador could not be located. . . . How class-conscious can you get?

The Russians, holding that Communism, which debases the individual, denying him all dignity and importance, thought they could force the masses to accept subservience. It is gradually becoming apparent that people cannot be brainwashed into being servants of the state. The individual wants recognition and is restive without it. It is here in America that a "people's capitalism" has, in a quarter of a century of peaceful liberalization, brought about the most nearly classless society in history.

We have accepted the *idea* of social equality, we have not yet accepted the *fact*. Most intelligent people have abandoned the notion that the Occidental is superior to the Oriental, the white man to the black man, a gentile to a Jew, an Englishman to an American, a lord to a laborer, a rich man to a poor man, a man to a woman, an adult to a child. We are beginning to recognize that all conflict is the result of insisting on the superiority of one human being or one group over another. Everywhere, on every front, from the home to international relations, it is being demonstrated that one group cannot with impunity dominate another. It would be wise at this point, where races and nations are prepared to prove their equality with the most lethal weapons, to decide to live as equals rather than to die as superiors.

The final test of any psychology is how much it helps us to understand ourselves and others and to live fully. To what extent can the system of psychology based on the inferiority complex, do that for us?

CHAPTER XI

No Man Is an Island

A YOUNG MAN walked with his mother toward her plane, carrying her suitcase. He kissed her good-bye and left the airport. Eleven minutes after the take-off, the plane exploded and crashed, killing all forty-four persons on board.

The cause of the explosion was twenty-five sticks of dynamite planted in a suitcase in the baggage compartment.

This is what the young man, John Graham, found it expedient to do in order that he might be the beneficiary of the $37,500 policy for which he had insured his mother's life. It seemed to him that all these people were expendable so that he might have what he wanted.

In a battle of the Civil War a Yankee captain stood over the body of his orderly. The boy had been burned to death while recovering his captain's sword, lost in battle.

"When I realized that he had died for love of me," said Captain Conwell later, "I made a vow that I would live, thereafter, not only my own life, but also the life of John Ring, that it might not be lost."

For sixty years Russell Conwell worked two days in

every one—eight hours for Conwell, eight for Ring. He had two law offices in Boston, one for Conwell, one for Ring. In addition he became a lecturer, a newspaper correspondent, a politician, a real estate operator, a newspaper publisher, a teacher, a minister. While commuting by train to his two offices in Boston, he learned to read five languages. He had already committed the whole of Blackstone to memory.

At one period he was the head of a large institutional church, a university, and three hospitals. On the side he wrote thirty-seven volumes of biography, travel, and legal treatises. He also founded Temple University and the Samaritan Hospital in Philadelphia.

Still it did not seem to him that he was fully repaying his debt to his dead orderly. So he prepared a special lecture. He called it *Acres of Diamonds* and it was about the opportunities which lie all around us, waiting to be picked up and polished into success. It was one of the most electrifying lectures ever written. Conwell delivered it over 6,000 times, sometimes for $9,000, sometimes for a chicken dinner. Hearing it, men went out and made themselves mayors, governors, successful business and professional men, ministers and teachers. All told, Conwell earned several million dollars with this lecture—and he gave it all away. He died a penniless millionaire.

Two men who gave two different meanings to life.

To one of them it meant: to get all I can.

To the other it meant: to give all I can.

To discover the meaning of life was Adler's lifelong goal. He did not see how he was going to help the sick mind get well until he could answer that question.

What then *is* the meaning of life?

Most people answer, "The religion I was taught as a child." They inquire no further.

But it is the nature of the scientist to doubt what he was taught as a child and to seek his own answer.

Einstein, asking himself, "What is the meaning of human life, or, for that matter, of the life of any creature?" answered:

"To know the answer to this question means to be religious. You ask: Does it make any sense, then, to pose this question? I answer: The man who regards his own life and that of his fellow creatures as meaningless is not merely unhappy but hardly fit to live. . . . The scientist's religious feeling takes the form of a rapturous amazement at the harmony of natural law, which reveals an intelligence of such superiority that, compared with it, all the systematic thinking and acting of human beings is an utterly insignificant reflection. This feeling is the guiding principle of his life and work, insofar as he succeeds in keeping himself from the shackles of selfish desire. It is beyond question closely akin to that which has possessed the religious geniuses of all ages."

That is an impressive answer.

Each scientist seeks an answer to this question in the field of his own special interest—Einstein as a physicist, Darwin as a naturalist, Schweitzer as a philosopher. Adler, a biologist and psychologist, argued as follows:

The primate baby comes into the world helpless and remains so for a long period, often for years. Mother and child must remain together during this period. Gradually the human male learned to stay more or less permanently with the female and their progeny in order to provide for and protect them. This was the beginning of the family.

But man, one of the weakest of animals, could not survive in so small a unit. Only the herd offered him defense, protection, a livelihood, survival. Gradually the family evolved into larger and more complex communities—the hunting band, the clan, the tribe, finally sovereignties and empires.

Thus, almost from his earliest appearance on earth, man has lived in communities. As a result, community feeling has always been basic in his psyche. Only if each individual subordinated himself to the group could the species survive.

There was more to it than just necessity. There was also the fact that man alone among animals could sense a future, man alone could feel fear in advance. Because of this he experienced a sense of insecurity, always present to his consciousness. So it was that he developed a brain superior to that of all other animals, one that could react swiftly enough to compensate for his physical deficiencies. His uninterrupted feeling of inadequacy developed in him foresight and precaution, and gradually his psyche expanded to the unparalleled organ of thinking, feeling and acting that it is today.

Because he perforce lived among his fellows, there came about the final miracle of speech. Speech would be absolutely unnecessary to an organism living alone.

And so from the first moment he draws breath a human being must reckon with the conditions of communal life. Through his dependence upon society he has developed all the qualities that make him man. It would seem that he owes society something.

"Civilization and culture, every good thing we have, was left us by men who contributed to human welfare," Adler argues. "And what has happened to those who asked only, 'What can I get out of life?' No trace of them is left. It is as if the earth itself had said, 'You are not fit for life. You are useless. Go!'

"In all religions we find this concern for the welfare of mankind. What I have called Individual Psychology arrives at the same conclusion in a scientific way. Science,

by proving the necessity we are all under to increase our
interest in the welfare of human beings, backs up religion.
. . . The oldest striving of mankind is for men to join
with their fellowmen. It is through our interest in our
fellowmen that all the progress of our race has been
made."

What is the meaning of life?

Either the answer must be, "Life has no meaning," or,
"The meaning of life is to contribute." If a man's answer
is the first, he owes the world nothing, he himself is the
be-all and the end-all. He is a John Graham. If it is the
second, he will do all he can for others. He is a Russell
Conwell.

Due to his helplessness and his consequent dependence
upon the community, two contradictory forces have developed in man's nature—competitiveness and co-operativeness. Both are the result of his feeling of insecurity and
his desire to compensate for it. He competes to get what
he needs. He co-operates so that others will co-operate
with him. These two principles are constantly at war,
making man the most inconsistent of living creatures,
consistent only in his inconsistency. He is ununderstand-
able to himself and inscrutable to all but the greatest
creative geniuses.

He does not know if he is good or bad. Western civilization has generally assumed that man is evil. Theologians
have insisted on original sin. They have been backed up
by scientists like Darwin who saw in our animal nature
only the struggle for life and the survival of the fittest,
and by Freud who saw the *id* as evil and the newborn
babe as a selfish little monster. The instinctivists in psychology hold that man is evil, civilization merely a system
of restraints to protect himself, and culture a veneer applied to make association with others tolerable.

Liberal schools of psychology, revolting against this

theory, maintain that the instincts are sometimes good or, at the very least, neutral, and that civilization developed, not merely as a means of holding man's animal instincts in check, but also to gratify his higher needs. True, man is an animal but there are good animals and animals with good instincts. And certainly many animals do co-operate. Naturalists tells us of a tiny field mouse attacking a five-foot racer snake to save its mate; of a gander tearing into a fox to rescue the hen; of the tiniest of all birds, the humming bird, unhesitatingly chasing an eagle that has invaded its territory. I myself have seen a sparrow, after unsuccessfully tugging at a string tied to a window, summon its mate so that both might pull together. And I have seen a starling walking ahead of its mate across the lawn, dragging worms from the earth and dropping them into the open squawking beak of the female. In Zurich, Switzerland, one year as winter approached and all the storks flew south to warmer climes, one male kept vigil beneath a bridge from dawn to dusk every day for his mate who never appeared. She had been killed by a high tension wire.

Co-operation is not a built-in reflex in humans as it is in some species of insects. This reflex is what accounts for the mound builders among the ants being the oldest social organization on earth, dating back some sixty million years. The colony expects every ant to do its duty—and every ant does, automatically. The queen, after the nuptial flight, plucks off her wings so that she will never be tempted to neglect her task of laying eggs for the next fifteen years. The nurses spend their lives licking fungi from the eggs; the honey-makers chemically process the flower juices in their own bodies into honey; servitors are assigned on hot days to air-condition the hive with fanning wings; and soldiers, when the mound is invaded, rush forth to engage in mortal combat.

No, it isn't that easy for man. Co-operation comes hard to him. He co-operates only because he must. After millions of years of co-operation he still doesn't like it. He infinitely prefers competition. Over the centuries he has shifted his ground from the struggle for life to the struggle for money, power and prestige, but it's still the same old competitive spirit. We are thoroughly at home down there in the arena slugging it out.

Man has schooled himself to be the most socialized animal—but he is also the most individualistic. He has surrendered everything to the community except his egotism. He allows himself to be disciplined only so that others will likewise be disciplined. Wearing a mask of humanitarianism, he continues to carry on the fierce struggle for domination. He is incorrigible.

And thoroughly inconsistent. For he can be as sublime as he is deplorable.

"The name cannot be disclosed—" read many reports of action on the front during the war. In one case the man cited was designated merely as a Royal Navy surgeon lieutenant, the medical officer in a British destroyer which picked up the survivors of a Canadian warship. Already crippled by one explosion, he was helping the survivors aboard the destroyer when a second underwater explosion shot both legs from under him, breaking them below the knee. He at once ordered three seamen to carry him among the wounded. Beside each cot he sat on the floor, examining, bandaging, prescribing. When all were cared for he had the men place him in a long chair, his broken legs stretched out before him. There he sat many more hours, prescribing treatment for the most serious wounded, until the destroyer reached Gibraltar. There they carried him off on a stretcher.

More than mere survival was at stake in this man's soul.

A man whose name is known to only a few was, on his death, credited by Major Walter Reed with an "exhibition of moral courage never surpassed in the annals of the Army of the United States."

In Havana in 1900, Major Reed, seeking the cause of yellow fever, called for volunteers to submit to the bite of the steyomyia mosquito, guaranteed to inoculate them with the deadly disease. John R. Kissinger volunteered. His reward (he refused money) was the Congressional Medal of Honor and a lifetime of severe physical disability. After his death an editorial commented:

"Kissinger . . . brought to life an ideal which, perhaps a little more than other forms of valor, is the buried treasure of democracy. He represents the unpredictable factor of greatness in our way of life which comes out of the ranks to meet emergencies with reasoned courage and the selflessness of high purpose, without expecting, or getting, his name written in capital letters across a page of fame."

This goes beyond self-preservation.

That some trace of this urge to co-operate is in almost all human beings, is proved by the selfless acts often performed by hardened criminals.

A Chinese darted into a blazing building in the Chinese quarter of a big city, rescued a sleeping child, then slipped away through the crowd, picking a pocket here and there, to continue on his rounds selling opium.

A volunteer from the Ohio State Penitentiary, about to be injected with live, growing cancer cells, asked why he had offered himself, shrugged and said, "I've been a stinker all my life. I thought I'd like to do something worthwhile for once."

The two principles are endlessly at war in the individual and in society. No doubt about it, men love to fight. They are as convinced that it is necessary to fight as it is to draw breath. They don't want to be told they don't need to fight. Only a fuzzy idealist with both feet firmly planted on a cloud would maintain that humanity is going to give up competition and go in whole-hog for co-operation. Are the Russians? Is the American businessman? Are you and that so-and-so who's after your girl? But a gradual increase in co-operativeness is possible—in fact has begun. One of the chief reasons we dragged our feet so long is that we are not aware of the great number of solutions for human problems other than fighting or yielding.

The meaning which Adler found for life was: to contribute.

"All failures—neurotics, psychotics, criminals, problem children, suicides, perverts and prostitutes—are failures because they are lacking in fellow-feeling and social interest. . . . The meaning they give to life is a private meaning: no one else is benefited by the achievement of their aims and their interest stops short at their own persons. . . . A private meaning is no meaning at all."

It follows from any such philosophy of life that, granting his goal, a purely personal superiority, the criminal has gone the best way about achieving it. His logic, that everything that serves his ends is permissible, is infallible. Only his goal is questionable.

The genius stands at the other extreme—not personal superiority but service to the community. Only those are called geniuses who have contributed greatly to mankind. They seek superiority, true, but only in order to serve their fellowmen. They are in the highest sense co-operative.

The character and behavior of many geniuses would seem to contradict this—Wagner, Nietzsche, Whistler, Poe, Schopenhauer, Gauguin. Often their attitude implies that they are not even slightly interested in co-operating and don't give a damn for their fellowman. Only when we look at the whole picture of their lives do we realize to what extent they have co-operated.

"It was not so easy for them to co-operate," says Adler. "They went a difficult way and they had many obstacles to contend with. But if we study their childhood and youth we see at once how hard they trained themselves for their task, how they sharpened their senses to make contact with the world and to understand its problems. . . . They strove and we are blessed. . . . Even genius is to be defined as no more than supreme usefulness; it is only when a man's life is recognized by others as having significance for them that we call him a genius. . .

"Life means—to contribute to the whole. We are not speaking here of *professed* motives. We are closing our eyes to professions and looking at achievements. The man who meets the problems of life successfully, acts as if he recognized, fully and spontaneously, that the meaning of life is interest in others and co-operation."

No minister of the gospel could be more fervent on this point than Adler. The commandment to "Love thy neighbor" is to him not only a religious doctrine but a scientific law. "The oldest striving of mankind is for men to join with their fellowmen. It is through interest in our fellowmen that all the progress of our race has been made." Science, by proving the necessity of fellow-feeling, backs up religion.

A human being can be judged by the proportion of self-interest to social interest in his attitude toward life. We have only to ask ourselves, "Does this individual manifest a high degree of social feeling and only a minor degree of striving for personal power and prestige—or is he (or she) predominantly egoistic, primarily interested in acquiring a sense of superiority over his environment?"

This is the point at which Adler passes from the science of psychology to the art of psychology, eventually embracing philosophy, ethics, pedagogy, even religion, territory where Freud refused to set foot. Considered as a "depth psychology," Adler's system did not go so deep nor was it so involved as Freud's. But whereas Freud emerged from his researches into the darkest depths of human nature with a wholesale indictment of man and no hope for him, here or hereafter, Adler returned with a not unfavorable opinion of the creature and an optimistic view of his possibilities. Jung likewise rejected Freud's instinctual drives, pansexuality, the pleasure principle, and so forth, and stressed instead the creative impulse in man, his intuition, idealism, and other spiritual qualities. Both Jung and Adler believed that, within the framework of the evolutionary process, man is striving toward a higher destiny, a possibility Freud refused to contemplate.

According to Adler the greatest difficulty in the way of progress is our reluctance to co-operate, to drop the struggle for personal superiority and to live with others on a basis of equality, which he believed is the only basis for living in peace.

Since Adler lived and wrote, men everywhere, in all their relationships, have begun to struggle for this equality. Adler did not initiate these great movements; he foresaw them, explained them, and insisted that they must be accepted psychologically before they can be accepted politically, economically, and socially.

The family and society were inextricably interwoven in Adler's psychology. "Sexuality," he said, "cannot be regarded as a private matter." The events in the individual's life are meaningless except as they relate to the collective lives of all. Our social relations and our social philosophy start with the family and work outward toward the community.

In the family, he was the first to point out, the chief cause of conflict is the striving for equality between the sexes, between parents and children and among siblings.

The change-over from an authoritarian patriarchy to a democratic unit, is the basis of most family dissension today. But the very confusion that reigns in the home, viewing which our own grandparents would thank God they hadn't lived to see the day, is in itself a healthy sign. No one holds the same position in the family they did even fifty years ago. Who is the head of the house—Dad or Mother? Should Dad wash the dishes—or shouldn't he? Should Mother go to business—or shouldn't she? Should boys make beds—or should only girls?

A thousand or more psychiatrists, psychologists, teachers, parents, and social workers, gather annually at the meeting of the Child Study Association of America to hash over these once unthinkable problems. In 1957 they devoted most of their time to the problem of the American male and his changing rôle in the family. Only in America and Australia, it seems, do they have this problem to contend with. In Germany, Japan, Switzerland, and the Middle East, men still manage to hold their own. Here in America, seeing their traditional "head of the family" status crumbling beneath them, they try to laugh it off, but their laughter has a slightly hollow sound. They realize that their autocratic rule is at an end. In adjusting to their new position, they should consider that society has always overemphasized masculine prerogatives and that in consequence women fear domination. When a man sees the girl who was a gentle and docile sweetheart suddenly, after the marriage, turn into a hostile and aggressive opponent, he should understand that this may well be because she fears he'll clap the handcuffs on the minute she quiets down. He should try to prove to her from the start that he does not consider himself her superior. For a happy marriage, Adler held, both partners must feel they are equal, irreplaceable, needed, valuable, and utterly loyal.

True equality between the sexes, he maintained, means monogamy. One partner to the marriage cannot take privileges denied the other. By nature human beings are neither polygamous nor monogamous. Nature has left that entirely up to them. But, comments Adler:

"This relation is one of such intimate devotion that any search for escape is sure to shape its fundamental basis. . . . In Europe I have found that psychiatrists for the most part think that personal welfare is the most important point generally. Therefore they recommend a sweetheart or a lover and think this might be the way to solve the problem. . . . They can only propose such a solution if they have not been rightly trained in the whole coherence of the problem and the way it hangs together with the other tasks of our life on this earth."

The attitude of the man as a father as well as a husband, was also due for a change. Children would no longer accept an autocratic rule. At first new psychologies and new theories of education brought in a laissez-faire school in child training. Fearful of the dire consequences of repressing the little libidos of their charges, warned by the Freudians of the frustrations and hostility that might follow severe disciplinary methods, mothers and teachers indulged and spoiled children to the point where they became veritable little monsters, silently cursed by one and all. One overwrought mother, goaded to the unspeakable act of spanking her small son, later confessed to her husband, "I finally took a strap and gave him something to tell his psychiatrist about later on."

Adler was no proponent of this lack of discipline, but equally he was unalterably opposed to the authoritarian father. From such a man boys acquire a false idea of what a man should be and girls come to see marriage as subjugation. The only teaching which has any lasting effect is that given in a friendly way on a basis of equality.

No human being, not even a child, can tolerate without disgust being treated like an inferior.

Dr. Rudolf Dreikurs follows Adler in his belief that the transition from an authoritarian to a democratic society is responsible for the general confusion and maladjustment of our time. We do not know how to live with each other, he holds, nor how to solve conflicts. This is as true of our relationships outside the family as within it—in the community, the nation, the world. Man, after all his thousands of years of experience in social living, has suddenly become completely illiterate in his social relationships. The explanation Dreikurs finds for this anomaly is that it is the mission of our generation to establish democracy in all human relationships and that the attempt to do this has brought about a state of upheaval in all phases of our lives.

From the family co-operation spreads to the community. Benjamin Fairless contrasts the management of a generation ago to that of today. Formerly, says the former president and chairman of the board of the United States Steel Corporation, one man founded, built up and ruled over a great industry. Today such companies are run by a corporate management with opportunities for anyone to rise to the top from the humblest job, as Fairless himself did.

"Modern management," he continues, "with its professional attitudes, its concern for the public welfare and public relations and generally humane attitudes toward business, is far better than the old system. Some critics . . . deplore the fact that all businessmen today seem to be modest and polite duplicates of one another instead of flamboyant 'characters' as in the old days. But . . . today's Man in the Gray Flannel Suit is ten times more efficient than his more colorful, more hot-tempered predecessor."

It seems obvious that the underlying psychological cause of most of the conflict in the world today, from the increasing rate of divorce to the Suez Canal crisis, from juvenile delinquency to the shrinking of the British Empire, is this universal effort to throw off inferiority complexes and to achieve equality in all our relationships. Individuals, races, nations all struggle to escape domination and to overthrow the old irregularities. The free world's international airlines could not operate without wiping out all racial and national barriers. Seldom has this ideal been better expressed than in a manifesto issued by them which in itself is a little sermon on the mount. Lacing the globe, invading all countries, being of all faiths and colors and nationalities, these men of the air had to find a common denominator. They found it in the dedication to human safety. Here are some of their articles of faith quoted from an article by Howard C. Kurtz, Jr. in *Flying:*

> Never from the cloudbank above London comes a pilot's voice saying, "Give way to the Union Jack."
> Never does a co-pilot cry into his microphone, "I demand priority landing in the name of the one true faith."
> Yet, if from that cloudbank comes perchance a call from an obsolete twin-engined plane flying the flag of some obscure little principality, then the great planes of the great flags give way at once and the objective of all concerned concentrates on bringing the little fellow safe to port. Each understands that his own safety would be jeopardized by another plane out of control in the cloud. Any rule less than the golden rule would be too dangerous a principle upon which to build air transportation. . . .
> Could it be perhaps that survival for all will emerge from a mutual concern for human safety?

. . . From our cockpits and desks and laboratories
and control towers we believe human nature is ready for
higher levels of cooperation.

We have, says Ashley Montagu, anthropologist, the
perfect example of these "higher levels of co-operation,"
constantly beneath our eyes. Mother love, he argues in his
book, *The Natural Superiority of Women,* is the ideal
type of human love. It does not dispense justice but
functions as though aware that justice is not enough. It
neither condemns nor condones. It never forsakes. It is
the purest and the most efficient form of love, the most
understanding, the least censorious, the most compas-
sionate.

To the extent to which men approximate this kind
of love in their relationships with others, do they approach
ideal human relations. "Women love the human race; men
are, on the whole, hostile to it." He holds that so long
as men continue to force upon women their ideas of how
to run the family and the community, relationships between individuals and nations will never improve.

"It is the evolutionary destiny of human beings so to
love each other. I believe that it is the unique function
and destiny of women to teach men to live as if to live and
love were one . . . The genius of woman is the genius
of humanity, and humanity is the supreme form of
intelligence."

They go in by different doors, the men of science
and the men of God, but they come out by the same
door: love or perish. As usual, it was a poet who said
this best.

"No man is an ilande intire to itselfe," wrote Donne,
"every man is a peece of the Continent, a part of the
maine. If a clod be washed away by the sea, Europe is
the lesse, as well as if a promontorie were . . . So any

man's death diminishes me, because I am involved in Mankinde; and therefore never send to know for whom the bell tolls; it tolls for thee."

Psychiatrists, being doctors of the sick mind, have made few researches into the sound mind. They are, as a group, morbidly inclined to believe that, at our best, we are "normally neurotic." But among the few studies that have been made in this field we find considerable unanimity on the following points:

That superior normal individuals (which we all like to think we are) are democratic, meeting all men on the same footing, judging the inner man, not his trappings, seeming to be unaware of distinctions of birth, money, position, color, race, religion.

That, though they are not apt to be orthodox in religion, even the agnostics and atheists among them are religious in the sense of being dedicated to spiritual values.

That, though their ethics may not always be the same as those of other people, they are nevertheless intensely moral.

That they are well adjusted but not in the sense of being adjusted to uniformity—they are never rubber stamps.

That they possess a deep feeling of oneness with the human race. They identify themselves with others, desire to help mankind and are invariably interested in some activity for the good of humanity.

Lacking all or most of these qualities, a person could scarcely be said to be normal. And when you have an individual in whom these qualities are carried to a high power, you have a human being so superior that we are drawn out of ourselves and lost in love and astonishment.

Such a man was John von Neumann, a Hungarian Jew, a scientist so brilliant that another brilliant scientist, physicist Edward Teller, said of him, "Von Neumann was one of those rare mathematicians who could descend to the level of the physicist." And Hans Bethe, director of the theoretical physics division at Los Alamos, remarked, "I have sometimes wondered whether a brain like von Neumann's does not indicate a species superior to that of man."

Von Neumann was one of the scientists chiefly responsible for the invention of the atomic bomb, the H-bomb, the electronic brain, the machine he named MANIAC, which was the prototype for the most advanced calculating machines in existence. His greatest work, the culmination of his whole life, was to be a treatise on the working of the human brain and how these concepts could be applied to electronic computers so that machines could perform most of the functions of the human brain and even reproduce themselves.

Yet when von Neumann lay dying of cancer, knowing he could either finish this great work or devote his remaining days to serving the United States, he did not hesitate. As a member of the Atomic Energy Commission, he traveled to meetings by limousine and wheelchair. When he finally was confined to Walter Reed Hospital, an Air Force officer worked full time assisting him, eight airmen were assigned to him on a 24-hour basis, cabinet members and military officials visited his bedside regularly for advice, and even the top brass of the Air Force gathered in his suite while there was still time to consult him.

Thus all chance of ever finishing the crowning work of his life was sacrificed to serving his country.

The surge of love and admiration we feel when we hear of such men as this is proof that they are the climax of humanity. It is their infinite capacity to serve their fellowmen that has made them what they are.

Now we come to the question: granting that a man decides he would like to make certain changes for the better in his character and personality, can he? Admitting that he has an inferiority complex or two and that he'd like to cash in on them, can he? Is it worthwhile for him to undertake the struggle to make these changes or is he destined to go out of this world very much the same as he came into it?

Let us look at the evidence on both sides.

CHAPTER XII

Am I the Captain
of My Soul?

ASSISI IN THE spring in the year 1200.

Never on earth has there been a more joyous spot in a more joyous time. Troubadours, carnivals, masquerades, jousts poured through the hill towns of Italy, and the Master of Revels in Assisi was the gay, the debonair young Francesco Bernardone.

Francesco was the son of a wealthy, self-made merchant. No amount of money was too much for the father to spend on the boy's pleasures for thus he mingled with the nobility and so made up to the old man for the contempt in which he himself had always been held by the aristocracy.

Francesco was a gifted debauchee, bringing real genius to his role of Master of Revels. After one more than usually brilliant banquet which he tendered his aristocratic friends, at which he was crowned King of Revels, the young blades all sallied forth into the streets in search of adventure. Suddenly Francesco was missing. Searching, his companions at last found him lying in a trance. From it he awoke Saint Francis of Assisi.

Soon after this event, he stood up in church one day in the presence of the Bishop and the Ecclesiastical Court, naked as he was born, as a symbol that he had renounced all worldly wealth and had nothing to give but himself. Thereafter he went about ministering to the sick, kissing lepers, comforting the poor, gathering disciples. He poured out inexhaustible love for all God's creatures. He preached to the birds, he communed with the trees, the flowers, the streams, addressing the forces of nature as brother Sun, sister Moon, brother Wind and sister Fire. He had visions and revelations, he received the stigmata, he became a saint.

His whole attitude toward life was unreasonable and utterly adorable. Even the sober Encyclopaedia Britannica quite loses its head over him.

"There is [in him] such a many-sided richness, such a tenderness, such a poetry, such an originality, such a distinction revealed by the innumerable anecdotes in the memoirs of his disciples, that his personality is brought home to us as one of the most lovable and one of the strongest of men. Probably no one has ever set himself so seriously to imitate the life of Christ. His enthusiastic love of poverty is certainly the keynote to St. Francis's spirit. Another striking feature was his constant joyousness."

It would seem impossible to deny that a major change had taken place in the personality of this man.

Or again—

When America was only a gleam in Columbus's eye, a boy was born in a castle in Spain who grew from spoiled child to spoiled young lord, with all the usual faults of an heir to vast estates. He was worldly, vain, a brawler, a drunkard, a lecher.

Then at twenty-two, convalescing from battle wounds, and requesting a romance to while away the time, he was

238   THE IMPORTANCE OF FEELING INFERIOR

given instead *The Life of Christ* and *Flowers of the Saints*. They were tough going. He sought distraction by dreaming up ways to ravish a certain young lady of his acquaintance.

Then one night, in full possession of his senses, he found himself thinking of a woman in a different way from what he had ever thought before. He saw a vision of the Virgin Mary with her divine Son. Suddenly a loathing for everything he had ever been or done swept over him.

Recovered from his wounds, he went direct to the Benedictine Abbey of Montserrat, gave his clothes to a beggar, placed his sword on the altar, and spent the night on his knees praying. The next day he began his life as a hermit and a saint.

Thus did Íñigo de Oñez y Loyola become St. Ignatius of Loyola, founder of the Society of Jesus, familiarly known as the Jesuits—or the "Jebbies." His *Book of Spiritual Exercises* has probably reformed—and kept reformed—more people than any other book penned by one man . . . Sometimes it almost seems as though it took a sinner to make a saint.

Certainly it cannot be said that such a man has not changed—and the question we are trying to answer here is: *can* we change?

Yes, you may say, these men have changed, but by divine intervention, by a miracle; or, if you do not believe in miracles, then by hysteria, a psychoneurosis characterized by emotional excitability. After all, look at the stigmata—pure hysteria! And no miracle, you may add, is going to change you, nor are you an hysteric.

Very well, take the case of Arthur Barry. If the great Raffles had a prototype in real life it was Barry. He was the detective-story writer's ideal of the gentleman crook—

tall, handsome, perfectly groomed, debonair, polished in manners and speech, and beyond the average, intelligent.

With this endowment Barry became the greatest jewel thief who ever lived. He amassed a fortune of between five and ten million dollars—and he was very choosy about whom he amassed it from. He wouldn't touch anyone not in the Social Register. His victims were the Rockefellers, the Harold Talbots, the Tommy Hitchcocks, the James P. Donahues, the Louis Mountbattens, the Jesse Livermores.

His particular pride was that he never used violence, never carried a weapon. His method was to don a dress suit and mingle with the guests at fashionable receptions and weddings, spot the genuine pearl necklaces and diamond tiaras and return later to pick them up. Or, in less formal but still elegant attire, he might enter a bedroom at night and make off with the family jewels. He made a point of never frightening his hosts if they awoke but persuading them that policy dictated quiet. In this manner he took in a half-million dollars a year, and became known during the 1920's as the king of the second-story men.

But finally, betrayed by a jealous woman, he was caught and sent to Auburn Prison for twenty-five years. He broke out and, wounded, fleeing—well, let him tell it.

"Have you ever tried to put on a pair of wet woolen socks, over a pair of broken toes, in the rain, with two bullets through you and your eyes full of broken glass? Let me tell you something. Right then and there was when I finally realized what a damned fool I had been all my life. I was cured. If I lived through this one I'd never steal again."

He lived and he went straight. For three years he went straight. And then, for no new crime, merely as a fugitive from justice, he was rearrested and sent back to prison for seventeen years, five of them in solitary. Even that couldn't dent his new-found honesty. Out again in 1949, he got a job as a counterman in a roadside restaurant in Worcester, Mass., his home town, at $50 a week, plus tips. Even the police bear witness that he is today an honest man and his neighbors, knowing his past, have elected him commander of a local veterans' organization. His own comment on his life is:

"When I was a young man I had many assets. I was not only intelligent, I was clever. I got along well with people on any level and, if I do say so, I had guts. I could have gone anywhere—to Wall Street, maybe—and made an honest fortune. So when you put down all those burglaries, be sure you put the big one at the top. Not Arthur Barry robbed Jesse Livermore, or Arthur Barry robbed the cousin of the King of England, but just—*Arthur Barry robbed Arthur Barry.*"

Here is a man changed, not by a miracle, not due to a psychoneurosis, but deliberately, by his own unaided efforts. But is he really changed?

It is the most natural thing in the world for a person to believe that he can change, once he makes up his mind. The alcoholic is convinced he can stop drinking; the ill-tempered shrew is sure that, once things stop going against her, she will become her own sweet-natured self; the thief believes implicitly he'll never steal again after he has a certain sum of money.

But can they? This is the age-old argument of free will versus predestination and everyone is in on the act— theologians, scientists, philosophers, right down to you and me. Theologians thunder about "original sin," the error of Adam inherited with all its consequences by all men, and about "predestination," the purpose or decree of God from eternity respecting all events. That seems to leave little chance for free will.

We are the product of our chemistry, say the biochemists, body and mind, heart and soul. The results they are obtaining today in changing the personalities of the insane by the use of drugs is just about the most impressive proof of their contention that has come our way in a long time. Nothing goes wrong with the mind, they claim, unless something first goes wrong with our chemistry—and only chemistry can set it right.

"The hell with psychoanalysis, psychosurgery, electric shock, insulin shock and all the rest of it," they say in effect. "Chemistry alone can save you."

One of our most renowned brain surgeons, Dr. Percival Bailey, director of the Illinois Psychopathic Institute, stood up before the American Psychiatric Association not long ago and blasted Freud and psychoanalysis root and limb. Human mental health and human psychology could only be helped, he said, by chemistry. As for Freud, he was no more scientific than the Delphic Oracle, his writings at best were "chirographic ruminations," his psychoanalysis has nothing to offer the mentally ill, his conception of infant and childhood sexuality and the Oedipus complex (the theory that guilt is generated in the young child by his wish to murder his father and to occupy the marital bed himself) is purely presumptive and entirely false . . . Many of the 1,000 psychiatrists who heard him, applauded wildly.

We are, say the biochemists, walking drugstores, a synthesis of various not-at-all-rare chemicals worth about 95 cents at the nearest drugstore. When we have abnormal substances in the system, we develop abnormal symptoms of behavior. These symptoms can, they claim, be removed by neutralizing the abnormal substances. Our behavior depends entirely upon our chemistry . . . Where then is free will?

Dr. Robert H. Felix, director of the National Institute of Mental Health, recently described to Congress a new type of electrode brain stimulation that has "almost frightening" potentialities for treating mental conditions. An angry, snarling monkey with one of those electrodes in his brain can, if we merely close the circuit, be transformed in a lightning flash into a creature so pleasant and friendly that he will crawl into your arms and stroke your cheek. A circuit in the brain which, stimulated, can cause good feeling, commented Dr. Felix, is there for a purpose.

When our personality can be manipulated by drugs and electric charges, when our conduct varies according to our chemistry, where is the opportunity for choice and for freedom of action? Where is the chance of making ourselves over—except through chemistry?

The naturalists, like Darwin, deny we have freedom of action, but for different reasons. They see no chance of escape from our animal nature. We live strictly according to our animal instincts, which we cannot alter nor evade.

The instinctivists among the psychologists hold with the Darwinians that we are the prisoners of our heredity and environment with no more power to change our course than a moth has to cease hurling itself against a flame.

The determinists among the philosophers go along with this view. What is to be is determined by what has been, with no loophole for chance. The universe, including man, is a totality and all that was or is or shall be has from eternity been there. There are never *two* possibilities, there is only one, and since only one, then no choice. All seeming acts of the will are the result of causes which determine them. We cannot change; we were predetermined from eternity to be what we are.

> With earth's first clay they did the last man knead,
> And there of the last harvest sowed the seed,
> And the first morning of creation wrote
> What the last dawn of reckoning shall read.

For Freud this was self-evident. He saw the working of this psychic determinism in all human beings. Psychoanalysis was a "scientific mechanistic cause-and-effect method" of explaining human nature. To Freud, whose psychology was based on Darwin's theory of evolution, it was obvious that, with the establishment of the Oedipus complex in early childhood, the fate of our libido and hence of our whole life was determined. Most psychiatrists, of whatever school, agree with him that our behavior pattern is set during the first five or six years of our lives and that thereafter it is difficult, some believe impossible, to alter it. To a similar situation we will react at forty just as we did at four. This would seem to leave us little more chance of change than does determinism.

Adler starts from the same premise.

"One's style of life is established in early childhood, generally between the third and fifth years," he wrote; and, "The goal of each human being is probably formed in the first *months* of life." And again: "The prototype is the original form of an individual's adaptation to life. This psychic prototype is a finished being by the time the child is four years old. It is the baby in the man or woman which never grows up any further but rules the whole life up to the end. It is the greatest power in human life."

An Adlerian, Dr. Leland E. Hinsie, writes: "Very few

individuals have ever been able to change the behavior
pattern of their childhood, though in adult life they have
found themselves in entirely different situations. A change
of attitude in adult life need not necessarily signify a
change in behavior pattern. The psychic life does not
change its foundation; the individual retains the same
line of activity in childhood and in maturity, leading us
to deduce that his goal in life is unaltered . . . The
hardest thing for human beings to do is to know themselves and to change themselves."

Hard, yes. Impossible? Human experience would seem
to show that it is not. Life appears to give the lie to
the biochemists, the instinctivists, the determinists. We
ourselves feel it in our bones that we have a choice of
actions. We can decide to walk in the sun or in the
shade, we can give a coin to a beggar or pass him by, we
can accept or reject a contract, we can marry the girl or
give her the gate.

And there are scientists who agree with us. Following
Darwin's discovery of the descent of man, scientists in
many fields, overwhelmed by its sweeping implications,
at first subscribed to the compelling power of heredity
and of our animal instincts. We were descended from
animals, and bad animals at that, or at least animals having bad instincts. These instincts were unmodifiable and
uncontrollable. We were putty in their hands.

Accepting this theory, a man might as well give up
without a struggle. "I was born that way," he shrugs. "I
look like my dad, I drink like my dad—what can I do
about it?" An appalling number of neurotics and failures
pronounce the fatal word, "heredity," and let it go at
that. Or accepting environment as the determining factor,
a man will claim that he was licked by his early sordid
surroundings, and forced by them into juvenile delinquency.

For many years these two factors, backed up by the heavy artillery of Freud, Pavlov, Thorndike, Watson, Lewin, Hall, Adolf Meyer, and others, were held to explain the whole nature and behavior of man.

But more recently, from various directions, has come a concerted attack on these theories. Ethnologists, psychologists, anthropologists and other scientists are claiming that too much emphasis has been put on the animal instincts, that they are not omnipotent, as originally supposed, but are opposed by powerful cultural forces in man's nature. Where the church with its "original sin" and Freud with his "id" held that man by nature was evil, these new men began to discover forces for good in his nature quite as strong as his instinctoid needs and his primitive impulses toward evil. Where Darwin and his followers could see only aggressiveness and competitiveness in his animal nature, they saw co-operation. These animal instincts may be omnipotent in frogs—they are not in man. Man's higher nature—and he has one, including conscience, reason, morality—is not a mere veneer over his animal nature; civilization is not merely a means of restraining his aggressive instincts. Man is not all animal. He has an essential nature of his own that marks him off from all other animals. He is different and he is more. He is more than the sum of his parts. He is more than his chemistry. There are forces in him, neglected by Freud but recognized by psychologists like Adler, Jung, Rank, Horney, Fromm, and others, which lead him to a higher destiny than that of any other animal. Men are not dumb, driven cattle. Their organism is far more self-directing and self-governing than the Darwinians believed, far more autonomous than the Freudians gave it credit for being. Heredity, environment, and the animal instincts are not the whole story.

There are indeterminists as well as determinists among

the philosophers. They hold that there is free will, that of two alternatives both may be possibilities, with one becoming impossible only when the other actually happens. Where determinists see only necessity on the one hand and impossibility on the other, indeterminists see a plurality of possibilities, an opportunity to choose and therefore to change. After the event, they say another event *might* have occurred. The determinists swear that no other event could possibly have occurred.

Adler, like any other scientist, acknowledged the influence of heredity and environment, although he thought too much stress had been put on them. Traits of character which appeared to be inherited were, he said, often actually acquired by the child in the effort to conquer his environment or by imitation of those around him or by a process of identifying himself with another person. This *looks* like heredity but is not. So far as psychic phenomena and character traits are concerned, heredity plays by no means so important a role as has been supposed. No worse mistake can be made in child training and education than to assume hereditary limits to intellectual development, and the belief in inherited character traits here is pure superstition. The most important factor in intellectual development is interest. It is by discouraging interest that we limit development.

In addition to heredity and environment, Adler saw a third factor—the reaction of the individual to these two factors. There is, he maintained, a margin for free will, small and uncertain, but still present. It is this third hopeful factor, not the pessimistic factors of heredity and environment, which must be emphasized in any attempt to change our way of life. This x that he postulates in man is what lifts him above the animal ruled by its instincts or reacting automatically to heredity and environment.

"If I believed," he said, "that man was controlled by

his drives—by hereditary factors—I would give up psychiatry. Instead I believe that by changing our opinion of ourselves we can change ourselves."

It was his belief in human responsibility that brought him to postulate this third factor. If man is responsible, he must possess a modicum of free will; he must be able to react to heredity and environment in an individual way. It was this belief that made Adler an ally of religion, an educator, and a sociologist, all things with which Freud had no patience as being no concern of a psychiatrist.

The prototype developed in childhood still remains the constant factor in our lives, Adler admits, "but we can improve its later manifestations to an indefinite extent when we come to recognize and understand it." True, the life plan is formed during the early years of childhood but since it is based on the child's estimate of himself and others, it can be altered at any time if his opinion is altered.

Is character unchangeable? In *What Life Should Mean to You*, Adler asks himself this question and answers it thus:

"Only those who have never found the right key to the situation can answer in the affirmative. The key is the meaning the individual gives to life. The original error which set him on a wrong path should be discovered. The only possibility for improvement lies in abandoning this false interpretation of life and training oneself to a more cooperative approach."

And Béran Wolfe, an Adlerian, in his book, *How to Be Happy Though Human*, states it thus:

"What is to be done with the inferiority complex? . . . Can it be cured? Can human nature be changed? Can the timid be made courageous, can the criminal be transformed into a philanthropist, can the hobo enjoy his day's work and the homosexual thrill to the love of a woman? The answer is yes! Mankind has said yes with civilization. Confucius, Isaiah, Christ have said yes in their preachings. Demosthenes, Beethoven, Darwin, Edison have said yes in their work. Socrates, with the keenest of psychological insight, said, 'Virtue can be learned!'"

Most psychiatrists would maintain that the *essential characteristics* of a human being never change. If there appears to be a change in his personality, it is not because these characteristics have changed but because they have been rearranged. A man who is essentially a fighter remains a fighter to the end although he is now a mountie instead of a gangster. A voluptuary remains a voluptuary although he may now be scourging himself in a monastery instead of climbing balconies at night. To the layman these seem to be actual changes of essential characteristics. To the psychiatrist they are rather such changes as we see in a kaleidoscope where the bits of glass remain always the same and only their arrangement is altered to form a new design. A man with his head growing between his legs would appear entirely different from a normal man. Still, it's only a rearrangement.

Perhaps, biased by their concentration on the psychotic, who is absolutely bound by his primitive, childlike drives, and the neurotic, who is strictly limited by them, the psychiatrists have allowed too little for the greater range and freedom of the normal individual. Whereas the mentally ill can deviate from their childhood pattern of behavior only with great difficulty backed up by enormous boosts of psychiatric treatment, normal persons are not so rigidly bound.

The position many psychiatrists take today is that our childhood pattern of behavior bears the same relation to our adult style of life that an artist's first rough sketch bears to the finished painting. The principal features are all there but the details remain to be filled in. We can't completely discard the early sketch but we can make sweeping alterations. The final portrait may bear little resemblance to the original sketch. As Adler put it: "People do not change their attitude toward life after their infancy though its expressions in later life may be quite different."

Why should we, when considering the possibility of change, disregard the *experience* of human beings and especially of outstanding human beings who have deliberately set about making alterations in their character? Men like Ben Franklin, for example?

When Franklin undertook to reform his whole character and way of life, he spoke of one vice in particular which he was determined to overcome—pride.

"There is, perhaps, no one of our natural passions so hard to subdue as Pride," he wrote. "Disguise it, struggle with it, beat it down, stifle it, mortify it as much as one pleases, it is still alive . . . I was determined endeavoring to cure myself, if I could, of this vice. I added humility to my list. . . . I cannot boast of much success in acquiring the *reality* of this virtue, but I had a good deal with regard to the *appearance* of it. I made it a rule to forbear all direct contradiction to the sentiments of others and all positive assertion of my own. I even forbade myself . . . the use of every word or expression in the language that imported a fixed opinion, such as 'certainly,' 'undoubtedly,' etc., and I adopted, instead of them, 'I conceive' . . . 'I imagine' . . . or 'so it appears to me at present.' . . . I soon found the advantage of this change in my manner; the conversations I engaged in went on more pleasantly. The modest way in which I proposed my opinions procured them a readier reception and less contradiction . . . And this mode, which I at first put on with some violence to natural inclination, became at

length so easy . . . that perhaps for these fifty years past
no one has ever heard a dogmatical expression escape me.
To this habit . . . I think it principally owing that I had
early so much weight with my fellow-citizens."

Could there be a better illustration of the theory that,
while the prototype never changes, its manifestations
can be improved to an indefinite degree—that although
the characteristics of the individual (here pride) may
remain the same, he appears to others to be a completely
different person?

This, indeed, would seem to be the answer to the
age-old problem of free will and the ability of human
beings to control their destiny.

In his discussion of this subject, William James says,
"My own belief is that the question of free will is in-
soluble on strictly psychological grounds . . . Taking the
risk of error on our head, we must project upon one of
the alternative views the attribute of reality for us . . .
The present writer does this for the alternative of freedom, but the grounds of his opinion are ethical rather
than psychological."

Actually the whole question of free will is as academic
as the old theological argument as to how many angels
could stand on the head of a pin. For no matter what we
think, we are forced to *act* as though free will existed.
Since we can't know in advance what we are predestined
to do we must go ahead and do what we (seemingly)
choose to do. We cannot know until after the event that
we were foreordained to fall in love with a particular
girl, get drunk on a certain night, forget an appointment.
Even if our belief in free will is an illusion, we are
forced to act as if it were an actuality.

Psychiatrists (even Freudians) no matter what they
think, still *act* as though they believed human beings
could change. Otherwise they wouldn't be psychiatrists—

they'd be quacks. They believe they can help even the neurotic, far less flexible than the normal person, to change his pattern of behavior.

"As a result of successful therapy," says A. H. Maslow, "people perceive differently, think differently, learn differently. Their emotions change, as do their intentions . . . Their interpersonal relations and attitude toward society are transformed. Their character (or personalities) change both superficially and profoundly . . . In some cases even the IQ goes up."

"At the same time that we understand a trait or behavior pattern in anyone, we acquire a lever with which we can modify that individual's behavior," says Adler.

Wendell Johnson, Director of the University of Iowa Speech Clinic, notes how quickly and easily a person with a personality problem can, given a little relevant information, a new point of view that sharpens his awareness of some of the little things that so often underlie big problems, have his problem solved and significant changes in behavior brought about.

Everyone is running to psychiatrists these days. On the theory that there must be something wrong with a person who goes to a psychiatrist when there's nothing wrong with him, these people probably need help. But a little courage and patience would enable them to avoid being couch cases. An increasing number of psychiatrists are coming to believe that we can handle our own emotional problems. Many, among them Rank, Steckle, Sullivan, Horney, Fromm, Blanton, maintain that, to a far greater extent than psychiatrists heretofore thought, we are self-directing and self-governing organisms. For decades after Freud's discovery of the unconscious, it was held that the unconscious was all, the conscious nothing. Today the tide is turning, and the conscious is being given back a little of its pre-Freudian importance.

"Human beings," says Maslow, "have within their own power greater possibilities than they realize for curing themselves of the multitude of mild maladjustments which are so common in our society . . . If the individual knows he should have his esteem needs fulfilled, he can *consciously* seek out these satisfactions. [Love, security, belongingness and so forth.] Everyone will agree that this is better than trying to make up for their lack *unconsciously* . . . I have seen deep character changes without the help of a technical therapist."

Dr. Smiley Blanton, a Freudian, in his book, *Love or Perish,* says, "I believe that it is possible to achieve an emotional change with the insight developed through books . . . Many people need personal counseling; but it is a fact that many can and do bring changes into their own lives through books."

On this question of *if, how* and *how much* we can change our character and control our destiny, Dr. Alfred Farau, a close friend and co-worker of Adler's, says:

"We must recognize what a large part courage and optimism play in Adler's psychology. He understood only too well the inherent tragedy of life. Life *is* difficult, life *is* dangerous, man *is* weak. *But* since he cannot know the limits of his potentialities he must continue to fight, even against impossible odds.

"Adler liked to quote Aesop's story of the two frogs who fell into a great pot of milk, one an optimist, the other a pessimist. The pessimist croaked, 'I'm finished,' and drowned without a struggle. The courageous frog, kicking like the very devil to get out, suddenly felt solid ground under him—he had churned the milk to butter. How much more do we humans know about the substance of the life into which we have fallen? We know a lot about the difficulties life presents, little about our own potentialities.

They may be unlimited. The nature of man does not follow mechanistic laws. A part of nature, it is itself dynamic, creating dynamic forces directed toward chosen goals."

The stumbling block is not the impossibility of changing, not even the difficulty of changing—it is that we don't want to change and don't even think we need to change. Let someone or something else change—then you'll see how well-adjusted *we* are. To most people there is nothing more upsetting than the idea that the difficulties they encounter require any improvements in themselves.

The very thought of change brings immediate conflict. We want to change—and we don't. We try to conceal this situation from ourselves since it is humiliating to admit that we want to cling to the things that are hurting us. So we compromise. We decide we'll change—but just as little as possible. We will not go even that far unless our case is desperate.

In all difficult situations our natural reaction is to blame the other fellow. Only in the most desperate situations will we ask ourselves, "What did *I* do to bring about this situation?" As soon as a person begins to explore his own ego he discovers attitudes he has always endeavored to conceal from himself and he realizes that the process of changing these attitudes is going to involve a number of major alterations he hadn't contemplated. He both fears and desires these alterations. He is appalled at the task before him.

In order to make these changes we must first change our interpretation of past events. If in childhood we formed the opinion that every man's hand is against us because our father's was and we have in consequence taken a hostile attitude toward the world, if we have been filled with self-pity because of some childhood disability or situation and feel that the world should protect us and forgive us for everything as our mother did—then we must now realize that this is a false interpretation of life and we must change it. Once we discover, with or without psychiatric help, the meaning we have given to life, we hold the key to our personality and the possibility of change. A problem is never solved by giving up, looking for the easy way out, trying to escape, throwing the burden on someone else, making a bid for special treatment or seeking revenge. Although at the end of his fifth year a child's personality has crystallized and the meaning he gives to life, the goal he pursues, the style of his approach to life, and his emotional disposition are all set, all these things can be changed in later life if he can free himself from the mistaken interpretations of his childhood. Once he is persuaded that co-operation, not competition, is the key to happiness, he has every chance of changing.

Let us suppose that an individual has reached a point where he earnestly desires to change. With what weapons is he to fight? The primitive drives which have brought him to this pass—sexual instincts, anger, fear—are the most powerful forces in human nature. They can only be fought with equally powerful forces. Illogical as it may sound, the elemental emotions of anger, fear and the sexual instincts must be opposed by *themselves*.

A very simple, very clear illustration of the way this works is the case of Rocco Graziano.

Rocco was the product of the slums, the gutter, the bawdy house, the reformatory, the jail. From childhood his only companions were thieves, gunmen, and gangsters, with all of whom Rocco associated enthusiastically. Drafted into the United States Army, he became a deserter. A prisoner in Fort Leavenworth, with the death house freely prophesied for him, he sat down one day and asked himself:

"Whose fault is it I'm here? Who is it I got to even the score with? The cops? The courts? The corporals? My old man? . . . Or is the fault in me? Me, who's got to be the big shot, the wise guy . . . the only person in the world I can't lick with my own two fists?"

In this desperate situation he made up his mind that, given another chance, he'd do things differently. Out of Leavenworth, he was still the same tough, angry guy, hating the world and hating himself, but resolved to channel all that hostility into new grooves. He became a prize-fighter.

"All I see is the patch of canvas shining under the lights, and this other guy who by now I've even forgotten he's got a name. He is the enemy. I am going to destroy him . . . I want to tear this guy's eyes out with my fingernails. I want to put a knife through his gut and rip everything out . . .

"Whatever the poison was inside me—whatever I picked up from the tar on the streets and roofs, from the rats that crawled through the Tombs, from the blood-caked rubber hose in the station house, from the bedbugs of the reform schools and the cans and the guardhouses—whatever it was, I had it beat out of me in the boxing ring. I didn't need to fight ever again. I wasn't sore at anybody in the world, not even myself. The poison and the hate were belted out of me."

He took on the best and beat them. When he was at the top, he was stunned to find how many "legitimate guys" there were up there, and even more stunned to discover that they could like him. He set himself a new goal—to be a legitimate guy himself.

Today Rocky Graziano is a well-to-do, happily married man, a father, a respected citizen and "a member with all dues paid up of the legitimate world . . . I did not really believe there was this many legitimate characters in the world."

No psychiatrist could have devised a better strategy for him than Rocky devised for himself. He just had to beat people up to pay back the human race, especially his old man, for what it had done to him. In the boxing ring he could do it legitimately. He finally licked himself with his own two fists.

The weapon he used was anger—primitive, elemental anger. In order to survive, primitive man had to fight. To fight, he needed anger. Today, whether it is a foe in battle, a competitor in business or a rival in love, it is still anger that is one of our best weapons. Reason, so recent an acquisition, is impotent without it. Reason does not generate energy. Only the emotions do that.

Originally the goal of anger was to kill. Often it still is. But today it assumes many other forms, not all lethal, such as aggressiveness, antagonism, hostility, hate, bitterness, scorn, defiance, disdain, competitiveness, irritability, frustration, indignation. There are also beneficent forms of anger—righteous indignation, scorn of evil, hatred of cruelty and oppression. It was with anger that Christ drove the moneylenders from the temple, that Gandhi passively resisted the British, that Schweitzer fought disease in the jungle. Under whatever form it appears, its value is that it inevitably incites aggressive action. A mere emotional outburst, an explosion of anger, is wasted energy. Only when consciously controlled and directed does it become effective power.

Anger is in itself neither good nor evil. It is a mighty motivating force, worthy or unworthy only according to its goal.

Alexander the Great was one of the greatest leaders of men who ever lived, adored by his armies. He was capable of titanic angers but these were directed with skill and wisdom against his enemies. Then, on occasion, they broke loose and swept toward their primordial goal of destruction and he murdered a beloved general, tortured an enemy, stabbed a bodyguard, ordered a massacre, destroyed a city. Anger, like all primitive emotions, is neutral, evil only when turned against humanity.

"Anger," wrote G. Stanley Hall, educator and psychologist, "in most of its forms is the most dynamic of all emotions. Anger and Power are near neighbors; they both imply the treading down of rivals."

To William James anger is the very foundation of the energetic character.

"One mode of emotional excitability is exceedingly important in the composition of the energetic character, from its peculiarly destructive power over inhibitions. I mean what in its lower form is mere irascibility, susceptibility to wrath, its fighting temper; and what in subtler ways manifests itself as impatience, grimness, earnestness, severity of character. Earnestness means willingness to live with energy, though energy bring pain . . . Nothing annihilates an inhibition as irresistibly as anger does it."

Life abounds in new stimuli and excitements which often bring about the most sudden and startling changes in character, altering a person's whole scale of values and outlook on life. To such stimuli we are highly vulnerable. They often have a tremendous impact on the personality.

I know a man whose whole life is strewn with enemies, all richly deserved. It isn't so much that he hates people as that he ignores them, than which there is no surer way of getting yourself disliked. As far as he is concerned, the men and women in his organization have no private lives, first names, or faces.

One day he was invited by a business associate to hunt with his club. Dawn—trailing mists—hunting horns—the baying of hounds—something got under his skin. He remembered a boy back home in England furiously pedaling a bicycle to keep up with the hunt, hanging over a stile, his heart filled with envy and despair, watching the damned British aristocracy flash by in all their intolerable arrogance . . . *This* was what he'd always wanted—to ride with them.

He joined the hunt club and found himself at the bottom of a hierarchy with the Master of the Hunt at the top. He was not permitted to wear a pink coat and a top hat, only a humble black coat and a derby. He could reach the top echelon only by proving himself in the hunting field to be "the right sort"—co-operative and courteous. This meant, in the beginning, learning never to cause delay, cut off a rider in front of a fence, talk in the checks; later to let down the bars for the juniors, help in case of mishap, wait at the fences to direct stragglers, open gates.

He was hell-bent on winning the symbols of sportsmen's acceptance—the right to wear a pink coat with the Master's buttons and insignia, the velvet collar, and the top hat. He performed every service expected of a new member— and he performed them with a smile. On several occasions he even lent his own mount to a member whose horse had suddenly gone lame, leading it back to the stables, *whistling* as he went. That first season he wasn't in at a single kill, sometimes because he simply didn't recognize the huntsman's "gone away!"

By some form of psychological osmosis this new-found kindliness seeped into his other relationships. He found himself being pleasant at home and at the office. Gradually he ceased being ashamed of being decent and even enjoyed it. By the time he had earned his pink coat, he was a changed man.

All his life, he had borne the world a grudge because

of an underprivileged childhood. Diverted into new channels, this inner rage against society worked a complete transformation. Obviously this could only take place in a strong personality, a nature capable of powerful emotions under the direction of an iron will.

Fear is another of the primitive emotions which can be used constructively or destructively. Like anger it is universal and basic in our psychology, and it is *all* energy. Of it, one of our foremost psychiatrists, Dr. Edward Strecker, says:

"The psychiatrist is constantly struck with the amount and ferocity of anger produced by domination and coercion. This being the case, it logically follows that the *danger of domination* should arouse the greatest amount of fear in people. And indeed such appears to be the case. The most extreme fear seen in people, the fear that totally incapacitates them, not for minutes or hours, but for months and years, seems to be most frequently traced to this cause. Fear of this type is usually referred to a loss of personality and means fear that one's ego will not survive, that one's free will will be lost."

Like anger, fear assumes many forms—physical cowardice naturally, but also apprehension, anxiety, worry, dread, panic, terror, horror, timidity, shyness. Physically we fear death and bodily injury. Psychologically we fear being slighted, misunderstood, disapproved. We fear loneliness, loss of prestige or power. We fear being thought inadequate. We fear becoming merely the instrument of another's will, an appendage to his personality. We fear we may not meet the danger bravely or insult with dignity. The real mission of fear is to prompt us to run from danger or to stand and fight.

At the turn of the century, Mary Morrill, a girl from Maine, went to China as a missionary. She was so timid a creature that the Board almost didn't appoint her. She herself said, "If the supreme call should ever come, my cowardice is so great I fear I shall run away."

She was in China when the Boxer Rebellion broke out. When the Boxers attacked the mission, Mary Morrill appeared alone at the gate to face the howling mob. Stunned, they stood silent as she pleaded, "Slay me but spare the others. I turn myself over to you to do with as you please."

Fear that she might fail in her duty gave her the courage to face death just as it has given it to men from the beginning of time.

The sexual instincts are powerful forces for or against us. In their many guises—love, pity, admiration, respect, adoration, kindness, sympathy, empathy, understanding— they can be our most powerful allies in the struggle to change our attitudes. Heredity gives us these primitive drives but heredity does not determine how we shall react to them. The sexual instincts can be allowed to run riot or they can be controlled and channeled into love of the human race, altruism, philanthropy, self-sacrifice. The primordial emotions have been transmuted by man into higher forms.

During the second World War a fortress was shot down by enemy fire. A ball-turret gunner was caught fast in the blister of the underside of the fuselage. Crew members tried but could not free him. As one by one they parachuted to safety they could hear his screams, then the voice of the gunner saying quietly, "Take it easy, kid, we'll take this ride together."

Such forms of love are not as rare as one might suppose. We may find it in ourselves at any time.

"If there is something peculiar in the blood and fiber of a hero," said the president of the Carnegie Hero Fund Commission, hero hunters, "it has not been discovered by the Commission in over thirty years."

In the snows of February last year a bus with sixteen passengers was stranded by a blizzard near the Texas–New Mexico border. The bus driver, John Herron, waited five hours for passing help. None came. At 2:30 P.M. he set out on foot to seek it. He staggered through waist-high drifts, making twelve miles in eight and one-half hours, heading for the tiny border town of Glenrio. He never made it. Snow-blind, frostbitten, almost hysterical, he fell into a drift only one hundred yards before he reached it.

He had one thing left—a feeble whistle. He whistled. Someone heard. Three highway patrol cars, following the path made for him through the drifts by a road grader, set out, finally located the stranded bus and rescued all sixteen passengers.

Courage is not something we have today and that is gone tomorrow. It is character. It is habit. Each time we react to a situation it is not a new act of volition. We don't make up our minds afresh each time whether to accept insult, to strike back, to save a life at the risk of our own. We do all these things as we have been in the habit of doing them. The important thing is to groove the desirable habits into our nervous system by constant practice so that in the hour of need the *habitual* action beats the instinctive action to the draw.

The elemental, primitive emotions—these are the weapons with which we must fight and the tools we must use in any endeavor to change our way of life or our attitudes. A mere transitory emotion is worthless. The emotions must be organized into a system of sentiments spearheaded by an idea. An idea has force only in proportion to the emotion it arouses and the emotions have force only if they are organized into sentiments behind the idea. Reason alone is impotent and unorganized emotion is mere waste.

Let us assume that you have reached the point where

you earnestly desire to make certain changes in your way of life. You are persuaded that the inferiority complex is the key to these changes. You realize that it is not, as you may have suspected, a liability but an asset. You have seen how it can make a president out of a railsplitter, an ambassador out of a soapboiler, a saint out of a roisterer. What it can do for you depends upon how much drive you are prepared to put behind it. It will be a hard fight. But never was there a flabby genius, a flaccid conqueror, an apathetic saint.

"If this life be not a real fight in which something is eternally gained for the universe by success," said James, "It is no better than a game of private theatricals from which one may withdraw at will. But it *feels* like a real fight—as if there were something really wild in the universe which we are needed to redeem. For such a half-wild, half-saved universe our nature is adapted."

The world is *not* a stage, life is not a play, men and women are not merely actors. Life is a battle, the world is a battlefield, we are the warriors, not to be excused until we draw our last breath.

Until this motivating force in human nature which, by lowering our self-esteem, drives us to prove our superiority, was discovered and named by Adler, we were like men fighting in the dark. Many used this force blindly and emerged victorious. Today anyone can use it with full knowledge of what he is doing—and there will be many more victors.

The time to start is *now*. With this key to understanding yourself and others, a whole new life can open up to you.

You doubt it? You have a feeling that the past *is* the future and that you will meet there the same old you, a little older, a little less attractive, and not much wiser?

Even if that were true, if there were no margin for free will, we still must struggle for we can't know what fate has been clamped upon us (if one has) by God or by chemistry. We are forced to act as if we were free men.

As free men we will at once undertake certain long overdue alterations in our way of life. We will refuse any longer to be scourged, humiliated, and generally bullied by an inferiority complex (probably plural). We will decide to put it to the use for which it was obviously intended and to which successful and happy people have always put it. We will no longer be ridden by it but will ride it, even if a little uncertainly at first, toward our future, our destination as individuals being a richer, fuller life; as a race to that higher, unknown destiny that awaits us at the end of the next few million years.

INDEX

265

Set in Linotype Caledonia
Format by James T. Parker
Manufactured by The Haddon Craftsmen, Inc.
Published by HARPER & BROTHERS, *New York*